Forty years ago I dreamed of teaching Gurukula students with Śrīla Prabhupāda's *Śrīmad-Bhāgavatam* serving as the central text. Toward realizing that goal, I had compiled the *Bhāgavatam* into its essential stories, for I trusted Śrīla Prabhupāda's words that such study would truly educate and prepare my students on every level for a satisfying and worthwhile life.

But Kṛṣṇa had a more wonderful plan. The opportunity to fulfill Śrīla Prabhupāda's desire – like a fragrant lotus in the form of this *Śrīmad-Bhāgavatam: A Comprehensive Guide for Young Readers* – has been carefully placed in the open hands of Mātājī Aruddhā Devī Dāsī and her team of parents and educators. May the fortunate children who take advantage of their love-laden offering gain a taste for this sweet, potent literature. May those children continue throughout their lives to taste and distribute to others what they have relished in their childhood and youth. May the *Śrīmad-Bhāgavatam* safeguard their rapid journey to the lotus feet of Śrī Kṛṣṇa. And may Śrīla Prabhupāda bless those who have sought to fulfill his desire by compiling this offering and placing it into his lotus hands.

– Bhūrijana Dāsa

Śrīmad-Bhāgavatam: A Comprehensive Guide for Young Readers, to our reading, and from all reports, is an unsurpassed resource for teachers of *Śrīmad-Bhāgavatam,* both in families and in schools. The variety of materials and amount of work that went into producing the book as a gift to Śrīla Prabhupāda are astonishing.

– Hanumatpreśaka Swami (Prof. H.H. Robinson)

As I travel around the United States, I get to personally witness how much devotee families have benefitted from Aruddhā Devī Dāsī and her homeschooling methods, which are completely based on Śrīla Prabhupāda's books and teachings. I am an ardent supporter of her and the models of education which she develops and promotes through her books and various homeschooling seminars.

It is very pleasing to note that she and her team have come up with a second project, *Śrīmad-Bhāgavatam: A Comprehensive Guide for Young Readers*. The series' main objective is to provide children with a *Bhāgavatam*-centered education, with lots of activities created by parents and teachers that are geared toward different learning styles, while meeting devotional, cognitive and language objectives of a growing child in Kṛṣṇa consciousness. This innovative and systematic compilation of various activities in book form is a great resource for any homeschooling parents who want their children to go deeper into the messages of *Śrīmad-Bhāgavatam*.

– Romapāda Swami

From my reading of Aruddhā Devī Dāsī's book on studying *Śrīmad-Bhāgavatam*, it is evident that she is fulfilling Śrīla Prabhupāda's desire that our children get the best Kṛṣṇa conscious education. As Śrīla Prabhupāda said in a lecture on *Śrīmad-Bhāgavatam* 1.5.13 given in New Vrindaban in 1969: "When one can understand *Śrīmad-Bhāgavatam* in true perspective, then it is to be understood that he has finished all his educational advancement. *Avadhi*. *Avadhi* means 'this is the limit of education.' *Vidyā-bhāgavatāvadhi.*"

This book gives the highest knowledge in an interesting way, so that children may access the *Bhāgavatam* on many levels, including higher-level thinking and application to their lives, as well as artistic, dramatic and journalistic approaches. I recommend this book for all parents who want to give their children a higher taste for reading Śrīla Prabhupāda's *Śrīmad-Bhāgavatam*.

– Nārāyaṇī Devī Dāsī

Śrīmad Bhāgavatam

– A Comprehensive Guide for Young Readers –

Canto 1, Volume 1

ŚRĪMAD BHĀGAVATAM

– A Comprehensive Guide for Young Readers –

CANTO 1, VOLUME 1

Compiled and edited by
ARUDDHĀ DEVĪ DĀSĪ

Krishna Homeschool

Library of Congress Cataloging-in-Publication Data

Srimad Bhagavatam : a study guide for children / compiled by Aruddha devi dasi.
282 pages
ISBN 978-1-7339272-1-5
1. Puranas. Bhagavatapurana--Textbooks. 2. Hinduism--Textbooks.
I. Aruddha, devi dasi.
BL1140.4.B436S745 2014
294.5'925--dc23
2014005526

Cover and book design by Robert L. Wintermute (Yamarāja Dāsa)

For more information, contact:

Krishna Homeschool

Contact the author at: aruddha108@yahoo.com

RAIVATA DESIGN
Designing with the Soul

Design: Raivata Dāsa
design@raivata.pro
www.raivata.pro

Contents

This book is a tribute to the spiritual master of the entire world, His Divine Grace A. C. Bhaktivedanta Swami Prabhupāda, who gave us the invaluable gift of *Śrīmad-Bhāgavatam*. Śrīla Prabhupāda spent hours each night translating this vast literature from Sanskrit to English, and writing his erudite purports. He emphasized that anyone who studies *Śrīmad-Bhāgavatam* will be liberated from misery and directly connected to Kṛṣṇa. It was Śrīla Prabhupāda's great desire that our children be educated in *Śrīmad-Bhāgavatam*.

Acknowledgments

My humble obeisances to my spiritual master, His Holiness Gopal Krishna Goswami, a dear and dedicated disciple of Śrīla Prabhupāda, who is untiring in his efforts to preach Kṛṣṇa consciousness throughout the world. He always encourages me to share my experiences regarding Kṛṣṇa conscious parenting with devotees.

My gratitude to my husband, Anantarūpa Prabhu, my sons, Rādhīkā Rāmaṇa and Gopāla Hari, and my daughter-in-law, Amrita Keli, who were very supportive of my efforts to bring this book to completion. They were patient and tolerant as I spent many months writing, coordinating and reviewing the work of the contributors.

And my profound thanks go to all the contributors who spent many hours creating resources for the 19 chapters of Canto 1. They hail from countries around the world:

Australia

Śrī Yaśodā Devī Dāsī for songs, plays and other hands-on activities.

Pṛśnī Devī Dāsī for creating comprehension activities.

New Zealand

Bhava Sandhī Devī Dāsī for composing songs, poems, puzzles, language and art activities.

Guruvāṇī Devī Dāsī for writing chapter activities.

Kāruṇā Pūrna Devī Dāsī for creating all the illustrations in the book. Her beautiful drawings brought the book to life.

Mānadā Devī Dāsī for creating language and general activities. She also assisted in compiling material to create the initial draft of the book.

Urjjeśvarī Devī Dāsī for doing the layout of the illustrations.

South Africa

Yamunā Jīvana Dāsa for facilitating the technical aspects of the project, such as creating a server for storing and accessing files. He also set to music many of the songs for each chapter.

United Kingdom

Śucirāṇī Devī Dāsī for developing a substantial amount of content, including comprehension questions, general activities and key messages. She also assisted in the reformatting and reorganizing of the book.

Sudevī Sundarī Devī Dāsī for chapter activities, sequence of events and character descriptions.

Svarṇa Rādhīkā Devī Dāsī, Braja Rāsa Devī Dāsī, Prāṇa Sakhī Devī Dāsī and Ashika Patel for selecting analogies from each chapter and then creating learning activities to explain their meaning.

Vṛndakiśorī Devī Dāsī for story summaries, comprehension, character descriptions, mind maps and songs.

Līlā Kāmala Devī Dāsī for checking the content after the chapters were completed.

United States

Nisha Madan for designing cryptograms and puzzles for all the chapters.

My gratitude to Sundarī Rādhīkā Devī Dāsī for reviewing multiple choice questions, to Parth Kashikar for improving formatting issues with an eye for detail, and to Arun Nair for adding diacritics throughout the manuscript. A special thanks to Rāgātmikā Devī Dāsī for proofreading the entire book with care and attention.

Finally, I am deeply grateful to my publisher, Advaita Candra Prabhu, who took up the project with enthusiasm and made it into a reality, and Yamarāja Prabhu, who spent countless hours doing the design and layout, making the book polished and attractive to children.

This book is the product of many hands, and it would not exist without the dedication of all these devotees. I am deeply indebted to them for taking time from their busy schedules to help create this valuable resource for children everywhere.

Introduction

While conducting seminars on homeschooling and Krishna conscious parenting throughout the world during the last seven years, I met many parents who wanted to teach their children *Śrīmad-Bhāgavatam*, but needed more guidance on exactly how to do it. It was then that I started doing workshops, during which we would sit together with their children and I would demonstrate how to guide a discussion in a way that evoked the child's curiosity about the nature of the world, God, the self, and the purpose of life. Together, we would read the translations of a chapter of *Śrīmad-Bhāgavatam* and discuss the stories, main themes, and great personalities. We would talk about the relevance of *Śrīmad-Bhāgavatam* in our own lives – how it provides spiritual solutions to material problems. Both the children and parents were thoroughly absorbed in the discussion.

When I explained at seminars how I taught my boys *Śrīmad-Bhāgavatam* through interactive reading and discussion, hundreds of parents were inspired to follow. However, I also realized that many parents who wanted to study the *Bhāgavatam* with their children were uncertain about how to do it. They needed a formal curriculum for studying *Śrīmad-Bhāgavatam*. I pondered how this would be possible, for it would take a long time to do this. This is when I decided to start a collaborative project, involving devotee parents from around the world. I formed an online Yahoo group in which approximately 15 parents – from Australia, New Zealand, South Africa, the United Kingdom and the United States – worked together to create study resources for each chapter of Canto 1. Every parent would send their creations to others in the group, who would use the material with their own children and offer feedback. I would go through all the materials, offering direction on content, organization, and activity design.

All of the parents brought special skills to the book. Our team included English teachers, musicians, artists and computer professionals. All of them have children of their own, with a strong motivation to give them a *Bhāgavatam*-centered education. The result? An innovative collection of material on every chapter of Canto 1. The creators used the curriculum with their own children as they designed it, seeing the results firsthand.

Of course, having all this material in email attachments is beneficial only to a certain extent – it had to be edited and organized and compiled. So we then began the painstaking task of putting together a book for use by parents anywhere. This book is primarily geared for children between the ages of 6 and 12, but much of the material can be adapted for children younger than 6, or older than 12.

WHY STUDY ŚRĪMAD-BHĀGAVATAM?
Śrīla Prabhupāda said that from the very beginning, children "should be taught Sanskrit and English, so in the future they can read our books. That will make them MA, Ph.D." Because the knowledge in these books is so advanced, children would be well-educated, happy, satisfied, and even go back home, back to Godhead (Jagadīśa, April 6, 1977).

As is evident in many of his lectures, Śrīla Prabhupāda desired that children in his *gurukula* schools read *Śrīmad-Bhāgavatam*. In 1974, speaking on *Śrīmad-Bhāgavatam* (1.16.22), Śrīla Prabhupāda confirmed that the *Bhāgavatam* would equip one to know any subject. Please read the following quotation carefully: "So in *Śrīmad-Bhāgavatam* you will find everything, whatever is necessity, for the advancement of human civilization, everything is there described. And knowledge also, all departments of knowledge, even astronomy, astrology, politics, sociology, atomic theory, everything is there. *Vidyā-bhāgavatāvadhi*. Therefore, if you study *Śrīmad-Bhāgavatam* very carefully, then you get all knowledge completely. Because *Bhāgavatam* begins from the point of creation: *janmādy asya yataḥ*." (July 12, 1974, Los Angeles)

By giving them this foundation, children become confident of their spiritual identity and also do well academically. Prabhupāda's books inspire critical reasoning and creative thinking, which are the main elements of academic education. *Śrīmad-Bhāgavatam* is pure and perfect and can equip one with the highest knowledge, both material and spiritual.

Parents and teachers who have taught their children *Śrīmad-Bhāgavatam* from their early lives have experienced how easily they pick up English language skills, especially reading, comprehension, and analytical reasoning. *Śrīmad-Bhāgavatam* is full of analogies, allegories, figurative speech, and metaphors. Even a seven-year-old child can understand difficult concepts because the subject matter of *Śrīmad-Bhāgavatam* encourages good thinking skills.

Śrīmad-Bhāgavatam is a wonderful book to teach from because it gives the philosophy of the *Bhagavad-gītā* through stories, and children love stories. These stories are not fictitious; rather, they are the lives of great saintly personalities and the pastimes of Kṛṣṇa and His *avatāras*. By reading these, one directly associates with the great personalities and their teachings. By such association, one begins to develop the character of these same personalities. As children grow older, they learn to appreciate the instructions given by Queen Kuntī, Prahlāda Mahārāja, Dhruva Mahārāja, Kapiladeva and so many others. In fact, many of the devotees described in the *Bhāgavatam*, such as Prahlāda and Dhruva, are children themselves, so our own children have perfect examples and heroes to follow.

The scriptures tell us that Śrī Caitanya Mahāprabhu heard the stories of Dhruva Mahārāja and Prahlāda Mahārāja hundreds of times while growing up, and still he was never bored. The example and instructions of these saints are so valuable that no other moral book can compare with them. Children develop good character, saintly qualities, and pure *bhakti* by reading *Śrīmad-Bhāgavatam*. Indeed, *Śrīmad-Bhāgavatam* is the very essence of Lord Caitanya's *saṅkīrtana* movement.

HOW TO USE THE BOOK

(A) *Discussion*

In my book, *Homeschooling Krishna's Children*, I emphasize the necessity of giving our children a Kṛṣṇa conscious education, based on Śrīla Prabhupāda's books. I explain my own experience of homeschooling my two boys with a curriculum based on *Śrīmad-Bhāgavatam*. I discuss the methodology of studying *Śrīmad-Bhāgavatam* through interactive reading and discussion – the most important element of the process. We sit in a circle and take turns reading only translations, pausing frequently for discussion. (For children who cannot read, they can listen as their parents read and paraphrase the translations). This method has been followed for thousands of years by the great sages of Vedic India, as we see in the *Bhāgavatam* itself.

Discussion is an important part of reading. For children it breaks up the monotony of reading, and can add both interest and challenge. By using *Śrīmad-Bhāgavatam* as our basic text, children can learn all aspects of language arts, composition, comprehension and vocabulary, along with critical thinking and analytical reasoning. The children often drive the discussion by asking questions, raising doubts, or making observations about what they read. By having the opportunity to express themselves, children will understand the material better, gain self-confidence and learn communication skills. Parents can pick up on their children's cues and ask questions of their own to encourage deeper understanding. Parents can also present their own realizations, play devil's advocate, and relate the stories to practical life, thus making the *Bhāgavatam* study a dynamic learning experience. Reading and discussion lead to good speaking, debate, and logical thinking. The nature of *Śrīmad-Bhāgavatam* is such that it encourages a person to ask questions, think critically, and work creatively because the *Bhāgavatam* is full of analogies, metaphors and figurative speech. For example, the analogy of the car and the driver that Prabhupāda uses to describe the difference between the body and the soul is practical and simple, but it allows a child to appreciate a foundational principle of Kṛṣṇa consciousness. Some analogies may be difficult for a four or five-year-old, but as he or she grows older, these analogies will become the basis for strong reasoning skills.

Before reading a chapter (translations) with their children, parents should read the chapter on their own and go through the discussion (higher-thinking) questions provided in this book. The discussion questions are meant to give parents some ideas of how to inspire discussion as they read with their children. Please remember, however, that the discussion questions are only for the purpose of stimulating ideas, not to create a highly structured "oral exam" atmosphere while reading. The key is to keep the discussion dynamic and student-driven, using the sample questions when needed and adapting/rephrasing them as appropriate for the age and personality of the child. In the course of a vibrant discussion, you and your child will, no doubt, come up with questions and topics that were not mentioned in this book. Here are some suggestions for raising interesting and thought-provoking questions:

- Take turns reading the translations, going in a circle. This keeps the child's attention, because children eagerly await their turn. If your child cannot read, you should read and pause frequently to paraphrase the story at the child's level. Ask your child to tell the story in his or her own words.
- Whenever possible, ask "why" and "how" questions rather than "what" (factual) questions, thus encouraging your child to think and reason.
- Don't be afraid to ask open-ended questions that do not have a clear-cut answer. These questions often lead to beneficial discussions.
- Analogies are good opportunities to connect the *Śrīmad-Bhāgavatam* to your child's experience and imagination. The *Śrīmad-Bhāgavatam* is full of vivid analogies and metaphors, so utilize these for your discussions.
- Frequently encourage your child to make comments and raise questions. When your child raises a question for which you don't know the answer, don't be afraid to say so. Discuss his or her question thoroughly, read through purports to find guidance, and you will see many fresh realizations arise.
- Try to relate the story to daily life: "Why did Parīkṣit Mahārāja not retaliate against the boy's curse?" "What can we learn from Parīkṣit Mahārāja's behavior?" However, don't put your child on the spot by pointing fingers: "How should you have behaved with your friend Johnny the other day?" Such finger-pointing destroys the discussion and intimidates the child.
- Draw connections with other stories from the scriptures that your child may already know: "The boy Śṛṅgi showed anger in an inappropriate way, but when is it okay to show anger? Can you give an example?"
- Some sections will be more interesting to a child than others. If a particular section doesn't raise discussion, don't worry – just keep taking turns reading until you come to a translation that raises a question or comment.
- Have a "realizations session" at the end of a chapter, where your child can tell you what they learned from the chapter, and you can tell your child what you learned. Or bring the family together and ask your child to give a short class on the chapter.
- Even if you have not read *Śrīmad-Bhāgavatam* before, that is okay. As a parent (or teacher), you have more life experience and you know your child, which will allow you to lead a discussion and engage your child.
- When you read with an older child (the specific age will vary based on the maturity of the

child), take the stance of a fellow reader and learner. This will help your child open up and feel comfortable. Of course, as the teacher, you will still need to correct a mistaken line of reasoning or raise points that are important, but try to do it as a partner rather than as a master.

• Consider these readings/discussions as your time with *Śrīmad-Bhāgavatam*. Stay focused and become absorbed in *Śrīmad-Bhāgavatam*. Just because your study partner is a 7-year old child does not mean that you will gain any less from studying *Śrīmad-Bhāgavatam*.

(B) *Written and Oral Exercises*

Once you have read a chapter of the *Bhāgavatam* translations together, you can use a variety of exercises provided in the book to teach language skills – including writing, comprehension, vocabulary and grammar – which will help in understanding the chapter. This book provides comprehension questions, key themes, character descriptions, word searches, language puzzles, and many other activities. There is also a section in each chapter dedicated to arts, crafts, and songs. The goal is to provide parents with a practical way to make *Śrīmad-Bhāgavatam* a central part of their children's education. Regardless of whether parents are homeschooling or sending their children to school, we hope they will find renewed confidence in studying this great literature.

Here are the different kinds of departments and activities you will find:

- Story Summary
- Key Messages and Character Descriptions
- Discussion Questions and Higher-Thinking Questions
- Language and Vocabulary Activities
- Puzzles, Games and Quizzes
- Analogy Activities
- Arts, Crafts, Drama and other Hands-On Activities
- Songs
- Answers (includes answers to questions and quizzes and solutions to the puzzles)

The instructions for each activity are addressed directly to the child, but we assume that parents will still need to explain and supervise the activities, especially if the child is younger.

LEARNING OUTCOMES

The book's main objective is to provide children from the ages of 6–12 with spiritual knowledge from the *Śrīmad-Bhāgavatam* and the opportunity for personal realization.

The primary process for doing this is by reading chapter translations with the children, discussing the stories and philosophical content of the chapter, and providing the children with the opportunity to make their own inquiries and share their personal experiences.

In addition, the activities in this book develop the key themes and philosophical points presented in each chapter, by accommodating a range of different learning styles, in a range of learning modes (visual, auditory and kinesthetic).

The activities also meet the following cognitive and language objectives:

Thinking skills (based on Bloom's *Taxonomy of Educational Objectives*):

- Acquiring knowledge
- Developing comprehension skills
- Applying knowledge
- Using knowledge to be creative
- Analyzing information
- Self-evaluating

Language objectives:

- Written language (includes reading and writing)
- Visual language (includes communicating through the visual arts, such as drama and static imagery)
- Oral language (includes communication through speaking)

This book works to supplement any existing curriculum that parents or teachers may use to teach language skills. This is not a course designed to teach reading and writing in itself, but it can work together with a formal curriculum to further develop language skills, while providing children with a resource for studying *Śrīmad-Bhāgavatam*.

Śrīmad-Bhāgavatam lies at the heart of Śrī Caitanya Mahāprabhu's philosophy and movement. I pray that this book will help children and their parents develop a lifelong love for this great literature, following in the footsteps of Śrīla Prabhupāda and our previous *ācāryas*. *Śrīmad-Bhāgavatam* is very profound, and this book only skims the surface. I humbly request the readers to forgive any faults and shortcomings herein.

Aruddhā Devī Dāsī
Rādhāṣṭamī, September 2, 2014
New Biharvan, Boise, Idaho
USA

1

Questions by the Sages

Story Summary

At the beginning of the *Śrīmad-Bhāgavatam,* Śrīla Vyāsadeva, the author, first offers his respectful obeisances to Lord Kṛṣṇa saying, "Before we begin this story, I bow down to Lord Kṛṣṇa with gratitude. He created this material world, although he eternally exists in the spiritual world. I think about how He is independent and the cause of all causes. He can place even the great sages and demigods into illusion. I meditate upon Him."

We can only understand the *Bhāgavatam* if we have a pure heart. The stories from the *Bhāgavatam* are true and blissful and by listening to them attentively we will meet our best friend, Lord Kṛṣṇa, Who is always in our hearts. These stories are like delicious fruits, and because Śukadeva Gosvāmī is the speaker, they have become even tastier, in the same way that a parrot pecks a mango, making it taste sweeter.

Once, in a holy place in the forest of Naimiṣāraṇya, many great sages, headed by Śaunaka Ṛṣi, gathered together to perform a sacrifice for one thousand years to please Kṛṣṇa and His devotees.

One day, after completing their morning duties, the great sages excitedly and respectfully offered Sūta Gosvāmī a seat. They said to him, "In this gloomy age of Kali, the people do not live for very long. They are lazy and misguided. They argue. They are also very unlucky. Above all, they are always disturbed."

The sages continued, "There are so many scriptures in the world that tell us to do so many different duties, which can only be learned after many years of study. Our dear Sūta Gosvāmī, please, therefore, explain the essence of all these scriptures so that people's hearts will be fully satisfied."

The sages approached the speaker, Sūta Gosvāmī, as he was sinless and knew all the scriptures. He was the eldest and knew the other learned sages also. Because Sūta Gosvāmī was submissive and listened to his spiritual master, he was blessed.

After the sages blessed Sūta Gosvāmī, they asked to learn about Lord Kṛṣṇa and His adventures because they knew that anyone who talks about or hears about Kṛṣṇa becomes uplifted and joyful. "Oh, wise Sūta!" they said. "We never tire of hearing about Kṛṣṇa's pastimes. Lord Kṛṣṇa and His brother Balarāma played just like normal human beings and so in this way They covered up Their many superhuman acts. We are eager to hear about His transcendental adventures in His different incarnations. Please tell us about these magnificent acts of the Lord, that great sages such

as Nārada Muni sing of so wonderfully."

Finally, the great sages said to Sūta Gosvāmi, "We are so grateful to have met you. Anyone who wants to cross this difficult ocean of Kali must come aboard this ship of hearing about Kṛṣṇa. Sūta Gosvāmī is our captain!"

Key Messages

In this section we have summarized the Key Messages in this chapter. Use this list as a quick reference guide to the verses listed. Have you looked them all up in your *Śrīmad-Bhāgavatam?* Using your own words, you can memorize these Key Messages and the verses supporting them so you will always know where to find what you are looking for in *Śrīmad-Bhāgavatam*. You can go through this list and discuss each topic further. Can you think of examples in your personal life that relate to these Key Messages?

Theme	References	Key Messages
Kṛṣṇa is the Supreme Personality of Godhead	1.1.1 1.1.12 1.1.20	Lord Kṛṣṇa is the Absolute Truth because He is the ultimate source of everything; He doesn't depend on anyone or anything else. He is the cause of all causes because nothing can happen without Him wanting it to happen. Although He creates the material world to put the spirit souls into illusion, He is free from illusion.
Disciplic Succession	1.1.1 1.1.3 1.1.5-9 1.1.13	By hearing the *Śrīmad-Bhāgavatam* from devotees who are in the disciplic succession and who have pleased their spiritual masters by their obedience and submission, one can ensure that the message that they receive is correct.
How to approach the *Bhāgavatam*	1.1.2 1.1.17 1.1.3 1.1.19 1.1.5 1.1.8 1.1.13	One should be very eager and excited to hear *Śrīmad-Bhāgavatam*, just like the sages were. They were so happy that a qualified speaker like Sūta Gosvāmī was there to speak to them. They approached him with respect and a humble service attitude. With this wonderful mood, Sūta Gosvāmī was pleased to speak the *Bhāgavatam* to them.
Ages and Yugas	1.1.10 1.1.22 1.1.14 1.1.16 1.1.21	The atmosphere of the age of Kali makes it very difficult to become devotees and it will get worse as time goes on. This is because people don't live for long, they are lazy, misguided, unlucky, always disturbed and they argue.
Devotees are compassionate	1.1.4 1.1.9 1.1.10 1.1.11	The sages met at Naimiṣāraṇya because they felt compassion toward the people of Kali-yuga. They asked Sūta Gosvāmī questions because they wanted to know how the people in the age of Kali can be helped. Thus Sūta Gosvāmī spoke the *Śrīmad-Bhāgavatam* for the ultimate and eternal benefit of all.

Character Descriptions

Have you heard of any of these characters before? What do you know about them? Share what you know with a partner, then read the descriptions below.

Śukadeva Gosvāmī

- He is a great devotee of Kṛṣṇa.
- He is the son and disciple of Śrīla Vyāsadeva.
- He spoke the *Śrīmad-Bhāgavatam* to Mahārāja Parīkṣit in seven days.
- He stayed in the womb of his mother for sixteen years.
- In the spiritual world he is Śrīmatī Rādhārāṇī's parrot.

Mahārāja Parīkṣit

- He is a famous king, who was cursed to die in seven days.
- He went to the River Ganges to meet Śukadeva Gosvāmī and heard the *Bhāgavatam* for his remaining seven days.
- He was protected by Lord Kṛṣṇa while in the womb of his mother and was therefore known as Viṣṇu Rāta.
- His name, Parīkṣit, means "examiner" because he would study all human beings in his search for that Personality Whom he saw before birth.
- He is the grandson of Arjuna and Subhadrā.
- He is the son of Abhimanyu and Uttarā.

Sūta Gosvāmī

- Sūta Gosvāmī was present when Śukadeva Gosvāmī recited the *Śrīmad-Bhāgavatam* to Parīkṣit Mahārāja.
- His full name is Ugraśravā Sūta.
- His father, Romaharṣaṇa Sūta, was killed by Lord Balārāma for being disrespectful.
- Sūta Gosvāmī took the place of his father as speaker in the sacrificial arena.

Śaunaka Ṛṣi

- He is a devotee of Lord Kṛṣṇa.
- He led the sages' inquiries to Sūta Gosvāmī about what he had heard when Śukadeva Gosvāmī originally recited the *Śrīmad-Bhāgavatam* to Parīkṣit Mahārāja.

Sequence of Events

Draw pictures on flash cards for each of the event sequences below and keep them in your pocket for when you are on the go. Your flash cards can be used as memory cards or story prompts to enact the pastime. Can you tell the whole story by just looking at your drawings? Try mixing them up and putting them back in the correct order. How fast can you do it?

1. Vyāsadeva pays his respectful obeisances to Lord Kṛṣṇa.
2. The sages gather in Naimiṣāraṇya to perform a great thousand-year sacrifice for the pleasure of the Lord and His devotees.
3. The sages offer Sūta Gosvāmī a seat and glorify him.
4. The symptoms of the people of Kali are described.
5. The sages ask Sūta Gosvāmī about Lord Kṛṣṇa and how the people of Kali-yuga can be helped.
6. The sages accept Sūta Gosvāmī as the captain of their ship.

Related Verses

Let's memorize these beautiful verses. As you learn the verses, you can engage your hands and body by thinking of movements that help to express each word in the verse. Another fun way to memorize *slokas* is to draw simple images or symbols as you speak. Remember to recite these *slokas* from your heart!

Bṛhan-nāradīya Purāṇa

harer nāma harer nāma
harer nāmaiva kevalam
kalau nāsty eva nāsty eva
nāsty eva gatir anyathā

In this age of Kali, there is no other way, there is no other way, there is no other way for self-realization other than chanting the Holy Name, chanting the Holy Name, chanting the Holy Name of the Lord.

Bhagavad-gītā 4.34

tad viddhi praṇipātena
paripraśnena sevayā
upadekṣyanti te jñānaṁ
jñāninas tattva-darśinaḥ

Just try to learn the truth by approaching a spiritual master. Inquire from him submissively and render service unto him. The self-realized souls can impart knowledge unto you because they have seen the truth.

Understanding the Story

Now it's time for you to check how well you understood the story by answering these multiple-choice questions. (Answers at the end of the chapter.)

1. Who is the author of the *Śrīmad-Bhagavatam?*
   a) Śukadeva Gosvāmī
   b) Śrīla Vyāsadeva
   c) Lord Kṛṣṇa
2. Who did he first offer his obeisances to?
   a) Śukadeva Gosvāmī
   b) Śrīla Vyāsadeva
   c) Lord Kṛṣṇa
3. What do we need in order to understand *Śrīmad-Bhagavatam?*
   a) A pure heart
   b) Lots of money
   c) An intelligent mind
4. What has been likened to delicious fruits?
   a) The sages
   b) Śukadeva Gosvāmī
   c) *Śrīmad-Bhagavatam*

5. What made the fruits even tastier?
   a) Spoken by Śukadeva Gosvāmī
   b) Heard by the sages
   c) Written by Vyāsadeva
6. What was the name of the forest where the sages gathered?
   a) Vṛndāvana
   b) Jhārikhaṇḍa
   c) Naimiṣāraṇya
7. Who recited the *Śrīmad-Bhagavatam* to the sages of Naimiṣāraṇya?
   a) Sūta Gosvāmī
   b) Śukadeva Gosvāmī
   c) Śrīla Vyāsadeva

8. Why was he chosen to recite it?
   a) He was the eldest, bossiest, and all other sages feared him.
   b) No other sage was brave enough to be the leader because they weren't intelligent enough.
   c) He was the eldest and sinless; he knew all the scriptures and the other learned sages as well.
9. Why was he blessed?
   a) He was well-behaved and submissive to his spiritual master.
   b) He was well-behaved and listened to his mother and father.
   c) He wasn't well-behaved, but listened to the sages.
10. How did the sages describe the people of Kali-yuga?
    a) They are lazy, misguided, short-lived, argumentative, unlucky, and always disturbed.
    b) They are happy, peaceful, and dedicated to helping others.
    c) They are well-behaved, honest, hard-working, and always looking for Kṛṣṇa.
11. What did the sages ask Sūta Gosvāmī?
    a) How to avoid the people of Kali-yuga.
    b) How to help the people of Kali-yuga.
    c) How to fight the people Kali-yuga.
12. What topic did the sages want to hear about?
    a) Lord Kṛṣṇa and the demigods.
    b) Lord Kṛṣṇa and the people of Kali-yuga.
    c) Lord Kṛṣṇa and His adventures.
13. When the sages got tired of hearing the stories of Lord Kṛṣṇa, what did they do?
    a) They went to sleep.
    b) They ate something.
    c) They never got tired.
14. What is the ship that crosses the difficult ocean of Kali?
    a) Sūta Gosvāmī
    b) Hearing about Kṛṣṇa
    c) Jaladūta
15. Who is the captain of the ship?
    a) Sūta Gosvāmī
    b) Śukadeva Gosvāmī
    c) Lord Kṛṣṇa

Higher-Thinking Questions

Now it's time to deepen your understanding of Chapter 1 by delving into Śrīla Prabhupāda's purports for this chapter and reflecting upon the following questions.

1. Sūta Gosvāmī was a good, qualified speaker of *Śrīmad-Bhāgavatam*. Why is it important to hear from the right person?
2. This chapter is called "Questions by the Sages." What questions did the sages ask? What are good questions? If you were among the sages in the Naimiṣāranya forest, what questions would you ask Sūta Gosvāmī? (Name at least three.)
3. What is more purifying, the water of the Ganges or the association of pure devotees? Explain why.
4. How did the sages of Naimiṣāraṇya show their compassion? What does true compassion mean?
5. What activities did Kṛṣṇa perform that are human-like? What activities did Kṛṣṇa perform that are superhuman?
6. What does sacrifice mean? Describe the different sacrifices for the different ages.
7. Why is *Śrīmad-Bhāgavatam* referred to as the "mature fruit" of Vedic knowledge?

ACTIVITIES

In this section you will find many exciting things to do! They will get you thinking, moving, drawing, acting, and most importantly, having loads of fun!

Action Activities . . . to get you moving!

VISIT YOUR LOCAL BOTANICAL GARDENS

Description: This activity can be done with a partner or in a group. Read through the description of Nārada Muni's travels while heading north. Visit your local gardens, perhaps a botanical or wooded section, and discuss some of the beautiful sights and sounds Nārada must have encountered on his travels.

You can play a quick memory game while out there by thinking of something Nārada Muni saw while he was traveling north. For example, you could say "While Nārada Muni was traveling north he went past/saw . . . some dangerous forests."

Then your partner/group member will repeat what you said and add something else. For example: "While Nārada Muni was traveling north he went past/saw . . . some dangerous forests and animal farms," etc.)

See if you can remember 6 or more things.

SCAVENGER HUNT IN THE FOREST & LORD IN THE HEART

Description: This activity can be done with a partner or in a group. Design a heart with a picture of Kṛṣṇa inside. Then take it with you to a forest of wooded trees. One person will hide the heart, while the others try to find it. You can extend this activity by making it into a treasure hunt with pre-prepared clues and hide each of the letters of Nārada Muni's name.

What a fun outing! End with a little *harināma* to benefit the insects and wildlife.

Analogy Activities . . . to bring out the scholar in you!

ILLUSIONS

"Śrī Vyāsadeva says herein that the manifested internal potency is real, whereas the external manifested energy, in the form of material existence, is only temporary and illusory like the mirage in the desert. In the desert mirage there is no actual water. There is only the appearance of water. Real water is somewhere else. The manifested cosmic creation appears as reality. But reality, of which this is but a shadow, is in the spiritual world. Absolute Truth is in the spiritual sky, not the material sky. In the material sky everything is relative truth." (Purport 1.1.1)

Instructions: For fun with lights and shadows, experiment with the position of an object, or the angle of the light source or the brightness of the light source and see what happens to the shadows. For fun with sun and shadows, go outdoors and discuss how sunlight creates shadows with various objects such as trees, houses and cars.

Resources: Any object, torch, dark room.

Learning Activity:
Children should be able to . . .
- Discuss how things are not what they seem.
- Begin to understand that the world we live in is a shadow of the spiritual world.

Prompt Questions:
- What happens if we move the object closer to the light? Further away from the light?
- Can the shadow exist without the object? Discuss further.
- Hold up a glass of water or a sandwich in the light – now try to quench your thirst or satisfy your hunger using only the shadow. Is it possible?

Conclusion (discuss):
- The shadow cannot exist without the original object. Similarly, this world that we live in wouldn't exist without the spiritual world.
- Further explore the point that the material world looks like it can make us happy, but that the real happiness is in the spiritual world.

MAKING A TREE COLLAGE

"Lord Viṣṇu is just like a great tree, and all others, including the demigods, men, Siddhas, Cāraṇas, Vidyādharas and other living entities, are like branches, twigs and leaves of that tree. By pouring water on the root of the tree, all the parts of the tree are automatically nourished. Only those branches and leaves which are detached cannot be so satisfied. Detached branches and leaves dry up gradually, despite all watering attempts. Similarly, human society, when it is detached from the Personality of Godhead, like detached branches and leaves, is not capable of being watered, and one attempting to do so is simply wasting his energy and resources." (SB 1.1.4 Purport)

Instructions: Collect small branches, twigs and a variety of leaves from outdoors. Make a big tree collage by glueing the items collected onto a large sheet of paper or card. Draw some roots in the lower part of the collage. Go through old *Back to Godhead* magazines or research online to find an image of Lord Viṣṇu, some demigods and some humans. For the humans you could also cut out old family photos. Glue the pictures and photos on different branches of the tree and put Lord Viṣṇu at the roots or on the trunk. Alternatively, you could draw the pictures.

Resources: Leaves, twigs, card/paper, glue, pictures.

Learning Activity:
Children should be able to . . .

- Explain why a plant only grows if its roots are watered.
- Understand that by serving Kṛṣṇa, everything else is taken care of.
- Discuss how we can only be happy when connected to Kṛṣṇa in loving service.

Prompt Questions:

- How do the leaves grow?
- Can the leaves on the ground still grow?
- Can we human beings be happy without Kṛṣṇa? Can our family be happy without Kṛṣṇa? Can our friends be happy without Kṛṣṇa?

Conclusion (discuss): No one can be happy without being connected to Kṛṣṇa.

GROW YOUR OWN PLANT

Instructions: Choose three of the same plants in three different pots. Water each plant every day for a week in the following different ways. Water only the roots in the first pot. Spray only the branches in the second pot and spray only the leaves in the third pot.

Resources: Plant pots, spray bottle, soil, and seeds or seedlings.

Prompt Questions:

- Which plant is growing well? Which are not?
- Why is that?

Conclusion (discuss):

- If we water the tree roots, the leaves will grow. In the same way, if we serve Kṛṣṇa, then everything and everybody will be taken care of.
- No one can be happy without satisfying or pleasing Kṛṣṇa.

Artistic Activities

. . . to reveal your creativity!

BHĀGAVATAM BOAT

Description: Make a boat! You can either research how to create an origami boat or you can make it in your own style by using different household articles such as a yogurt pot for the boat base, a triangular piece of paper as a sail and a popsicle stick to hold the sail in place. Fill up a basin with water and place your boat inside. Create waves to show how in the age of Kali it is not easy to cross over the material ocean, but if you have a good captain like Suta Goswami, you can easily cross over it.

Follow-up Discussion: Kali-yuga is compared with the ocean, the *Śrīmad-Bhāgavatam* with a boat, and Sūta Gosvāmī to the captain, traveling from the shore of the material world to the shore of the spiritual world. Discuss how when you have a good boat and a qualified captain, you can cross the difficult "ocean" of Kali.

AGE OF KALI – DRAW IT!

Description: Quick fire "draw it" game. One person will draw the symptoms of the people of Kali-yuga, and a partner can guess what it is.

Follow-Up Discussion: The people of Kali-yuga have short lives, are quarrelsome, lazy, misguided, unlucky and are always disturbed. How can these qualities make it difficult for people to understand the real aim of life?

SACRIFICIAL FIRE

Description: Build a mini fire *yajña* using matchboxes. (But don't use the matches!) Decorate with mini-fruits, moulded out of marzipan or clay. Decorate the boxes and make a fire with some red, orange and yellow tissue paper. You can also decorate with tiny leaves as well.

Follow-Up Task: Investigate the significance and purpose of fire sacrifices. How have they been used in the past? How are they being used in the present day?

ŚUKA THE PARROT

Description: Print the parrot picture (see **Resource 1** at the end of this chapter) and color it in. Now draw and color in a picture of a ripe mango. Then, carefully cut out the parrot. Pin the parrot onto a pinboard, using a single pin. Now add the mango to the pinboard close to the beak of the parrot. You can now create a pecking motion to show the parrot pecking at the fruit.

Follow-up Discussion: The mango is Vedic knowledge, and the parrot is Śukadeva Gosvāmī. Śukadeva not only repeated the knowledge without changing it, but he also made it easier to understand for all types of people by making it sweeter (like a parrot who cuts a ripened mango with his beak, thus enhancing its sweet flavor).

Critical Thinking Activities

. . . to bring out the spiritual investigator in you!

VERSE MIND MAP

Description: Let's gain a deeper understanding of the first verse of this chapter. An effective technique is to use a mind map (also known as a spider diagram) to help you understand all of the aspects of the verse. Try to put it in your own words. A mind map is a diagram used to visually outline information. It is often created around a single word or text, placed in the center, to which related ideas, words and concepts are added. You can find many examples on the internet. Your central bubble can be "SB 1.1.1 – Lord Kṛṣṇa the Absolute Truth." Then you can branch off by adding the qualities of Lord Kṛṣṇa that are mentioned in the verse.

Can you think of any examples to support the attributes of Lord Kṛṣṇa that it discusses? For example – "By Him even the great sages and demigods are placed into illusion" – Lord Brahmā was put into illusion when he tried to steal the cowherd boys.

ŚRĪMAD-BHĀGAVATAM INVESTIGATION

Description: This is a great way to start off your study of *Śrīmad-Bhāgavatam*!

You will be researching the glories of the *Śrīmad-Bhāgavatam*. You can use the following prompts to guide you:

- How and when was it first spoken?
- Which personalities glorify it?
- Which scriptures glorify it?
- What do the scriptures/personalities say about the *Śrīmad-Bhāgavatam*?

Now you can present your research in any, or all, of the following:

- A leaflet about the glories of the *Śrīmad-Bhāgavatam.*
- A mind map that visually shows the glories.
- Compile an index of verses in glorification of the *Śrīmad-Bhāgavatam.*
- Cut out a flower shape and write *Śrīmad-Bhāgavatam* in the middle in fancy writing. Then select the quotes/verses that you are most inspired by and write them on each petal.

WHAT IS THE NEED FOR ANY OTHER SCRIPTURE?

Description: Verse 2 discusses how the *Śrīmad-Bhāgavatam* is sufficient in itself for God realization.That means that there's no need for any other scripture. But there are so many other scriptures!

Conduct an investigation about various scriptures of the world. Use the following prompts to guide you:

- Who wrote it? Why did they write it?
- What religion considers it sacred?
- How did it originate?
- Where did it appear? In which country and place?
- When was it written/spoken?
- What process does the scripture recommend for God realization?
- What is the overall conclusion/essence of the scripture?
- Is the message still completely intact? How was that ensured?
- Do you agree with the conclusion of the sages of Naimiṣāraṇya?

Compile your research in a report. The basic structure for a report should be:

- Title and suitable headings
- Introduction
- Findings/outcomes
- Conclusion/recommendations

Remember to include:

- Factual information
- Formal language
- Diagrams and charts

Introspective Activities

. . . to bring out the reflective devotee in you!

TRUE COMPASSION

Description: The sages of Naimiṣāraṇya were so compassionate that they sat down to perform a 1000-year sacrifice!

What is compassion? How do you express your compassion? Do you wish that you were a little bit more compassionate?

Write an action plan about how you can be more compassionate in all aspects of your life. You can start off by writing down a list of things that you already do to show compassion to everyone around you. Then look at the list to see if your compassion will give the person eternal benefit or temporary benefit. For example, if you show compassion to the birds by feeding them bread, this may be temporary. However, if the bread is Kṛṣṇa *prasādam*, then that benefit will be eternal.

Try to steer your compassionate efforts to give those around you eternal benefit.

SPIRITUAL GOALS

Description: So you have taken on a wonderful challenge of studying the *Śrīmad-Bhāgavatam*! Now it's time to focus on setting goals so that you can get the most out of your study.

You can use the prompts below to guide you:

- What do you hope to get out of this? What is your main goal?
  - — To show off how much I know.
  - — To worship the Lord in His form as the *Śrīmad-Bhāgavatam*.
  - — So that my parents will stop bugging me.
  - — To gain a systematic understanding of the *Śrīmad-Bhāgavatam*.
- What steps do you have to take to get there?
  - — Read for a fixed amount of time each day.
  - — Study a chapter each week.
  - — Fill in a chart to monitor your progress.

- Effective goals are SMART:
  - **S** – Specific
  - **M** – Measurable
  - **A** – Attainable
  - **R** – Relevant
  - **T** – Time-bound

Now that you have set your goals, compose a prayer to the *Śrīmad-Bhāgavatam* asking for the Lord to reveal Himself to you through your study.

DEAR DIARY

Description: Monitor your progress of the study of *Śrīmad-Bhāgavatam* by keeping a diary, addressing the Lord. Make sure that at the end of each day you write down what you have learned and how it will impact the way you lead your life.

Quick-Fire Activities

. . . to bring out the all-rounder in you!

Music

Before devotees read *Śrīmad-Bhāgavatam* they chant a beautiful invocation with prayers to the guru and Kṛṣṇa to invoke auspiciousness and request their blessings to enter into *Śrīmad-Bhāgavatam*. This is followed by the mantra *oṁ namo bhagavate vāsudevāya*. There are many different ways to beautifully chant and sing these auspicious mantras. Learn them all by heart and sing them to your favorite melody or meter.

History

A quick-fire project on lifespan! In previous ages, according to the Vedic scriptures, what were the lifespans of humans? What does material science say about lifespans years ago and now? What factors affect lifespan?

Preaching

To start your study of *Śrīmad-Bhāgavatam*, begin with a mini book marathon of your own! Aim to distribute as many First Cantos of *Śrīmad-Bhāgavatam* as you can. Be imaginative! Distribute to friends, family, on *harināmas*, at festivals, in libraries and hotels – you could even try at your doctor's or dentist's offices! As you study this first chapter, you can take notes of all the good spiritual reasons why reading this *Śrīmad-Bhāgavatam* is the best thing that anyone can do with their life. *Saṅkīrtana-yajña kī jaya!*

Geography
A quick-fire project on mango trees! Do you know what one looks like? Discover how and where they are best grown all over the world, and what is the sweetest variety. Complete this quick-fire project with a mango feast!

Math
A quick-fire mathematical memory activity! How many chapters are there in the entire *Śrīmad-Bhāgavatam*? How many cantos are there? How many chapters are there in each canto? How many verses are there altogether? If you have learned all the numbers, you can start with the chapter names. A fun way to help yourself remember these is to make your own memory cards with the canto and chapter number on one side of the card, and the name and a simple illustration from the chapter on the other side. You can play all sorts of memory games with these cards and learn the whole *Bhāgavatam* while you're at it!

Cooking
Orange jelly boats! Cut 4 oranges in half and scoop out the fruit, keeping the peel "cups" whole. Fill your cups with your favorite vegetarian jelly or ice cream. Once the filling is set, add a little sail to your boats made from cut-out triangular pieces of paper stuck to toothpicks. Place your boats on a tray decorated as the ocean of Kali, with waves made from piped whipped cream, which can be colored blue with food coloring if you wish. Don't forget to add Sūta Gosvāmī as the captain of your boat!

Writing Activities . . . to bring out the writer in you!

POETIC LANGUAGE – USING SIMILES

Description: A *simile* compares two different objects, using the words *like* or *as,* to create a picture in the reader's mind. For example, *Her hand felt as cold as ice.* Or, *Kṛṣṇa's eyes are like lotus petals.*

Exercise (oral or written): For each of the objects or actions below, make a comparison of your own. Using the five senses of sight, sound, touch, taste, and smell will help you make comparisons. What does it look like? Feel like?

1) The fruit of the *Bhāgavatam* tastes as sweet as______________.
2) Sūta Gosvāmī's *vyāsāsana* was as soft as________________.
3) The lazy Kali-yuga people are like ______________.
4) The quick flow of the sacred Ganges waters is like_____________.

WORD SEARCH

Description: Create your own word search! Start off by identifying some key words that appear in this chapter. Then write them in the tables at the bottom of **Resource 2** and the grid above the tables. Once you have arranged them in a grid, remember to make a copy so that you have the solution. Finally, you can fill in random letters around your words so that they are hidden. Give the word search to a friend to solve.

RHYMING WORDS

Description: Circle the word in each line across that DOES NOT rhyme with the other two words.

1)	hear	fear	trip
2)	glories	Kali	stories
3)	bliss	sages	ages
4)	sacrifice	soul	vice

READING & COMPREHENSION 3-2-1

Description: After reading this chapter, use this reading strategy to summarize key events, to focus on important points, and to clarify areas that you may be unsure about.

3 things you found out   2 interesting things and why   1 question you still have

NAIMIṢĀRAṆYA WORD GAME

Description: What other words can you make out of the phrase "The sages of Naimiṣāraṇya"? Write the phrase "The sages of Naimiṣāraṇya" on a whiteboard/sheet of paper. Use either individual letters or letters that are together to make up new words (examples: is, name, there, etc.) Print the words on the whiteboard/paper. You can play this with a partner or in a group. The winner is the one who ends up with the most number of words.

KEYWORDS

- Define the following keywords from the story.
- Use each word in a sentence (either in oral or written form).
- Complete a New Word Map* at the back of the book for any new words.

KEYWORD	DEFINITION
illusion	
pure	
scripture	
hear	
explain	
essence	
sacrifice	
submissive	
attentive	

*A New Word Map is a visual tool useful for exploring new words. A New Word Map template is located at the back of this book for photocopying.

CROSSWORD

ACROSS

1) The place where the *Śrīmad-Bhāgavatam* was recited by Sūta Gosvāmī
2) One of the symptoms of people in the age of Kali
3) Another symptom of people in the age of Kali
4) Bathing in the ____________ once is not as purifying as being in contact with sages who have taken complete shelter of Kṛṣṇa's lotus feet.
5) In which chapter are the above points discussed in the *Śrīmad-Bhāgavatam*?

DOWN

6) Who was leading the sages?
7) The fruit that the *Bhāgavatam* is compared to
8) People in the age of Kali can be immediately freed upon doing what (even unconsciously)?
9) One of Sūta Gosvāmī's key qualities that allowed his spiritual masters to bestow great blessings upon him

Theatrical Activities

. . . to bring out the actor in you!

VERSE MIME

Description: Choreograph a mime based on verses SB 1.1.1 and SB 1.1.2. Miming involves using your facial expressions, arms, hands and whole body to communicate.

Play some background music or have someone read the verses. You can set up a simple stage and wear a costume or a mask if you like.

Research more about miming and use a mirror to practice getting your technique perfect. Then perform your mime to an audience!

KALI-YUGA ROLE-PLAY

Description: Quick-fire role play the symptoms of *Kali-yuga*: lazy, misguided, unlucky, always disturbed and arguing. The class/a partner can guess which characteristic you are role-playing.

THE ŚRĪMAD-BHĀGAVATAM

Śrīmad-Bhāgavatam is as bright as the sun.
Listen to it carefully and your hearts will be won.

Deep in the forest of Naimiṣāraṇya,
The sages were having a spiritual *yajña*.

Spoken to Śaunaka and the sages,
Of Kṛṣṇa's pastimes throughout the ages.

Sūta Gosvāmī told the history,
Of Śukadeva's narration of Kṛṣṇa's mysteries.

Listen attentively to the stories,
And grow in love of Kṛṣṇa's glories.

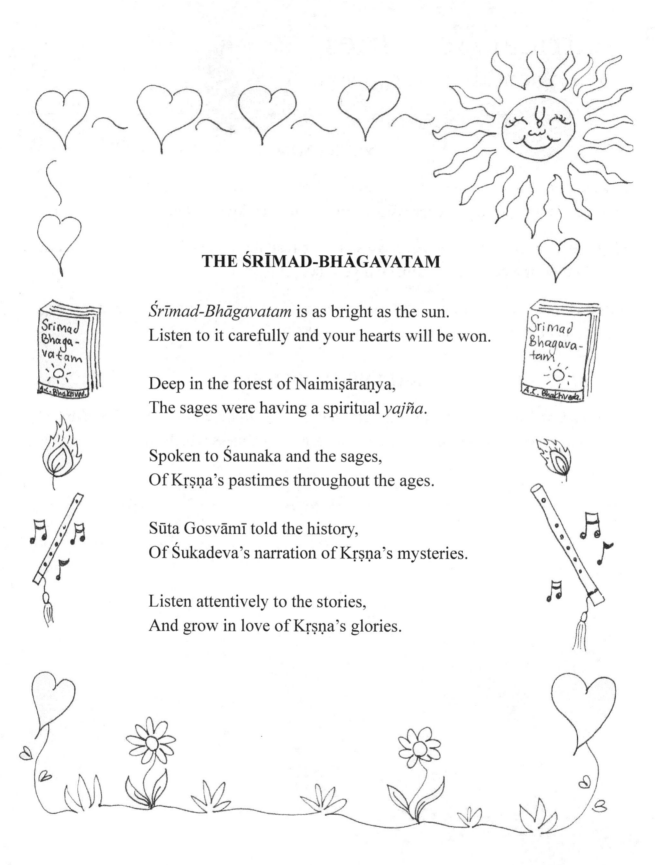

CREAM OF THE VEDAS

Many great devotees came
To hear from Śukadeva
As he spoke *Śrīmad-Bhāgavatam*
In just seven days!

Śukadeva Gosvāmī spoke
The *Śrīmad-Bhāgavatam*
To King Parīkṣit while Sūta
Gosvāmī listened on . . .
The sages of Naimiṣāraṇya
Came to discuss about Kṛṣṇa
They asked Sūta Gosvāmī to speak
Śrīmad-Bhāgavatam so sweet!

Many years had passed, but Sūta
Still knew word for word
Śukadeva's *Śrīmad-Bhāgavatam*
Just as he heard!

That cream of the *Vedas* flowed
Straight from Sūta's heart
In eighteen thousand verses he taught
How to love Kṛṣṇa!

Śrīla Prabhupāda came to us
In *paramparā*
To give us *Bhāgavatam* like
Śukadeva and Sūta!

Prabhupāda gave his life
To give us *Bhāgavatam*
So, as we turn each page,
we will learn
How to love Kṛṣṇa!

On and on around the world
The *Bhāgavatam* has gone
If you want to help Prabhupāda
Please spread this message on!

Hare Kṛṣṇa Hare Kṛṣṇa
Kṛṣṇa Kṛṣṇa Hare Hare
Hare Rāma Hare Rāma
Rāma Rāma Hare Hare

Resource 1

ŚUKA THE PARROT

Resource 2

WORD SEARCH

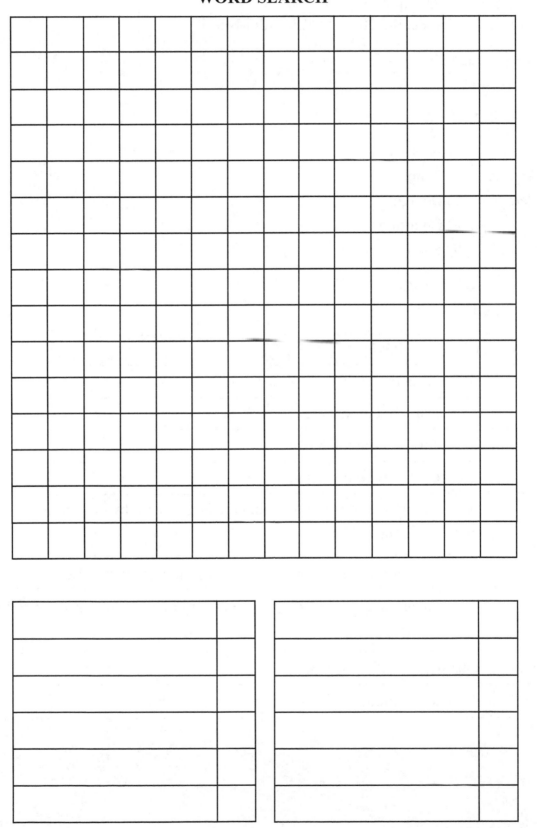

ANSWERS

"Understanding the Story" (pages 7–8)

1b, 2c, 3a, 4c, 5a, 6c, 7a, 8c, 9a, 10a, 11b, 12c, 13c, 14b, 15a

Rhyming Words (page 20)

trip, Kali, bliss, soul

Crossword (page 22)

ACROSS	DOWN
1) Naimiṣāraṇya	6) Śaunaka
2) Misguided	7) Mango
3) Lazy	8) Chanting
4) Ganges	9) Submissive
5) One	

Keywords (page 21)

KEYWORD	DEFINITION
illusion	Something that appears real, but is not
pure	Free from contamination
scripture	Holy books about God
hear	The act of perceiving sound
explain	A statement that makes something understandable by describing it in greater detail
essence	The core nature of something or the most important qualities of it
sacrifice	To make an offering to God (the sages' offering was hearing and talking about God)
submissive	Obedient, ready to learn
attentive	To listen without getting distracted

2

Divinity and Divine Service

Story Summary

Sūta Gosvāmī smiled at the sages with great satisfaction. He was very pleased with their questions. The sages had asked Sūta Gosvāmī what the people of Kali-yuga should do to become fully happy in the heart.

"This is a perfect question, thank you!" exclaimed Sūta Gosvāmī. "But before I reply to you, I must offer my obeisances to Śukadeva Gosvāmī. He left his home even while his father Vyāsadeva was running after him crying, 'Oh my son!' But he didn't care because he had tasted the secret of the scriptures and, due to his great compassion, really wanted to share it with those who were struggling in this material world."

After pausing for a moment, Sūta Gosvāmī continued, "Actually, anyone who is about to recite the *Śrīmad-Bhāgavatam* should also offer obeisances to Nārāyaṇa, Nara-Nārāyaṇa Ṛṣi, mother Sarasvatī (the goddess of learning) and Vyāsadeva, the author of the *Śrīmad-Bhāgavatam*."

"Do you know why your question is so worthy?" asked Sūta Gosvāmī to the sages. "It is because it has to do with Lord Kṛṣṇa and, therefore, is relevant for the ultimate benefit of everyone. Only topics related to Lord Kṛṣṇa can make one completely content. Listen carefully as I explain ..."

The sages all leaned forward in anticipation. They really wanted to know what the people of Kali should do to become fully satisfied in their hearts. With so many Vedic scriptures, the poor, unfortunate people of Kali-yuga might get confused and not understand them properly. So Sūta Gosvāmī began to explain, "You see, the people of Kali-yuga perform so many different activities just so they can be happy, but they never actually become satisfied because they forget to nourish their souls!" The sages knew what Sūta Gosvāmī meant. They understood that the body is like a cage and the soul is like a bird. The people of Kali-yuga try to polish and clean the cage as much as they can to make the bird happy, but the bird isn't happy because he is just hungry for food!

"To feed our souls and become really happy," Sūta continued, "we must lovingly serve and glorify Lord Kṛṣṇa. All day and all night, whatever we do, we must think, 'I want to do this to please Lord Kṛṣṇa; I want to do that to please Lord Kṛṣṇa; if I do this, will it please Lord Kṛṣṇa?' So if the people of Kali-yuga always think in this way and never stop thinking about what will please Lord Kṛṣṇa, then they will feel so overjoyed, and their hearts and souls will be dancing in happiness. They should desire a healthy life so that they can fully focus on the Lord. Therefore, everything you do, do it to please Lord Kṛṣṇa!"

"Let me explain more," continued Sūta Gosvāmī to the sages. "You see, if we always hear about Kṛṣṇa, talk about and remember Him, worship Him and always serve His dear devotees, we will begin to feel something very special happening in our hearts. We will begin to feel, 'I love Kṛṣṇa! I just want to serve Him always! All I want is to hear His glories and His messages!' At that moment, Lord Kṛṣṇa who is situated in everyone's heart as the Supersoul, will clean our unclean hearts of all those unwanted, selfish desires that say, 'I want this, and this, and this, for ME! And I want it right now!'"

The sages understood that, though the desire to want things was very hard to get rid of, with the special help and mercy of the Lord anything was possible. In fact, all that troubled the hearts of the people of Kali-yuga could be destroyed simply by regularly hearing the *Bhāgavatam* and serving the Lord's pure devotees. In this way loving service to Lord Kṛṣṇa takes over in the heart, and replaces all the undesirable things such as foolishness and inactivity that are due to the influence of passion and ignorance. Devotional service is so exciting and enlivening that the devotee, when in the mode of pure goodness, becomes completey happy.

Sūta Gosvāmī continued, "Lord Kṛṣṇa will personally scrub, and scrub, and scrub until our hearts are left squeaky clean and filled with happiness. Then, when we serve Lord Kṛṣṇa with our clean hearts, without envy, respecting everyone; the tight knot that binds us to this material world will immediately be cut and, all of a sudden, we will be free. This is why devotees like to lovingly serve Kṛṣṇa. It's so exciting and it brings our souls back to life!"

Key Messages

- Look them up in your *Śrīmad-Bhāgavatam.*
- Put them in your own words to help you memorize them.
- Discuss each one further.
- Apply them in your life.

Theme	References	Key Messages
Offering obeisances.	1.2.2 1.2.3 1.2.4	By offering obeisances to Lord Kṛṣṇa and the devotees, who are the representatives of the Lord, we recognize and appreciate that they are guiding us as they give us transcendental knowledge in the form of the *Śrīmad-Bhāgavatam* so that we can understand Kṛṣṇa.
The purpose of human life is self-realization, not material advancement.	1.2.6 1.2.13 1.2.8 1.2.9 1.2.10	The human form of life is very valuable so we need to make sure that we use it wisely and don't waste this rare opportunity. If we just use our life to perform material activity, then we are just wasting our time, as it won't benefit us spiritually.
Devotional service & the four-step secret to success.	1.2.6 1.2.14 1.2.22	There are four main devotional practices that are very powerful. They are hearing about, glorifying, remembering and worshiping the Lord. By performing these we can actually become freed from all our past sinful habits and advance very quickly in devotional service
Service leads to eagerness to hear.	1.2.12 1.2.16 1.2.18	This eagerness to hear is a gift that is given to us when we serve the pure devotees of the Lord. When we become eager to hear, Lord Kṛṣṇa, Who is sitting in our hearts, acts from within by purifying our hearts and gives us knowledge so that we may easily go back to Him.
The Lord helps us when He sees us trying.	1.2.17 1.2.21 1.2.34	The Lord, Who is sitting in our hearts, personally takes charge of cleaning our hearts when He sees that we are eager to know about Him and serve Him. Although it is very difficult to get rid of selfish desires, when the Lord helps, the whole process becomes easy.
The three modes of material nature.	1.2.19 1.2.20 1.2.23 1.2.34	It is possible to understand Kṛṣṇa when we are freed from the modes of material nature: goodness, passion and ignorance. We should rise to the platform of the mode of pure goodness to get to the stage of devotional service, which is above the three material modes.

Sequence of Events

Remember your flash cards!

1. Sūta Gosvāmī is pleased with the questions from the sages about how the people of Kali-yuga can be helped.

2. He prepares to speak by paying obeisances.

3. The unfortunate people of Kali-yuga must utilize the human form of life for their eternal spiritual benefit.

4. When we hear and talk about, and also remember and worship Lord Kṛṣṇa, all of our selfish desires will disappear.

5. Kṛṣṇa personally cleans our hearts when we hear about Him and serve the devotees.

6. We become free from the influence of material energy in the form of the material modes and become completely pure.

Related Verses

- Remember to use your body and mind to help you to memorize these.
- Don't forget your drawings too!

Śrīmad-Bhāgavatam 1.2.6

sa vai puṁsāṁ paro dharmo
yato bhaktir adhokṣaje
ahaituky apratihatā
yayātmā suprasīdati

The supreme occupation [dharma] for all humanity is that by which men can attain to loving devotional service unto the transcendent Lord. Such devotional service must be unmotivated and uninterrupted to completely satisfy the self.

Śrīmad-Bhāgavatam 1.2.17

śṛṇvatāṁ sva-kathāḥ kṛṣṇaḥ
puṇya-śravaṇa-kīrtanaḥ
hṛdy antaḥ-stho hy abhadrāṇi
vidhunoti suhṛt satām

Sri Kṛṣṇa, the Personality of Godhead, who is the Paramātmā [Supersoul] in everyone's heart and the benefactor of the truthful devotee, cleanses desire for material enjoyment from the heart of the devotee who has developed the urge to hear His messages, which are in themselves virtuous when properly heard and chanted.

Understanding the Story

Now it's time to check how well you've understood the story with these questions. (Answers at the end of the chapter.)

1. Was Sūta Gosvāmī pleased with the sages' question?
2. What did the sages ask?
3. Who did he offer obeisances to first?
   a) The sages
   b) Vyāsadeva
   c) Śukadeva Gosvāmī
4. Anyone who is about to speak *Śrīmad-Bhāgavatam* should offer obeisances to which of the following?
   a) Vyāsadeva
   b) Nārāyaṇa
   c) Nara-Nārāyaṇa Ṛṣi
   d) Mother Sarasvatī
   e) All of the above

5. The people of Kali-yuga perform so many different activities just so they can be happy, but they never actually become happy because they forget to feed their
   a) dogs
   b) souls
   c) children
6. To feed our souls and become happy we must
   a) lovingly serve Lord Kṛṣṇa
   b) lovingly serve ourselves
   c) lovingly serve the demons
7. Everything we do, we must do it to please
   a) ourselves
   b) our friends
   c) Lord Kṛṣṇa
8. When will Kṛṣṇa clean our unclean hearts? When we
   a) hear about Him
   b) talk about Him

c) remember Him
d) worship Him
e) always serve His devotees
f) all of the above

9. What will we be left with?
   a) Happy and clean hearts
   b) Unclean hearts
   c) Sad and lonely hearts
10. If we respect everyone with our new happy, good hearts, what will happen?
   a) The tight knot that binds us to the material world will be tightened and tangled more.
   b) The tight knot that binds us to the material world will be cut free.
   c) There will be more tight knots binding us to the material world.

Higher-Thinking Questions

Now it's time to deepen your understanding of Chapter 2 by delving into Śrīla Prabhupāda's purports for this chapter and reflecting upon the following questions.

1. The Story Summary points out that people in the age of Kali-yuga do so many things to become happy, so many things to please their *bodies,* but they neglect to attend to their souls' needs. List some examples of the things people in society do to please their bodies and their minds. Discuss some problems that come about as a result of these activities.
2. What are Kṛṣṇa's three features? (See verse 1.2.11). Draw a diagram showing these three features of Kṛṣṇa and their attributes.
3. Name the three modes of material nature. Discuss the different activities in the different modes. Create a poster with three divisions representing each mode, and cut out and paste – or draw – pictures from magazines showing activities in each mode.
4. When we are eager to hear about Kṛṣṇa, how does He help us?
5. In verse 1.2.18, studying the *Śrīmad-Bhāgavatam* and rendering service to the devotees are said to be the best ways to clean one's heart. How does reading and serving devotees help clean one's heart of all the lusty desires?
6. Explain how the Lord enters into everything as the Supersoul (Paramātmā). What does He do as the Supersoul?

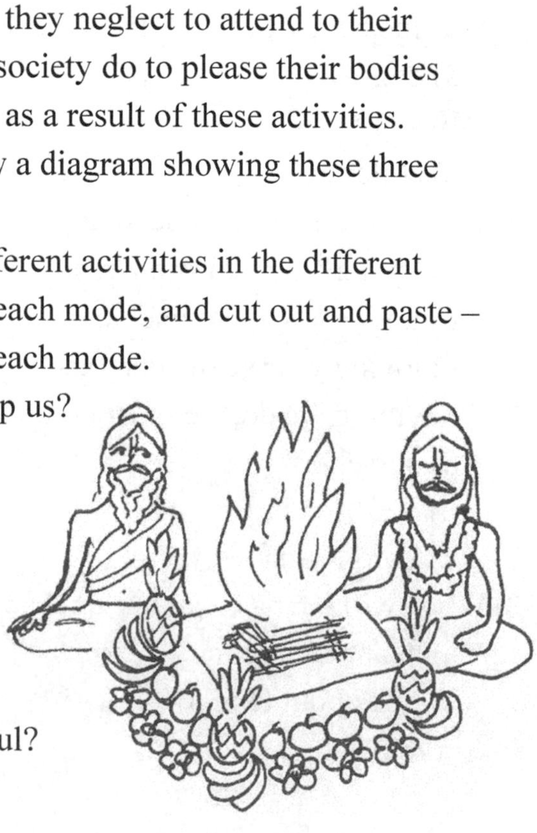

ACTIVITIES

In this section you will find many exciting things to do! They will get you thinking, moving, drawing, acting, and most importantly, having loads of fun!

Action Activities . . . to get you moving!

SECRET SEVĀ!

Description: Serving Kṛṣṇa's devotees is the key to nice devotee relationships. Write down a list of different service ideas that you could do for Kṛṣṇa and His devotees. Cut each idea into a strip of paper, fold and keep in a jar. Choose a different activity every day for a week.

Follow-up Discussion: What is described in this chapter as the result of serving devotees?

BHĀGAVATAM CLASS RESEARCH

Description: Prepare to give the *Bhāgavatam* class! The first step is to see how it is done. Go along to the *Bhāgavatam* class at your local center. Take notes while you are there about the structure of a *Bhāgavatam* class.

1. What *bhajan* is recited before it starts?
   - Do you know all of the words to the *bhajana* and the translation?
   - Do you know the accompanying *mṛdaṅga* beat or harmonium cords?

2. What prayers are recited before the class starts?
   - Do you know them and their meaning?
   - What procedure is followed for reciting the Sanskrit and English?
   - Why is the speaker's seat called a *vyāsāsana*?
   - How did the speaker end the class?

You can also hear some classes online at www.iskcondesiretree.com from different speakers – Did you find a favorite speaker?

GIVE ŚRĪMAD-BHĀGAVATAM CLASS!

Description: Plan and deliver a *Srimad-Bhāgavatam* class based upon this chapter. Choose a particular verse within the chapter to focus on and study the purport.

1. CONTEXT: Read the whole chapter – just translations, to get an idea of the context of the verse.

2. VERSE: Read the verse a few times to understand the main points. Note them down as you go along in the form of a mind map.

3. PURPORT: Read the purport a few times to understand the main points. You can extend the mind map of the verse by noting down how Śrīla Prabhupāda has expanded on each point in the purport.

4. EXAMPLES AND ANALOGIES: For each main point, look for any examples or analogies that Śrīla Prabhupāda has given. You can also make up your own that bring the philosophical point across in a way that the audience can relate to.

5. SCRIPTURES AND VERSES: Try to find any other scriptural references or verses that back up the main points.

6. PERSONAL EXPERIENCES: Think of any personal experiences that you, or a person that you know, has had to illustrate the main points. You can also refer to events in the media.

7. AUDIENCE: Make sure the content that you have prepared is appropriate for the people you are speaking to. Are the listeners primarily old? Young? Experienced devotees? Newcomers to Kṛṣṇa consciousness?

8. LIFE APPLICATION: Suggest how the main points can be applied to the audience.

9. CONCLUSION: Sum up the main points.

These are some additional points to consider while giving class:

- *Stick to the verse and purport* – Try not to go off the point; the purpose of the class must be to deepen the understanding of the text and Śrīla Prabhupāda's purport.
- *Questions* – Answer questions honestly and to the best of your ability, but don't be afraid to say "I don't know." The audience will appreciate that, more than you trying to speculate.

HEALTHY LIFE & SELF-PRESERVATION

"Life's desires should never be directed toward sense-gratification. One should only desire a healthy life or self-preservation, since a human being is meant for inquiry about the Absolute truth. Nothing else should be the goal of one's work." (SB 1.2.10)

Description: Think of some new activities that you can do to keep your body and mind healthy so that all of your focus can be directed to the real goal of life! This can be a new sport, or yoga, or anything to keep you active and healthy! Allocate yourself a day, or part of a day, to do this, and get a buddy to monitor you. How do you feel after a week of sticking to your routine?

Follow-up Activity: This chapter also discusses the three modes of material nature. Think about how a person in each mode would lead a "healthy life." Match up each mode below with the type of activity you would expect a person situated in that mode to do, by drawing a line between them.

Transcendental Mode	Very lazy; no endeavor; mostly sleeping or watching TV. No motivation to do anything.
Goodness	Sporadic endeavor; pushes themselves too much, then not at all; inconsistent in habits of eating and sleeping; goes to the gym excessively, or to zumba dance classes, or takes part in dangerous sports that may cause injury.
Passion	Maintains a healthy body and mind by eating healthy *prasāda* and regularly exercising, with a view that by looking after one's body one can serve the Lord effectively for a lifetime.
Ignorance	Steadily follows a routine and is regulated; remains determined; will do *yoga* practice and other peaceful non-strenuous activities.

Extension Task: A nutritious and balanced diet is also key to keeping healthy. Find out what types of foods are in different modes from the *Bhagavad-gītā*. Then use this information to plan out a healthy diet for yourself.

Analogy Activities
. . . to bring out the scholar in you!

THE BIRD AND THE BIRDCAGE

"The spirit soul's needs must be fulfilled. Simply by cleansing the cage of the bird, one does not satisfy the bird. One must actually know the needs of the bird himself."

(Purport 1.2.8)

Learning Activity 1 (Topic: Fun with the Bird):

Children should be able to . . .

- Describe the different needs, and identify the most important needs that animals may have.
- Discuss why people may not be happy.
- Begin to understand that the body and the mind are coverings to the spirit soul

Instructions: Visit your local zoo, farm or even the pet store. If this is not possible, find an image of a bird and birdcage (see online). Facilitate a discussion based on the prompt questions below.

Prompt Questions:

- Who is this (pointing to the bird)? What is around the bird (pointing to the cage)?
- Should we clean the cage? If we cleaned the cage would the bird be happy? What else does the bird need?
- What would happen if we cleaned the cage but forgot to feed the bird? Who is inside the cage?
- How would you feel if you had a nice house, but nothing to eat?
- What are the needs of the bird?
- Do you know what your needs are?
- What are the needs of your body? What are the needs of your soul?
- What makes you happy?
- How would you feel if you only had a bath, but you were not given any food?

Conclusion (discuss):

- The bird is happy when it has been fed water and seeds. Nothing else will make the bird happy.

- The soul is happy when it is in contact with Kṛṣṇa; that's why we sing and dance in *kīrtana* and eat Kṛṣṇa *prasāda*.

* * *

"In the Vedic literatures (*śruti*) it is said that there are two birds in one tree. One of them is eating the fruit of the tree, while the other is witnessing the actions. The witness is the Lord, and the fruit-eater is the living entity. The fruit-eater (living entity) has forgotten his real identity and is overwhelmed in the fruitive activities of the material conditions, but the Lord (Paramātmā) is always full in transcendental knowledge." (Purport 1.2.31)

Learning Activity 2 (Topic: Two Birds in a Tree):
Children should be able to . . .

- Begin to understand the concept of the soul and the Supersoul.
- Explain why the Lord is compared to the witness in the above analogy.

Resources: Card, tissue paper (optional), internet and printer, PVC glue, play dough (search online for homemade recipes) or marzipan, scissors, pens, pencils.

Instructions: On the internet, find, print, and cut out images of a small and large bird. Using play dough or marzipan, mold some of your favorite fruits. On a large sheet of cardstock draw or paint a tree with branches. For a creative touch, bring the tree to life with green tissue paper or pipe cleaners. Using PVC glue, attach the fruits to the tree and attach the smaller bird nearer to the large bundles of fruit, and the larger bird a little further away, maybe near the top of the tree.

Prompt Questions:

- What is the little bird doing?
- What is the big bird doing?
- Does the little bird know that the big bird is watching?
- Kṛṣṇa is like the big bird, He sits in our hearts and always sees everything that we do. So we are never alone as He is always with us.

Conclusion (discuss):

- Even if the little bird is busy eating the fruit, the big bird will always watch and look out for the little bird.
- Kṛṣṇa is like the big bird. He sees and knows everything. He is our best friend.
- Even if we can't see Kṛṣṇa, Kṛṣṇa can always see us.

Artistic Activities

. . . to reveal your creativity!

CLEAN HEARTS & DIRTY HEARTS – WALL HANGINGS

Description: On cardstock, make two hearts. On one heart, place a picture of Kṛṣṇa in the center with written comments around the picture on how to have a happy clean heart, such as worship Kṛṣṇa, serve devotees, serve Kṛṣṇa with love, hear about Kṛṣṇa, talk about Kṛṣṇa, and remember Kṛṣṇa. Decorate with brightly colored paint or decorative paper and other decorations of your choice. On the other heart, put the word SELF in the center and write down words and phrases that show what happens when we forget Kṛṣṇa. Decorate with dirt, dark-colored paper or paint, and even brown-colored spices to create a dirty appearance. Display both hearts so you can always check to see if you have a happy, clean heart. Make changes if you don't!

PROCESS OF PURIFICATION

Description: Read verses 1.2.14 to 1.2.21 and identify the key stages of purification of the heart that a person can go through. What does the process start with, and if executed properly, what does it result in? Use the small boxes on **Resource 1** (end of chapter) to note down the stages, and use the large boxes to draw pictures that symbolize each stage.

BHĀGAVATAM BOOK COVER

You will need: Fabric, scissors, thread, a needle, measuring tape, and of course, your copy of the *Śrīmad-Bhāgavatam!*

Description:

1. Measure the length and width of the wide-open book.
2. Cut your fabric the correct length and width of the book, allowing a 1-inch border all the way around. You will also need to allow an extra 3 inches in length on each side as a "pocket" that will be used for each side of the cover of the book to slot into.
3. Hem the short ends of the cover. Then turn the fabric over and fold the 3-inch pockets, sewing them into place. Hem the remaining fabric between the pockets.

Critical Thinking Activities

. . . to bring out the spiritual investigator in you!

MODES & DEMIGODS

"Those who are serious about liberation are certainly nonenvious, and they respect all. Yet they reject the horrible and ghastly forms of the demigods and worship only the all-blissful forms of Lord Viṣṇu and His plenary portions." (SB 1.2.26)

Description: Investigate which demigods are worshipped by those in different modes. Find out some details about each demigod such as:

- What they look like
- What their purpose is
- Who they are an expansion of
- The types of benedictions they give
- The method of worshipping them

Compile the information you find out in a mini fact file.

THREE ASPECTS OF GOD

"Learned transcendentalists who know the Absolute Truth call this nondual substance Brahman, Paramātmā or Bhagavān." (SB 1.2.11)

Description: Investigate each of the worshippers of these aspects.

- What are the worshippers called?
- What do they believe?
- What form does their worship take?
- What is their possible destination after death?
- Of the three aspects, which is the highest? Hint: Check *Bhagavad-gītā.*

Can you think of any analogies that Śrīla Prabhupāda gives to illustrate the three aspects of the Lord? Can you try to think of your own? Now identify the attributes of each of the aspects of God in **Resource 2**. Color in the attributes of Bhagavān in red, Paramātmā in orange, and Brahman in yellow.

GLORIFICATION

Description: Read and discuss verse 1.2.14 and its purport. Śrīla Prabhupāda points out that the four processes of glorifying, hearing, remembering, and worshiping are general tendencies in life. What does it mean to "glorify" someone? Who are the people glorified in modern society today? Give some examples. Draw up a chart and compare glorifying an unqualified person with glorifying the "actual object of glorification," the Supreme Personality of Godhead. What are the effects of both?

Introspective Activities

. . . to bring out the reflective devotee in you!

POWERFUL PROCESS

Description: Some of the most powerful secrets of devotional service have been given in this chapter. Now it's your turn to put the theory into practice by applying the instructions to your life, to the best of your ability, for one week.

Start by filling in the first column "Devotional Activities." The main instructions have been listed in this column. Under each heading you need to write down exactly how you personally will execute each instruction. For example under "Hearing" you could commit to hearing a lecture, hearing yourself reading a scripture aloud, or even hearing the Holy Name with greater concentration during *kīrtana* and *japa*.

When you have set your specific targets under each heading, you can start putting them into practice. Monitor yourself for a week.

(See **Resource 3**.)

OFFERING OBEISANCES

Description: Follow in the footsteps of Sūta Gosvāmī by writing some heartfelt prayers to your spiritual authority, Śrīla Prabhupāda, and the glorious personalities that Sūta Gosvāmī offered his obeisances to.

Investigate why it is important to offer obeisances and prayers. Can you think of any prayers that are usually recited before one recites or studies scriptures?

Quick-Fire Activities

. . . to bring out the all-rounder in you!

Music

Learn the *mṛdaṅga* beat and harmionium cords for the *bhajana* "Jaya Rādha Mādhava."

Geography

In which states of India are different forms of the Lord in different modes mainly worshipped? Investigate how the worship of that god became established.

Science

Śrīla Prabhupāda describes Kṛṣṇa consciousness as a very scientific process. Study verses 1.2.7–1.2.21. Try to break them down into a format of a science experiment.

- What is the hypothesis?
- What is the apparatus?
- What is the method?
- What is the result?
- What is the conclusion?

Cooking

Bird-in-a-cage soul food! Make a mixture of your favorite seeds and nuts, and lightly toast them. After they cool, mix in a selection of dried fruits and pieces of carob. Mix everything together and offer to Kṛṣṇa. This can be packaged and distributed to friends and family as a tasty, loving exchange, or kept as a nutritious snack for yourself.

Preaching

Now that you know the secrets of devotional service, don't keep them to yourself! Tell at least five people what they need to do so that Lord Kṛṣṇa will personally clean their hearts!

Out and About

Find out about the various types of knots. Remember you'll also need to know how to release them! Do you remember how to release the knot in the heart?

Technology

You will create and perform a puppet show in the drama section. Create a video of your drama and select suitable background music for it.

Writing Activities . . . to bring out the writer in you!

SUMMARY STORY

Description: Write a summary of this chapter in 100 words.

WHOSE LANGUAGE IS IT?

Description: In an animated way, retell, in another language, the process of how Kṛṣṇa cleanses the heart of the devotee who serves and hears, as stated in texts 1.2.7 to 1.2.21. It may be in your mother tongue or in a language that you are learning.

Perform before an audience of speakers of the same language. Make sure that you get their feedback about how well your choice of words accurately described the story, and how well your performance was as a whole.

WORD GAMES

Description: What other words can you make out of the phrase "Kṛṣṇa cleanses our hearts"? Write the phrase on a whiteboard/sheet of paper. Use the individual letters to make up new words (examples: sun, clean, earth, etc.) Print the words on the whiteboard/paper. If you are playing with others, the winner is the one who can come up with the most number of words in a set period of time.

READING AND COMPREHENSION 3-2-1

Description: After reading this chapter, use this reading strategy to summarize key events, to focus on important points of interest, and to clarify areas that you may be unsure about.

3 things you found out 2 interesting things and why 1 question you still have

TO OR TOO?

Description: Do you know when to use "to" and "too"? Find out the difference between them, and state examples of when each of them is appropriate. Read the following sentences, and put the right word (to or too) in the blank spaces.

1. What should the people in the age of Kali do _______ become happy?
2. Sūta Gosvāmī said, “I must offer my obeisances _______ Śukadeva Gosvāmī.”
3. Śukadeva Gosvāmī had tasted the secret of the *Bhāgavatam* and wanted everyone in this world to taste it ________!
4. Only topics having _______ do with Lord Kṛṣṇa can make one completely happy.
5. If we always hear about Kṛṣṇa, talk about Kṛṣṇa, remember Kṛṣṇa, worship Kṛṣṇa and always be the servant of His dear devotees ________, then we will begin _______ feel something very special happening in our hearts!

KEYWORDS

- Define the following keywords from the story.
- Use each word in a sentence (either in oral or written form).
- Complete a New Word Map at the back of the book for any new words.

KEYWORD	DEFINITION
remember	
talk	
serve	
worship	
about	
always	

WORD SEARCH

P	O	I	Y	T	I	E	W	Q	G	F	D	A	S
A	D	T	R	L	G	H	J	K	L	C	B	M	E
S	E	G	A	J	H	E	A	R	T	Z	X	C	R
D	V	K	O	H	Q	S	F	G	I	Q	O	K	V
F	O	S	Y	G	W	H	G	D	O	K	B	N	E
R	T	C	H	F	R	E	E	S	Y	R	E	G	F
E	E	V	J	D	A	S	D	C	H	G	I	L	C
M	E	B	Q	U	E	S	T	I	O	N	S	T	Z
E	S	K	L	H	D	V	C	A	X	Z	A	G	I
M	F	U	N	Q	H	A	P	P	Y	Q	N	D	O
B	G	J	A	O	C	V	I	J	H	K	C	S	Y
E	H	B	D	S	T	T	O	H	Q	R	E	C	H
R	J	C	L	E	A	N	Y	G	W	G	S	P	O
I	K	O	Q	W	A	S	D	F	G	E	S	T	I
O	L	N	U	R	H	E	A	R	B	D	V	C	U

HEART	
KALI	
KNOT	
DEVOTEES	
HEAR	
SERVE	

OBEISANCES	
FREE	
QUESTION	
REMEMBER	
CLEAN	
HAPPY	

Theatrical Activities
. . . to bring out the actor in you!

Perfect Questions & Perfect Answers

— A Puppet Show —

You will need . . .

A Puppet Theater
You can make your own puppet theater from things like cardboard boxes, chairs, tables, and sheets, etc.

Puppets
Puppets can be made especially for the puppet show, or toys can be dressed up to play the part of the characters. For this show, you will need puppets of Sūta Gosvāmī and the sages of Naimiṣāraṇya.

Backdrop
Paint a scenic backdrop of the Naimiṣāraṇya forest.

Lighting
Flashlights, Christmas tree lights, candles, room lights – set and change the scene as you desire.

Background Music and Sound Effects
Music and sound effects can be created from the following: Singing, making noises on cue, playing music from a CD, and finding instruments or objects around the house to make any particular sound you want.

SCENE ONE: Introduction

NARRATOR: Once upon a time, many years ago, the sages of Naimiṣāraṇya forest asked the great and powerful sage, Sūta Gosvāmī, what the people of Kali-yuga should do to become fully happy in their hearts. Sūta Gosvāmī gave such a wonderful answer to the sages, that it became famous for all time. Do you want to know what Sūta Gosvāmī said? Then please listen closely to our play to hear the answer.

SCENE TWO: Perfect Questions

SAGE 1: Wise Sūta Gosvāmī, please tell us what the people of Kali-yuga should do to become fully happy in the heart?

SAGE 2: There are so many Vedic scriptures; the people of Kali-yuga might get confused and not understand them properly!

SŪTA GOSVĀMĪ: My dear sages, thank you for your wonderful question. Do you know why your question is so nice?

SAGES: No Sūta Gosvāmī, why is that?

SŪTA GOSVĀMĪ: Because it is about Lord Kṛṣṇa! Only topics about Lord Kṛṣṇa can make us completely happy. Please listen carefully as I explain. But first, let us chant together . . .

SŪTA AND SAGES (*chanting*): *Oṁ Namo bhagavate Vāsudevāya* (call and response x3)
nārāyaṇaṁ namaskṛtya
naraṁ caiva narottamam
devīṁ sarasvatīṁ vyāsaṁ
tato jayaṁ udīrayet

(*Singing**)
Before reciting *Śrīmad-Bhāgavatam*
Four special things must always be done
To offer my obeisances
Unto these personalities!

First is to Nārāyaṇa – the supreme Lord,
Second is Nara – the best human of all!
Third is mother Sarasvatī, the goddess of learning,
And fourth is to the author, Vyāsadeva!

Hare Kṛṣṇa Hare Kṛṣṇa
Kṛṣṇa Kṛṣṇa Hare Hare
Hare Rāma Hare Rāma
Rāma Rāma Hare Hare

---

* For complete song lyrics, see end of chapter.

SCENE THREE: Perfect Answers

SAGES: Please tell us, Sūta Gosvāmī, what should the people of Kali-yuga do to always be happy in the heart?

SŪTA GOSVĀMĪ: The body is like a cage, and the soul is like a bird inside the cage. In Kali-yuga, people will try to polish and clean the cage, but will forget to feed the bird inside. If you were a bird, would you feel happy if your owner forgot to feed you?

SAGES: No! We would be starving!

SŪTA GOSVĀMĪ: So, our soul is like the bird, but this bird has a special diet. People need to feed it with loving devotional service to Kṛṣṇa and Kṛṣṇa's dear devotees. Always remember Kṛṣṇa and never forget Him! (*With emphasis*) In this way the people of Kali-yuga will feel so happy that their hearts and souls will dance with joy.

SAGES: Hari Hari bol!

SŪTA GOSVĀMĪ: This is why devotees like to serve Kṛṣṇa: it's so exciting and it brings our hearts back to life.

SAGE 1: Thank you, Sūta Gosvāmī! Just hearing you speak about serving Kṛṣṇa makes our hearts feel squeaky clean.

SAGE 2: And non-envious, too.

SŪTA GOSVĀMĪ: Kṛṣṇa is so kind that when we serve Him, He cleans our unclean hearts and fills them with happiness.

SAGES: Scrub scrub scrub!

SŪTA GOSVĀMĪ: Then, if we serve Kṛṣṇa with our fresh clean hearts, the tight knot that binds us to this material world will be cut and we'll be free! But what do we have to do?

SAGES: *Always remember KṚṢṆA and never forget Him!*

SŪTA AND SAGES: Hari Hari Bol!

SCENE FOUR: The End

NARRATOR: Thank you for watching our play.
Our request before you leave this day:

Remember Kṛṣṇa in your heart,
And today make a fresh new start!

PUPPETS & PUPPETEER: (*Bow to audience.*)

TEMPLE OF THE HEART

Before reciting *Śrīmad-Bhāgavatam,*
Four special things must always be done.
To offer my obeisances
Unto these personalities!

First is to Nārāyana – the supreme Lord.
Second is Nara – the best human of all!
Third is mother Sarasvatī, the goddess of learning.
And fourth is to the author, Vyāsadeva!

Hare Kṛṣṇa Hare Kṛṣṇa
Kṛṣṇa Kṛṣṇa Hare Hare
Hare Rāma Hare Rāma
Rāma Rāma Hare Hare

Śrīmad-Bhāgavatam – bright as the sun!
Śrīmad-Bhāgavatam – saves everyone!
Śrīmad-Bha-ga-vaaa-tam!
What should I do and what should always be done?

Think of Kṛṣṇa day and night! Alright!
Scrub your heart to make it fresh – and bright!
In your heart there's a temple, so turn on the light!
And Kṛṣṇa will dance in there with you all the time!

Hare Kṛṣṇa Hare Kṛṣṇa,
Kṛṣṇa Kṛṣṇa Hare Hare,
Hare Rāma Hare Rāma,
Rāma Rāma Hare Hare.

Resource 1

Resource 2

Resides in the Heart

Localized Aspect

Full Wealth

Overseer

Effulgence

Permitter

Light

Sat

Supreme Absolute Truth

Full Fame

Full Strength

Full Beauty

Include All 3 Aspects

Full Renunciation

Shining Rays

Sat, Cit, and Ananda

Impersonal

Yogī

Sanctions

Full Knowledge

Sat and Cit

Bhakta

Brahmavādī

Witness

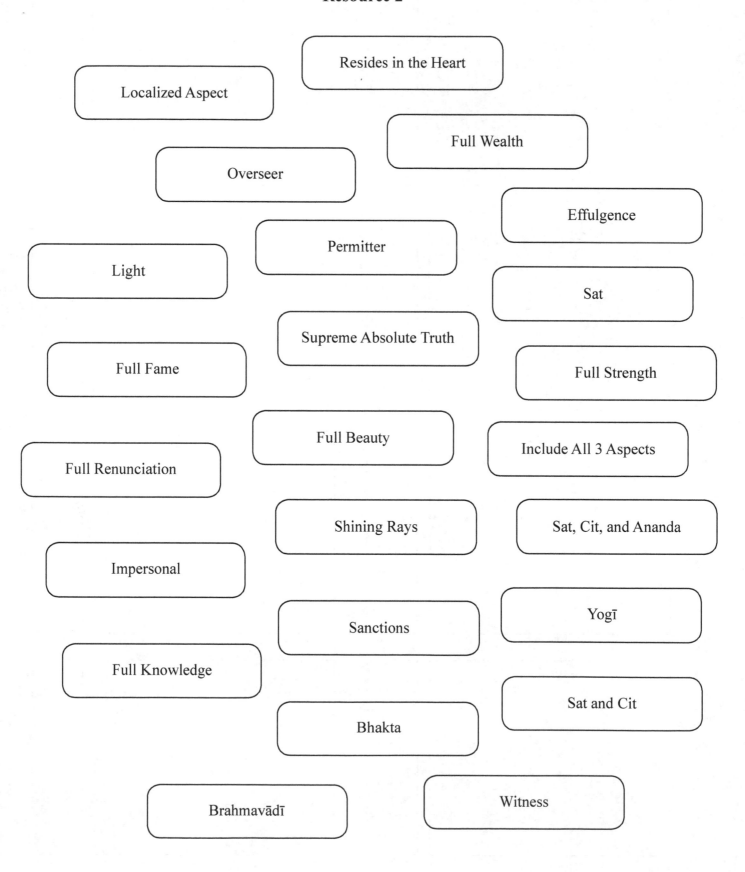

Resource 3

Devotional Activities	Monday	Tuesday	Wednesday	Thursday	Friday	Saturday	Sunday
Hear about Kṛṣṇa							
Talk about Kṛṣṇa							
Remember Kṛṣṇa							
Worship Kṛṣṇa							
Serve Kṛṣṇa's Devotees							

ANSWERS

"Understanding the Story" (pages 35–36)

1) Yes

2) What should the people of Kali do to become fully happy in the heart?

3) c, 4) e, 5) b, 6) a, 7) c, 8) f, 9) a, 10) b

To or Too? (pages 46–47)

1) to

2) to

3) too

4) to

5) too, to

Solution to Resource 2:

Brahman	**Paramātma**	**Bhagavān**
Light	Resides in the Heart	Full Wealth
Effulgence	Overseer	Full Fame
Impersonal	Permitter	Full Beauty
Shining Rays	Sanctions	Full Strength
Brahmavādī	Localized Aspect	Full Knowledge
Sat	Witness	Full Renunciation
	Yogī	Includes All 3 Aspects
	Sat and Cit	Supreme Absolute Truth
		Bhakta
		Sat and Cit and Ānanda

Keywords (page 47)

KEYWORD	DEFINITION
remember	Bring to awareness something that one has already seen or heard
talk	Give information or express feelings by using spoken words
serve	Perform duties or services for someone or something else
worship	An act of showing reverance
about	On the subject of
always	For all future time; forever

Word Search (page 48)

					I								S
	D			L									E
	E		A		H	E	A	R	T				R
	V	K									O		V
	O										B		E
R	T			F	R	E	E				E		
E	E										I		
M	E		Q	U	E	S	T	I	O	N	S		
E	S	K									A		
M			N		H	A	P	P	Y		N		
B				O							C		
E					T						E		
R		C	L	E	A	N					S		
					H	E	A	R					

3

Kṛṣṇa Is the Source of All Incarnations

Story Summary

Sūta Gosvāmī continued to speak to the sages . . .

"One day," he began, "in the spiritual world, which is far far away from here, Lord Kṛṣṇa did something very spectacular. He expanded Himself into another person. This form of Kṛṣṇa had four arms and was none other than Mahā-Viṣṇu. Now, Mahā-Viṣṇu wanted to lie down somewhere to meditate, so He looked around the spiritual world and saw the Kāraṇa Ocean."

"'Aaah! This is a nice place!' thought Mahā-Viṣṇu as He lay down on the waters of the Kāraṇa Ocean. He then half-closed His eyes and began to meditate. While lying on the Kāraṇa Ocean, Mahā-Viṣṇu, Who is also known as Kāraṇodakaśāyī Viṣṇu, saw a tiny cloud in a corner of the spiritual world. This cloud was the material sky, and just by His glance, immediately the ingredients for the material world were created, and from this many universes formed like bubbles. These bubbles came out of Mahā-Viṣṇu's skin holes and rested on His body, but His body always stays spiritual; it never becomes material like the universe bubbles."

Wouldn't this be exciting to see? All those universes on the spiritual body of Mahā-Viṣṇu. We *can* see this. Yes, Sūta Gosvāmī had told the sages this was possible if we lovingly serve Lord Kṛṣṇa and become His pure devotees; we will get the spiritual eyes to see.

Sūta Gosvāmī continued to speak:

"Mahā-Viṣṇu then entered each of these universe bubbles as Garbhodakaśāyī Viṣṇu."

"'Hmmm, these universes are just filled with darkness and space,' thought Lord Viṣṇu as He looked around, 'and there's no resting place.' So immediately, He filled each of these universes halfway with water from His own perspiration, and this became an ocean. This ocean was called the Garbhodaka Ocean."

"'Aaah! This is a nice place,' thought Lord Viṣṇu, as he lay down on the waters of the Garbhodaka Ocean. At that very moment, a lotus stem began to sprout from His navel, and a beautiful lotus flower grew at the top. Amongst the petals of the lotus flower, Lord Brahmā, the master engineer of the universe, was born. He would create everything else in the universe bubble, using Lord Kṛṣṇa's powers. This creation is maintained by Kṣīrodakaśāyī Viṣṇu, Who also enters every living being and even every atom, as Paramātmā or Supersoul."

"When the demons in this material world disturb the devotees, Lord Kṛṣṇa comes from the spiritual world as different incarnations to protect His devotees. These incarnations all come from Viṣṇu on the Garbhodhaka Ocean in the universe bubbles. Some of these incarnations are Lord Kṛṣṇa Himself, and some are saintly persons with Lord Kṛṣṇa's special powers."

"Lord Kṛṣṇa comes so many times in different forms that you can't even count how many times He comes. But the *Śrīmad-Bhāgavatam* tells us about some of them, and if we talk about these different forms of Kṛṣṇa everyday in the morning and in the evening, and lovingly serve Lord Kṛṣṇa at the same time, then we will never be miserable. You see, to become spiritually successful one must listen very carefully to these stories and ask many questions, just like you sages have, then we will start to love Him so much that we won't have to take birth in a material body again . . . do you know why? Because the *Śrīmad-Bhāgavatam* is an incarnation of Kṛṣṇa, too, and it is all-blissful and perfect, and meant for the ultimate welfare of all people. It is as brilliant as the sun and gives light to those who are blinded by the darkness of ignorance in the age of Kali. Now listen carefully as I repeat what I have heard and realized from Śukadeva Gosvāmī who spoke to King Parīkṣit, as he was about to die on the bank of the Ganges."

Key Messages

- Look them up in your *Śrīmad-Bhāgavatam.*
- Put them in your own words to help you memorize them.
- Discuss each one further.
- Apply them in your life.

Theme	References	Key Messages
Purūṣa-avatāras	1.3.1–5	Kṛṣṇa expands Himself into 3 principle forms of Viṣṇu to create the universes. First, Kāraṇodakaśāyī Viṣṇu lies down in the Kāraṇa or Causal Ocean, from His skin holes the universe bubbles appear. Within each of the universes the Lord enters as GarbhodakaśāyīViṣṇu. He is lying within the half of the universe which is full with the water from His own body. From the navel of Garbhodakaśāyī-Viṣṇu has sprung the stem of the lotus flower where Lord Brahmā appears. KṣīrodakaśāyīViṣṇu then appears to enter every living being and each atom, as well.
Līlā-avatāras	1.3.6–28	Kṛṣṇa comes in innumerable forms to perform His wonderful pastimes. He appears to protect His devotees, to kill the demons, to teach us about Him, and to attract us so that we can meditate upon His pastimes.
Kṛṣṇa is the source of all incarnations.	1.3.28	Even though Kṛṣṇa incarnates so many times, He is still the original Lord. He still remains the same Supreme Lord, just like an actor in the theater who plays many parts.
The *Bhāgavatam* is Kṛṣṇa.	1.3.40 1.3.43	In this difficult age of Kali-yuga, Kṛṣṇa has incarnated as the book *Śrīmad-Bhāgavatam*. The *Śrīmad-Bhāgavatam* is not only a book about Kṛṣṇa, it is Kṛṣṇa Himself. One can worship this incarnation of Kṛṣṇa by carefully hearing and discussing about the Lord as stated in the *Bhāgavatam*. One should also ask questions to find out more, just as Parīkṣit Mahārāja and the sages did.

Sequence of Events

Remember your flash cards!

1. The appearance of the *puruṣa-avatāras* at the beginning of creation is described.

2. A description of 22 *līlā-avatāras,* beginning with the four Kumāras and ending with Kalki *avatāra,* is given.

3. Lord Kṛṣṇa, as the source of all incarnations, is explained.

4. The *Śrīmad-Bhāgavatam* is described as the literary incarnation of the Lord.

Related Verses

- Remember to use your body and mind to help you to memorize these.
- Don't forget your drawings too!

Śrīmad-Bhāgavatam 1.3.28

ete cāṁśa-kalāḥ puṁsaḥ
kṛṣṇas tu bhagavān svayam
indrāri-vyākulaṁ lokaṁ
mṛḍayanti yuge yuge

All of the above-mentioned incarnations are either plenary portions or portions of the plenary portions of the Lord, but Lord Śrī Kṛṣṇa is the original Personality of Godhead. All of them appear on planets whenever there is a disturbance created by the atheists. The Lord incarnates to protect the theists.

Bhagavad-gītā 4.7

yadā yadā hi dharmasya
glānir bhavati bhārata
abhyutthānam adharmasya
tadātmānaṁ sṛjāmy aham

Whenever and wherever there is a decline in religious practice, O descendant of Bharata, and a predominant rise of irreligion – at that time I descend Myself.

Understanding the Story

Now it's time for you to check how well you understood the story with these questions. (Answers at the end of the chapter.)

1. Who did Lord Kṛṣṇa expand Himself into?
    a) Mahā-Viṣṇu
    b) Lord Śiva
    c) Lord Brahmā
2. In which ocean did Mahā-Viṣṇu lie down to meditate?
    a) Garbhodhaka Ocean
    b) Kāraṇa Ocean
    c) Material Ocean
3. Where do the universe bubbles rest?
    a) The heavenly planets.
    b) On Lord Brahmā's body.
    c) On Mahā-Viṣṇu's body.
4. What flower grew from Garbhodakaśāyī-Viṣṇu's naval?
    a) Rose
    b) Lotus
    c) Campaka
5. Where do the incarnations of Lord Kṛṣṇa come from?
    a) Garbhodakaśāyī-Viṣṇu
    b) Mahā-Viṣṇu
    c) Lord Brahmā
6. Where does the water that Garbhodakaśāyī-Viṣṇu lies on come from?
    a) The rain
    b) His own perspiration
    c) His tears
7. How many times does Lord Kṛṣṇa come?
    a) Twice in a *yuga*
    b) Innumerable times
    c) Ten times
8. To become free from miseries, how often should you recite the appearances of the Lord in His various incarnations?

a) Once in a week
b) In the evening before bed
c) In the morning and the evening

9. When the demons disturb the devotees, what does Lord Kṛṣṇa do?
10. Does Kṛṣṇa always come Himself or does He sometimes give His special powers to a saintly person?
11. Who breathes many universes from the pores of His skin in creating the material world?
12. Who is Lord Brahmā and what does he do?

Higher-Thinking Questions

Now it's time to deepen your understanding of Chapter 3 by delving into Śrīla Prabhupāda's purports for this chapter and reflecting upon the following questions.

1. What is stated that we should do in the morning and in the evening? What is the result?
2. Kṛṣṇa's incarnations are either His plenary portions or portions of His plenary portions. ("Plenary" means complete.) With the example of the candle and flame discuss how Kṛṣṇa is always the Original Person and never loses any of His powers when he incarnates.
3. Why do some souls want to leave the spiritual world? What does Lord Kṛṣṇa do when some souls insist on leaving?
4. Discuss at least three reasons why the Lord comes to the material world.
5. What does this chapter title, "Kṛṣṇa is the Source of All Incarnations," mean?
6. If you were to meet one of the incarnations listed, Who would it be and why?

ACTIVITIES

In this section you will find many exciting things to do! They will get you thinking, moving, drawing, acting, and most importantly, having loads of fun!

Action Activities . . . to get you moving!

UNIVERSAL BUBBLES

Lesson Objectives: Understand the creation of the material universes as coming from Mahā-Viṣṇu's breathing.

Description: Blow some universal bubbles! Mix together liquid soap, water, and glycerine in a container. Look at the picture of Mahā-Viṣṇu with the universes coming from His body. These universes are like bubbles coming from Mahā-Viṣṇu. Blow some bubbles (especially big ones if you have a big blower). The person blowing can be Mahā-Viṣṇu, and others can run around Mahā-Viṣṇu, catching "universes," or looking for the biggest universes.

CHURNING TUG-OF-WAR

Description: Churn like the demigods and demons did when Lord Kūrmadeva appeared! Form two groups of even numbers. One side will be the demigods and the other side will be the demons. To make it really fun, the demons can dress in black and draw moustaches on their faces, and the demigods can dress colorfully. The demons will hold one side of a thick rope while the demigod group holds the other side. When a signal is given, both sides will pull the rope as hard as possible to see who wins!

Analogy Activities

. . . to bring out the scholar in you!

THE CREAM OF THE VEDAS

"It is compared to the cream of the milk. Vedic literature is like the milk ocean of knowledge. Cream or butter is the most palatable essence of milk, and so also is *Śrīmad-Bhāgavatam*, for it contains all palatable, instructive, and authentic versions of different activities of the Lord and His devotees." (SB 1.3.41 Purport)

Children should be able to . . .

- Understand how to get the cream of the milk.
- Begin to explore why the *Bhāgavatam* is compared to the cream or butter.

Resources: bowls, spoons, crushed ice, ice cream, crushed watermelon, water, glasses, pens and paper, refrigerator.

Instructions: With a spoon, mix together in a bowl the crushed ice and crushed watermelon. Put the mixture into individual glasses and refrigerate. Next, with a spoon, mix together in another bowl some soft ice cream and crushed watermelon. Put the mixture into individual glasses and refrigerate. Offer both preparations to Kṛṣṇa. Once offered, first try the ice/melon mixture. Then try the ice cream/melon mixture.

Prompt Questions (ask the children):
(After tasting the ice/melon mixture)

- Did you like the taste of that bowl of icy fruit?
- Describe the taste. Was it sweet? Was it creamy?
- Try to remember this taste.

(After tasting the ice cream/melon mixture)

- Did you like the taste of the ice cream?
- Describe the taste. Was it sweet? Was it creamy?
- Try to remember this taste.
- Which was your favorite, the ice fruit or the ice cream?

Conclusion (discuss): The cream is the tastiest – it has the best part. In the same way, *Śrīmad-Bhāgavatam* has the best part of all the *Vedas*.

Artistic Activities

. . . to reveal your creativity!

CREATION MOBILE

You Will Need: Cardboard, Mahā-Viṣṇu picture (**Resource 1**), glitter, glue, aluminum foil, colored paper, two sticks, string/wool, scissors.

Description: Create a hanging mobile, depicting the creation of the material universes with Mahā-Viṣṇu at the center.

1. Photocopy and color in the picture of Mahā-Viṣṇu.
2. Draw and cut out round shapes as universes from the colored paper.
3. Glue all onto cardboard.
4. Decorate with glitter, aluminum foil, colored paper, or any other decorations.
5. Make a hole in each image.
6. Tie some string or wool through each hole.
7. To make the frame, find two sticks and place one over the other to create a cross, and then tie the sticks together.
8. Now hang Mahā-Viṣṇu from the center of the sticks and hang the universes on the middle and ends of the sticks. (Four universes per stick = eight universes in total.)
9. Hang from the ceiling.

INCARNATION POSTER

Learning Objective:

- Gain knowledge of a specific incarnation.
- Begin to understand how color can represent moods and ideas.

Description: Choose one of the incarnations of the Lord from the chapter. Paste or draw a picture of the incarnation on paper.

1. Using the descriptions from **Resource 2**, and your own research of the incarnations, discuss the key features (special powers) of each incarnation, and the reason for His appearance. Write these descriptions in simple form – single

words or short sentences – anywhere on the poster. (For example: Vāmana = fame.)

2. Decorate the space around the incarnation. Think about how color can be used to portray mood or ideas. (For example: red = angry; green = peace, etc.) How can color help to show a particular incarnation's special features or qualities?

Critical Thinking Activities

. . . to bring out the spiritual investigator in you!

QUIZ TIME

Description: Create an Avatāra Quiz! Collect facts about the incarnations mentioned in this chapter. You can use **Resource 2** to help you. This is a great game to be played with a group of people. You can organize different levels of questions from Level 1 (easiest), Level 2 (moderate), and Level 3 (hardest). Award points to the team that answers the most questions correctly.

AVATĀRA DEBATE

Description: Some people claim to be an incarnation. How can you prove that someone is or isn't an incarnation of the Lord? Set up a debate with a fictional god. Both sides will have to do some research to prove their side. The debate can be structured like this:

1. Begin with the pro "incarnation" side speaking first for five to seven minutes, introducing their arguments.
2. Repeat step number 1 for the opposing side.
3. Give three minutes to confer.
4. Begin the rebuttals with the opposing side and give them three minutes to speak.
5. Repeat step 4 for the pro side.

AVATĀRA MEMORY GAME

Description: Test your memory with this fun game. It can be played with a partner or in a group. One person will start by saying, "When Lord Kṛṣṇa incarnated, He came as

Matsya." The next person will continue by repeating the incarnation already mentioned and adding one more incarnation, for example, "When Lord Kṛṣṇa incarnated, He came as Matsya, then Kūrma." See if you can remember all of them in the correct order!

INCARNATION JUMBLE

Description: Three incarnations have been jumbled up in **Resource 3**. Find out who They are and identify all of the boxes that are related with the pastime of Their appearances, by choosing three different colors and coloring in the boxes.

Introspective Activities
. . . to bring out the reflective devotee in you!

PRAYER

Description: Which is your favorite incarnation? Why? Write a prayer to your favorite incarnation. You can put verse SB 1.3.29 into practice by reading the pastime of His appearance in the morning and in the evening for a week. You can also dedicate all of your activities during the week to Him.

ŚRĪMAD-BHĀGAVATAM

Description: Wow, can you believe that *Śrīmad-Bhāgavatam* is actually an incarnation of the Lord Himself? Write down a list of ways that you can worship this wonderful incarnation. Make sure that they are practical ideas that can be done. Now put them in order of priority. When you have your plan sorted, you can buddy-up with someone so they can see how you are progressing. Remember that even when all of the incarnations mentioned in this chapter appeared, not everyone took advantage of Them. You are so fortunate that *Śrīmad-Bhāgavatam* has appeared, and that you can take advantage of this most merciful incarnation in this lifetime.

VĀMANA DISCUSSION

Learning Objective: Discuss a range of important messages from the pastime and give examples to show understanding.

Description: "One should be satisfied with whatever he achieves by his previous destiny, for discontent can never bring happiness. A person who is not self-controlled will not be happy, even with possessing the three worlds." (SB 8.19.24)
Read and discuss the description of Lord Vāmana given in **Resource 2**. You may also wish to look up SB 8.19. 21–24 for further information on the pastime, and then discuss verse 24 and the points below:

Points for Discussion:
- Everything in this world belongs to Kṛṣṇa.
- We should take care of things that we get.
- Be satisfied and happy with what we have.
- There are many more people in the world with less than what we have.
- Be grateful for what we have and use it nicely.
- Share these things with our friends.

Quick-Fire Activities
. . . to bring out the all-rounder in you!

Music
Learn the Daśāvatāra Stotra *bhajana.* You can also take this opportunity to pray to the Lord in His different Līlā-avatāras.

Health and Safety
Learn how herbs are good for you and what their healing properties are.

Cooking
1. Universal rolled fruit balls! Create the entire Vedic universe out of sweets!
   2 cups mixed dried fruits
   2 cups raw mixed chopped nuts and seeds
   ⅓ cup raw sesame seeds
   Mix together in a food processor, then roll into balls!
2. Create Lord Dhanvantari's nectar by blending together your favorite fruits to make a delicious fuit smoothie!

Preaching
Pick three different incarnations and analyze Their pastimes to find out key morals. Tell three people about how they can apply these morals to their lives.

Technology
Create a powerpoint presentation about the Lord's different incarnations. Try to make it really dramatic with suitable background music.

History
Using Vaiṣṇava resources, do some research into the Vedic version of how we came to be, versus Darwin's theory of evolution and the Big Bang Theory. How do they compare to the understanding of *Śrīmad-Bhāgavatam*?

Writing Activities . . . to bring out the writer in you!

KṚṢṆA'S QUALITIES

Adjectives: Adjectives are words that describe *nouns*. They make what we say or write more interesting. Kṛṣṇa, the source of all incarnations, has sixty-four main attributes (qualities) that He has in full. His expansions or incarnations have some percentage or portion of these qualities.

Exercises (oral or written):

1. Use each of the following *adjectives*, describing Kṛṣṇa's qualities, in a sentence: beautiful, young, strong, intelligent, grave, grateful, heroic, gentle, truthful
2. Choose two or three of these qualities and think of some pastimes in which Kṛṣṇa shows these qualities.

PASTIME

Description: Pick an incarnation of your choice and write the full story of Their appearance in your own words.

INCARNATION WORD JUMBLE

Description: Unjumble the words below to reveal the incarnation!

JUMBLED	UNJUMBLED
URARPASAMA	
ANVANTADHRI	
PIAALK	
ALKIK	
ADANAR	
MAKUR	
AMVAAN	
ARUAKMS	
RAAHVA	
DHBAUD	
MRAA	
TAMYSA	

CONNECTIVE WORDS

Connectives are words that link sentences together or make a sentence longer.
Learning Objective: To extend sentences and use connective words.
Task: For each sentence, select a joining word from gray area below, and then finish the sentence in your own words. You will usually add a comma before the connective word, unless it is at the beginning of the sentence. The first one is done for you as an example (the added part is underlined).

and	so	but	when	because

1. Mahā-Viṣṇu wanted to lie down somewhere in the universe and meditate, **so** He found the Kāraṇa ocean and lay down.
2. Bubbles came out of Mahā-Viṣṇu's pores and rested on His body________________
____
3. Mahā-Viṣṇu saw the universes were filled with just darkness and space, with no resting place________________________________
____
4. ____, Lord Kṛṣṇa comes as His different incarnations to protect His devotees.
5. Some of the incarnations are Lord Kṛṣṇa Himself ________________________
____
6. We will never be miserable, nor will we take birth again in this material world, if we listen to stories from the *Śrīmad-Bhāgavatam* ________________________
____

KEYWORDS

- Define the following keywords from the story.
- Use each word in a sentence (either in oral or written form).
- Complete a New Word Map at the back of the book for any new words.

KEYWORD	DEFINITION
Lord	
form	
creation	
universe	
world	
incarnation	
material	

CRYPTOGRAM

Directions: At the top there is a KEY that lists all the letters from A to Z with a box below. Each of the letters has a corresponding number. Below the KEY is a secret phrase. Each blank has a number beneath it. Fill in the letters that correspond to the numbers below the blanks to solve the phrase.

A	B	C	D	E	F	G	H	I	J	K	L	M	N	O	P	Q	R	S	T	U	V	W	X	Y	Z
10	19	8	22	25	11	6	24	26	5	17	1	20	16	4	9	7	12	3	18	13	15	2	14	23	21

T H E _
18 24 25 3 13 9 12 25 20 25 25 16 5 4 23 25 12 4 11 10 1 1

_ _
3 10 8 12 26 11 26 8 25 3 10 8 8 25 9 18 25 22 18 24 25

_ _ _ _ _ _ _ _ _ _ _ _ _ _ _ _ _ _
26 16 8 10 12 16 10 18 26 4 16 4 11 10 19 4 10 12

Theatrical Activities

. . . to bring out the actor in you!

AVATĀRA CHARADES

Description: Act out the main characteristics or pastime of an incarnation while a partner or group tries to guess who it is.

DRAMA

Description: Pick an incarnation and write a drama about Him. Use the points below to guide you:

Setting

- Decide where the scene will take place.
- Write an introduction that describes the place. You can have the narrator describe the scene.

Characters

- Decide who the characters will be.
- Write a short description of each character.
- Keep the number of main characters as small as possible.
- Give the characters distinctive features.

Story

- Know the story before you begin.
- Have the different scenes in mind.
- The dialogue, or the narrator, has to tell the story.
- Keep the story line simple.

Layout

- Set the scene (Write a short paragraph).
- Start a new line each time a new character speaks.
- Put the name of the speaker in a left hand margin, followed by a colon (e.g. Brahmā:)
- Give instructions to the character in brackets (*often in italics*). (e.g. Opening the door to let sages in.) The words in parentheses are <u>not</u> spoken.

MAHĀ-VIṢṆU SONG

My name is Mahā-Viṣṇu, I'm lying down
In the Kāraṇa ocean, with disc and crown,
Lotus, conch and golden mace,
Sleeping soundly in outer space.

Universe bubbles come from My skin,
I create the worlds to rid souls from sin.
From Me comes Garbhodakaśāyī Viṣṇu,
From His navel a lotus grew.

Lord Brahmā was born from there,
Approaching the Lord with humble prayer,
To give him the power to create
men and demigods small and great.

Lakṣmīdevī takes her seat
At His transcendental feet.
Kṣīrodakaśāyī Viṣṇu then appears,
To enter the universal spheres.

Every single atom He then pervades,
As the Supersoul at everyone's aid.

So these are the Viṣṇus one, two, three,
Kṛṣṇa expansions, to set us free!

THE AVATĀRA SONG

(Based on Jayadeva Gosvāmī's *Daśāvatāra Stotra*)

Who's that swimming in the water,
With a long horn pulling a little boat?
Who's that swimming in the water,
Who came to keep the *Vedas* afloat?
Who came to keep the *Vedas* afloat?

Matsya! Hari Hari Bol!

keśava dhṛta-mīna-śarīra,
jaya jagadīśa hare!
jaya jagadīśa hare!
jaya jagadīśa hare!

Who's that lying in the ocean of milk,
With Mandara Mountain churning on His back?
Who's that lying in the ocean of milk,
Who has a hard shell for His back?
Who has a hard shell for His back?

Kūrma! Hari Hari Bol!

keśava dhṛta-kūrma-śarīra,
jaya jagadīśa hare!
jaya jagadīśa hare!
jaya jagadīśa hare!

Who's that fighting Hiraṇyākṣa?
With a long snout and two sharp, curled tusks,
Who's that fighting Hiraṇyākṣa?
Who lifted the earth from the Garbhodaka?
Who lifted the earth from the Garbhodaka?

Varāha! Hari Hari Bol!

keśava dhṛta-śūkara-rūpa,
jaya jagadīśa hare!
jaya jagadīśa hare!
jaya jagadīśa hare!

Who's that fighting Hiraṇyakaśipu,
With wonderful claws and a very loud roar!
Who's that fighting Hiraṇyakaśipu,
Who came to save Prahlāda Mahārāja?
Who came to save Prahlāda Mahārāja?

Nṛsiṁhadeva! Hari Hari Bol!

keśava dhṛta-narahari-rūpa,
jaya jagadīśa hare!
jaya jagadīśa hare!
jaya jagadīśa hare!

Who took big steps, one, two, three!
With a water pot and *japa* beads?
Who took big steps, one, two, three!
Over earth and the universe then, Bali?
Over earth and the universe then, Bali?

Vāmanadeva! Hari Hari Bol!

keśava dhṛta-vāmana-rūpa,
jaya jagadīśa hare!
jaya jagadīśa hare!
jaya jagadīśa hare!

Who's that holding a powerful axe?
With *kṣatriya* arms and a *brāhmaṇa* thread!
Who's that holding a powerful axe?
Who came to teach the *kṣatriyas* respect?
Who came to teach the *kṣatriyas* respect?

Paraśurāma! Hari Hari Bol!

keśava dhṛta-bhṛgupati-rūpa,
jaya jagadīśa hare!
jaya jagadīśa hare!
jaya jagadīśa hare!

Who's that holding a golden bow
With lotus eyes and greenish skin?
Who's that holding a golden bow
With Sītā, Lakṣmaṇa, and Hanumān?
With Sītā, Lakṣmaṇa and Hanumān?

Rāma! Hari Hari Bol!

keśava dhṛta-rāma-śarīra,
jaya jagadīśa hare!
jaya jagadīśa hare!
jaya jagadīśa hare!

Who's that holding a mighty plough?
With whitish skin and reddish eyes!
Who's that holding a mighty plough?
Who plays with Kṛṣṇa all the time?
Who plays with Kṛṣṇa all the time?

Balarāma! Hari Hari Bol!

keśava dhṛta-haladhara-rūpa,
jaya jagadīśa hare!
jaya jagadīśa hare!
jaya jagadīśa hare!

Who came to teach compassion?
Meditating under a Bodhi tree,
Who came to teach compassion?
To every living entity!
To every living entity!

Buddha! Hari Hari Bol!

keśava dhṛta-buddha-śarīra
jaya jagadīśa hare!
jaya jagadīśa hare!
jaya jagadīśa hare!

Who's that holding a shining sword
Riding high upon a horse?
Who's that holding a shining sword
Who comes at the end of Kali-yuga?
Who comes at the end of Kali-yuga?

Kalki! Hari Hari Bol!

keśava dhṛta-kalki-sarīra,
jaya jagadīśa hare!
jaya jagadīśa hare!
jaya jagadīśa hare!

Matsya, Kūrma, Varāha, Nṛsiṁha
Vāmana, Paraśurāma, Rāma,
Balarāma, Buddha and Kalki
Are Kṛṣṇa's ten *avatāras!*

Hare Kṛṣṇa Hare Kṛṣṇa,
Kṛṣṇa Kṛṣṇa Hare Hare!
Hare Rāma Hare Rāma,
Rāma Rāma Hare Hare!

Resource 1

Resource 2

Incarnation Character Descriptions

(*Number indicates place in appearance.*)

Kumāras (1)

Description: The Kumāras are the first four sons (Sanaka, Sanātana, Sanandana, and Sanatkumāra) of Lord Brahmā. They are born from his mind and are called *mānasa-putras*. They are young boys of about 5-years-old and they don't wear any clothes. They are empowered incarnations.

Main Features: Austerities and transcendental knowledge.

Reason for Coming: "They are the incarnations of the knowledge of the Supreme Lord, and as such they explained transcendental knowledge so explicitly that all the sages could at once assimilate this knowledge without the least difficulty." (SB 2.7.5)

Activities: Lord Brahmā told them to get married and have children, but they didn't want to. Instead they decided to stay as children forever because life gets more complicated as children grow into adults. They knew that the best thing for them to do was to become self-realized devotees. One day the four Kumāras decided to go to Vaikuṇṭha. When they arrived at the gates, they were stopped by the gatekeepers, Jaya and Vijaya, who refused to let them in. The Kumāras became very offended that they had been prevented from entering Vaikuṇṭha and cursed Jaya and Vijaya to be born on Earth as enemies of the Lord. Lord Viṣṇu then appeared and, when the Kumāras smelled the Tulasī leaves from the Lord's lotus feet, they became great devotees. Previously they were attached to the Lord's Brahman feature, but after smelling the Tulasī leaves they were attracted to the Lord's personal form and became great devotees.

References: Śrīmad-Bhāgavatam: 3.12.4–7, 3.15.12–50, 1.3.5, 2.7.5

Varāha (2)

Description: Lord Varāha is the boar incarnation. (A boar is a wild pig.) He is a direct incarnation of the Lord.

Main Features: He has tusks and a club. He appears in different millenniums, once in a white form and again in a reddish form.

Reason for Coming: He is born from the nose of Lord Brahmā when the Earth needs to be saved from the bottom of the Garbhodaka Ocean.

Activities: When the Earth falls into the Garbhodaka Ocean, Lord Varāhadeva appears from the nose of Lord Brahmā to rescue it from Pluto's region of filthy matter. Picking up something from a dirty place is done by a boar, so the Lord descends Himself to save the Earth from the bottom of the Ocean. When arising from the waters, He is challenged by the powerful demon Hiraṇyāksa. He fights with Hiraṇyāksa, using His club, and then finally kills the demon by slapping him at the root of his ear.

References: Śrīmad-Bhāgavatam: 3.13.18–33, 1.3.7

Nārada Munī (3)

Description: Nārada Muni is the chief sage among the demigods – the principle *devarṣi*. He is an empowered incarnation of the Lord, and is always broadcasting the names and glories of the Lord. He is a *brahmacārī.*

Main Features: He travels all over the universe chanting and playing his stringed instrument, the *vina*.

Reason for Coming: He comes to spread devotional service all over the cosmos and is one of the twelve Mahājanas, or great authorities on eternal truth.

Activities: He always chants the names and glories of the Lord. He acts as an instigator in many of the Lord's pastimes, such as when he instilled fear in the heart of Kaṁsa that any of Devakī's children might be his enemy. He also dispels the confusion of Vyāsadeva and tells him to write the *Śrīmad-Bhāgavatam*. He is the spiritual master of Vyāsadeva, Vālmīki, Prahlāda Mahāraja, Dhruva Mahāraja, the Pracetās, Citraketu, and many other prominent personalities in Vedic history. He is the author of the *Nārada-pañcarātra*, which is the exposition of the *Vedas,* particularly for the devotional service of the Lord.

References: *Śrīmad-Bhāgavatam*: 1.3.5, 1.3.8, 1.9.6–7

Nara and Nārāyaṇa (4)

Description: Nara and Nārāyaṇa are the Supreme Lord's dual incarnation. Nārāyaṇa is the Lord himself, and Nara is a part of the Lord. They are forms of Kṛṣṇa and Arjuna. They are the twin sons of Dharma and his wife Mūrti, the daughter of Dakṣa.

Main Features: "One of Them is of a whitish complexion, the other blackish and They both have four arms. They wear garments of black deerskin and bark, along with the three-stranded sacred thread. They carry a mendicant's waterpot, straight bamboo staff, and lotus-seed prayer beads, as well as the all-purifying *Vedas* in the symbolic form of bundles of *darbha* grass. Their bearing is tall and Their yellow effulgence, the color of radiant lightning." (SB 12.8.33–34)

Reason for Coming: "He appeared at Badarikāśrama, to favor His devotees by teaching them religion, knowledge, renunciation, spiritual power, sense control, and freedom from false ego. He engages in executing austerity until the end of this millennium." (SB 5.19.9)

Activities: Nara and Nārāyaṇa engage in self-denial to teach the people of the world how to achieve self-realization. They teach by example that *tapasya* (austerity) is the duty of the human being, and that by controlling the senses we can realize Kṛṣṇa and engage in His service.

When Nara and Nārāyaṇa were performing penances in Badarikāśrama, Indra became fearful that, with the power from Their austerities, They would take over his heavenly kingdom. Indra decided to send Cupid with beautiful women to disturb Their penances. Nara and Nārāyaṇa weren't disturbed at all by the beautiful women. Although the demigods had created an offense, Nara and Nārāyaṇa didn't get proud or angry. By Their own mystic power They showed the demigods many beautiful women. The demigods bowed their heads in shame and were very regretful of their offense. Nara and Nārāyaṇa were merciful to them by relieving them of their false pride. They then asked the demigods to choose one of the beautiful ladies, Urvaśī, to take back to heaven with them. The servants of the demigods then went back to Indra to explain to him the offense and the glories of the Lord.

References: Śrīmad-Bhāgavatam: 5.19.9, 11.4.7–16, 12.8.33–34

Kapila (5)

Description: Lord Kapila becomes the spiritual master of His own mother, Devahūti, after His father, Kardama Munī, leaves home.

Main Features: Transcendental knowledge, Sāṅkhya philosophy, *aṣṭāṅga-yoga*. "He has golden hair, His eyes are just like lotus petals and His lotus feet, which bear the marks of lotus flowers, will uproot the deep-rooted desire for work in this material world." (SB 3.24.17)

Reason for Coming: Lord Kapila appears as the son of Kardama Muni and Devahūtī for the purpose of preaching the godly Sāṅkhya philosophy, which is a combination of mysticism and devotional service. Lord Kapila speaks the Sāṅkhya philosophy, whereby the material entanglement is analyzed and found not to be the true condition of the spirit soul.

Activities: "Lord Kapila is the highest authority on *yoga*, and explained the *yoga* system known as *aṣṭāṅga-yoga*, which comprises eight different practices, namely *yama, niyama, āsana, prāṇāyāma, pratyāhāra, dhāraṇa, dhyāna,* and *samādhi.* By all these stages of practice one must realize Lord Viṣṇu, who is the target of all *yoga*. *Aṣṭāṅga-yoga* is therefore part of Vaiṣṇava practice because its ultimate goal is realization of Viṣṇu." (SB 3.28.1 pp.)

Reference: Śrīmad-Bhāgavatam: SB 3.25–33

Matsya (10)

Description: He is the fish incarnation of the Lord.

Main Features: He has a beautiful golden form and a horn. He is eight million miles long.

Reason for Coming: Matsya avatāra appears first when the *Vedas* are stolen by the demon Hayagrīva from the mouth of Lord Brahmā. He again appears in another millennium to favor His great devotee King Satyavrata, and to save everyone from an upcoming universal flood.

Activities: Once, while King Satyavrata was offering oblations of water in the river, a small fish appeared in his palms. When he threw it back into the water, the fish appeared to be frightened, and pleaded with the king to provide shelter. So the king took the fish and placed it in a jug. When he did this, the fish expanded, so the king transferred it to a well. However, it expanded again to the size of the well, so he transferred the fish to a lake. Very quickly it grew to the size of the lake, and then to the size of a reservoir into which it was placed. Even the ocean was too small to hold this ever-expanding fish. Understanding that this must be the Supreme Personality of Godhead, King Satyavrata offered his obeisances and inquired as to the reason for the Lord's

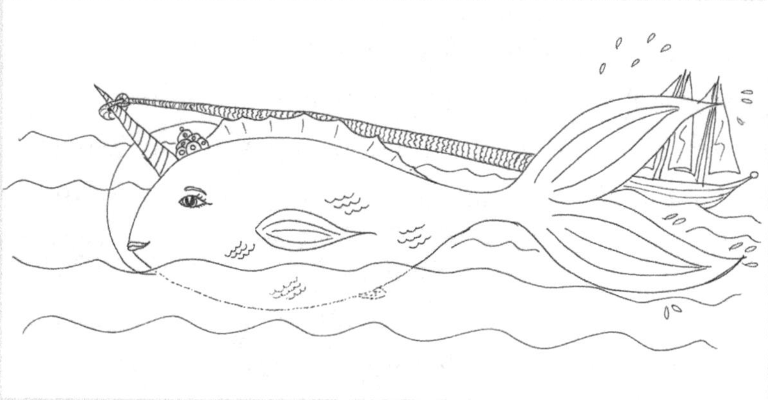

descent. The Lord instructed the king to gather together in a boat the sages, herbs, and seeds, along with each kind of living being. He would save them from an impending universal flood. It rained for seven days throughout the world, causing the great flood, and Lord Matsya appeared on the scene to rescue the king's boat. The king anchored his boat on the horn of Matsya, using Vāsuki as a rope, and offered prayers to worship Him. The Lord delivered Vedic knowledge to King Satyavrata, and He guided the boat until the rainstorm and the flooding stopped.

Reference: Śrīmad-Bhāgavatam: 8.24.5–61

Kūrma (11)

Description: He is the tortoise incarnation of the Lord.

Main features: When the Mandara Mountain rests upon Lord Kūrma's shell, He seems like a huge island, eight-hundred thousand miles wide.

Reason for Coming: To keep the Mandara Mountain steady while it is being used as a churning rod to churn the ocean of milk by the demigods and demons.

Activities: The demigods and demons uprooted Mandara Mountain to use as a churning rod and requested Vasuki, the king of the serpents, to serve as the churning rope. With

the churning, the mighty, golden Mandara Mountain began to sink slowly into the ocean of milk. The demigods and demons became discouraged and didn't know what to do. Then the Lord took the form of a tortoise, known as Kūrma-avatāra. He entered the water and held the great mountain on His back. The mountain moved back and forth with the churning motion, scratching the back of Lord Kūrma, who, while partially sleeping, was experiencing a pleasing itching sensation.

Reference: Śrīmad-Bhāgavatam: 8.5.10–25

Dhanvantari (12)

Description: Dhanvantari is the incarnation of Lord Kṛṣṇa who inaugurates the medical science. The ancient Vedic literature deals with all types of knowledge, material and spiritual. It includes a scientific system of medicine, known as *Āyurveda,* to cure the diseases of embodied living beings.

Main Features: "He was strongly built like a lion with very good features. His neck resembled a conch shell and his eyes were reddish. He looked very young and his complexion was blackish. He was garlanded with flowers and dressed in yellow garments. He was decorated with brightly polished earrings made of pearls, bangles, and various ornaments. In his hand he carried a jug filled to the top with nectar." (SB 8.8.32–33)

Reason for Coming: He comes to deliver nectar from the churning of the ocean of milk.

Activities: When the milk ocean had been churned by the demigods and demons, Dhanvantari rose slowly from the ocean, holding a jug containing nectar. When the demons saw this, they quickly snatched it from Him. The demigods became very frightened and prayed to the Lord. The Lord created a quarrel amongst the demons, and they started fighting over who should drink the nectar first. The Lord then incarnated as a beautiful female form called Mohinī Mūrti to bewilder the demons and take back the nectar for the demigods.

Reference: Śrīmad-Bhāgavatam: 8.8.31–40

Mohinī Mūrti (13)

Description: Mohini Mūrti is the form of the Lord as an enchanting beautiful woman.

Main Features: Her complexion resembles a newly-grown blackish lotus in color, and every part of Her body is beautifully balanced. She has a thin waist and wears a beautiful *sari*. She is decorated with many precious ornaments such as bangles, earrings, necklaces, and ankle bells. She smells of a wonderful fragrance and Her hair, which is extremely beautiful, is garlanded with *mallikā* flowers.

Reason for Coming: The Lord becomes the form of an extremely beautiful woman to bewilder the demons and to take back the nectar that is stolen from Dhanvantari and deliver it to the demigods.

Activities: Mohini Mūrti came after the churning of the milk ocean. When Dhanvantari rose from the milk ocean, carrying the jug of nectar, the demons snatched it. The demigods, being frightened, prayed to the Lord for help. So the Lord created an argument amongst the demons, and then appeared as Mohini Mūrti. She had an exquisitely beautiful form that completely bewildered the demons. She took the pot of nectar to distribute it amongst them all. Bewildered by Her charming ways, they accepted. However, She chose to divide it – but She tricked them by giving the nectar to the demigods. Rāhu noticed what She was doing, sat in between the demigods, and managed to take a sip of the nectar. Just then, Mohinī Mūrti killed Rāhu with Her *sudarśana* disc, cutting off his head. Rāhu's head became immortal, having been touched by the nectar.

References: Śrīmad-Bhāgavatam: 8.9 Summary, 8.8.41–46, 8.9.1–26

Nṛsiṁha (14)

Description: Nṛsiṁhadeva is the half-man, half-lion incarnation of the Lord.

Main Features: Lion-like. His nails are His weapons.

Reason for Coming: He appears from a pillar to protect His dear devotee Prahlāda, who is being bothered by his demoniac father Hiraṇyakaśipu.

Activities: The great demon Hiraṇyakaśipu performed severe austerities to become immortal because he wanted to be the absolute ruler of the universe. Hearing about his austerities, Lord Brahmā went to see him to award him a benediction. When Hiraṇyakaśipu requested the boon of immortality, Lord Brahmā explained that he could not grant this because even he is forced to die. Instead, Hiraṇyakaśipu asked that he should never be killed in the day or in the night, inside or outside, on land or in the air, by man or beast or demigod or by any weapon. Hiraṇyakaśipu thought that these boons would make it impossible for anyone to kill him.

Hiraṇyakaśipu had a son named Prahlāda who was a great devotee of Lord Viṣṇu. He became a devotee while still in the womb of his mother, because he had the opportunity to hear about the glories of the Lord from Nārada Muni. His father hated the fact that he was a devotee and so he tried to kill him in many ways. Every attempt he made failed because the Lord protected Prahlāda. Finally, in a fit of rage, Hiraṇyakaśipu himself was ready to attack his son, but Lord Nṛsiṁhadeva appeared from a pillar to save his dear devotee Prahlāda and kill his demoniac father. Hiraṇyakaśipu was not killed on the land or in the air, but on the lap of the Supreme Lord. He was not killed during the day or the night, but in the twilight. He was not killed by beast or man, but by the Lord's lotus hands. He was not killed with weapons, but with the nails of Lord Nṛsiṁhadeva. And he was not killed inside or outside, but in the doorway of the assembly hall. Thus Hiraṇyakaśipu's benediction from Lord Brahmā remained unbroken.

Reference: Śrīmad-Bhāgavatam Canto 7

Vāmana (15)

Description: Vāmanadeva is Lord Kṛṣṇa's incarnation as a dwarf *brāhmaṇa*.

Main Features: "He wore a belt made of *muñja* straw, an upper garment of deerskin, and a sacred thread. He carried in His hands a *daṇḍa*, an umbrella and a *kamaṇḍalu* (waterpot)."

Reason for Coming: Lord Vāmana appears as the son of Aditi and Kaśyapa Muni. During a period of intense conflict between the demigods and demons, the demons assume control and send the demigods into hiding. Vāmanadeva appears to return the demigods back to their posts.

Activities: As a trick to return the demigods to their administrative posts, Vāmanadeva begged three paces of land in charity from the leader of the demons, Bali Mahārāja. Bali Mahārāja was warned by his spiritual master that the *brāhmaṇa* was none other than Lord Viṣṇu Himself in disguise. However, as Bali had already offered charity to Vāmanadeva, he thought it not fair to take back his offer. When Bali granted His request, Lord Vāmana assumed such a gigantic form that, with two steps, He covered the earth and then the entire universe. For the third step, Bali Mahārāja was then pleased to receive the Lord's lotus foot on his head.

Reference: Śrīmad-Bhāgavatam: 8.18 Summary

Paraśurāma (16)

Description: Paraśurāma is Lord Kṛṣṇa's incarnation who rids the world of sinful warriors.

Main Features: He uses an axe, which was presented by Lord Śiva, to kill *kṣatriyas*.

Reason for Coming: Paraśurāma appears in Tretā-yuga to kill all the *kṣatriyas* twenty-one times, because they become arrogant and rebel against the *brāhmaṇas*.

Activities: When the powerful warrior, Kārtavīryārjuna, stole the Kāmadhenu cow from Paraśurāma's father, Jamadagni, Paraśurāma sought revenge by killing Kārtavīryārjuna. Jamadagni disapproved of this action and chastised Paraśurāma; he told him to go on pilgrimage to purify himself.

Once when Reṇukā, the wife of Jamadagni, went to the bank of the Ganges to get water, she saw the King of the Gandharvas and became attracted to him and failed to remember that the time for the fire sacrifice had passed. When she returned to the hermitage, Jamadagni understood his wife's adulterous mind and told his sons to kill their mother. But the sons did not carry out his order, so he ordered his youngest son, Paraśurāma, to kill his brothers and his mother, who had mentally committed adultery. Lord Paraśurāma killed them immediately. Being pleased with Paraśurāma, Jamadagni allowed him to ask for any benediction he liked. Lord Paraśurāma asked that his mother and brothers be brought back to life and forget that they had ever been killed by him.

Once while Lord Paraśurāma went to the forest with his brothers, the sons of Kārtavīryārjuna decided to retaliate by beheading Jamadagni. Just like cowards, they did this while the holy sage was in meditation.

Lord Paraśurāma and his brothers heard the piercing cries of his mother and returned to the *āśrama*. When Lord Paraśurāma understood what had happened he became very angry and vowed to kill the *kṣatriya* race twenty-one times. He then armed himself with an axe, and a bow and arrows, and set off to roam the earth, killing *kṣatriyas*.

Reference: Śrīmad-Bhāgavatam: SB 9.15.14–22

Lord Rāma (18)

Description: Lord Rāma is the son of King Daśaratha and Queen Kauśalyā. His wife is Sīta and His brother is Lakṣmaṇa. He has a faithful servant called Hanumān.

Main Features: Bow and arrows.

Reason for Coming: Lord Rāma appeared as an ideal King.

Activities: On the day that Lord Rāma was going to be coronated as King, he was banished to the forest by his stepmother, Kaikeyī, who wanted her own son, Bharata, to become King. Upon hearing Kaikeyī's request, he went with His chaste wife, Sītādevī, and younger brother, Lakṣmaṇa, to reside in the forest.

An evil king, named Rāvana, heard about the beauty of Rāma's wife and wanted Her for himself. So he kidnapped Sītā, with the help of a mystic, called Mārīca, who disguised himself as a golden deer.

Rāma and Lakṣmaṇa set off for Rāvaṇa's kingdom to rescue Sītā. On the way, they made alliance with an army of monkeys headed by Hanumān. Rāvaṇa lived on the is-

land of Laṅkā and, in order to get there, Lord Rāma had to cross the ocean, so He constructed a bridge over it by throwing into the water mountain peaks, which mystically floated.

Rāma and His army of monkey soldiers attacked and defeated the soldiers of Rāvaṇa, which made Rāvaṇa very angry. Rāvaṇa then tried to personally attack Lord Rāma, and so, Lord Rāmacandra fixed an arrow to His bow, aimed at Rāvaṇa's heart and killed him. After giving Vibhīṣaṇa, the brother of Rāvaṇa, the power to rule the population of Lanka, Lord Rāmacandra placed Sītādevī on an airplane decorated with flowers and returned to Ayodhyā.

References: Śrīmad-Bhāgavatam: 9.10 Summary; 9.10

Balarāma (19)

Description: Balarāma comes directly from the spiritual planet, Goloka Vṛndāvana. He is the first expansion of Lord Kṛṣṇa and is Kṛṣṇa's older brother. Balarāma is married to Revatī.

Main Features: He sometimes holds a plough. He is very expert in fighting with a club. Balarāma's complexion is whitish, like the moon, and He is very strong.

Reason for Coming: He is the son of Rohiṇī and Vasudeva. He comes to attract everyone by His wonderful pastimes as the brother of Lord Kṛṣṇa.

Activities: He performed many wonderful pastimes in Vṛndāvana with His brother, Lord Kṛṣṇa. Balarāma killed demons like Pralambāsura and Dhenukāsura and taught Duryodhana and Bhīma how to fight with a club.

"One day Lord Balarāma became intoxicated by drinking liquor and began wandering about the forest in the company of the *gopīs*. He called out to the Yamunā to come near, so He could sport in her waters with the *gopīs*. The Yamunā ignored his command, so He started to pull the Yamunā with the end of His plow, splitting her into hundreds of tributaries. The goddess Yamunā was very sorry. She fell down at Lord Balarāma's feet and prayed for forgiveness. The Lord forgave her and then entered her waters with His girlfriends to sport for some time. When they rose from the water, the goddess Kānti presented Lord Balarāma with beautiful ornaments, clothing and garlands." (*Śrīmad-Bhāgavatam* 10.65 Summary)

Reference: Śrīmad-Bhāgavatam: 10.65 Summary

Lord Kṛṣṇa (20)

Description: Lord Kṛṣṇa comes directly from the spiritual planet, Goloka Vṛndāvana. He is the source of all incarnations.

Main Features: Flute, peacock feather, yellow *dhotī*. His complexion is bluish, like a dark rain cloud.

Reason for Coming: He is born as the son of Devakī and Vasudeva in Mathurā, and is later cared for by His foster mother and father, Yaśodā and Nanda Mahārāja in Vṛndāvana. Kṛṣṇa comes to attract everyone by his wonderful pastimes. He also comes to protect his devotees and kill the demons.

Activities: Kṛṣṇa played just like a child with his parents Yaśodā and Nanda Mahārāja, stealing butter and herding cows. He protected the residents of Vṛndāvana by killing many terrible demons that were sent by His uncle, Kaṁsa. He sheltered the residents of Vṛndāvana from the devastating rains sent by Lord Indra by lifting Govardhana Hill. Kṛṣṇa performed many loving pastimes with the young cowherd maidens of Vraja, especially Śrīmatī Radhārāṇī. He spoke the *Bhagavad-gītā* to His close friend Arjuna on the Kurukṣetra Battlefield. He also arranged for His dynasty to be destroyed by a family war.

Reference: Śrīmad-Bhāgavatam: Canto 10

Lord Buddha (21)

Description: Lord Buddha is an empowered incarnation of the Lord.

Main Feature: Sits in meditation.
Reason for Coming: Lord Buddha appears in the beginning of Kali-yuga as the son of Añjanā, in the province of Gayā. "At the time when he appeared, the people in general were atheistic and preferred animal flesh to anything else. On the plea of Vedic sacrifice, every place was practically turned into a slaughterhouse and animal-killing was indulged in unrestrictedly.

Lord Buddha preached nonviolence, taking pity on the poor animals, he rejected even the animal sacrifices sanctioned in the *Vedas*." (SB 1.3.24 pp)

Activities: In his early life, he was known as Siddhārtha Gautama. He was a noble prince, and in his youth he was sheltered from the miseries of life. When the prince traveled out of his kingdom for the first time and saw a dying person, a person giving birth, a diseased person, and an aged person, he asked his servant if such hardship or suffering was common. His servant responded by telling him that these troubles afflict men during their lives. Buddha was deeply affected. He realized that, in light of the inescapable miseries of material existence, no one could be truly happy. Ultimately, he came to realize the state of *nirvana*, or that existence beyond the cycle of repeated birth and death.

Reference: Śrīmad-Bhāgavatam: SB 1.3.24

Lord Kalki (22)

Description: Kalki appears to rid the earth of the sinful population of Kali-yuga and the sinful men that have dressed as kings.

Main Features: Kalki rides a fast horse called Devadatta and carries a sword which he uses to kill thieves who have dared to dress as kings.

Reason for Coming: When the age of Kali has almost ended, the Supreme Personality of Godhead will incarnate. Lord Kalki will appear in the home of the most eminent *brāhmaṇa* of Śambhala Village, the great soul Viṣṇuyaśā. As the age of Kali progresses, all good qualities of men diminish and all impure qualities increase. Atheistic systems of so-called religion become the strongest, replacing the codes of Vedic law. The kings become just like highway bandits, the people in general become dedicated to low occupations, and all the social classes become just like *śūdras*. Kalki takes birth to protect the principles of religion and to relieve His saintly devotees from the reactions of material work.

Activities: "He will mount His horse, Devadatta, and ride around the earth with great speed, taking His sword in hand, displaying His unequaled effulgence, and will kill by the millions those thieves who have dared dress as kings. Then the signs of the next Satya-yuga will begin to appear. When the moon, sun and the planet Bṛhaspati enter simultaneously into one constellation and conjoin in the lunar mansion Puṣyā,
Satya-yuga will begin."

References: Śrīmad-Bhāgavatam: 12.2 Summary, 12.2.17, 6.8.19

Resource 3

Poison	Rāvaṇa	Demigods and Demons
Kumbhakarṇa	Śūrpaṇakhā	Churning
Hanumān	Garbodhaka Ocean	Mohinī Mūrti
Earth	Ayodhyā	Sītā
Lakṣmaṇa	Boar	Four Kumāras
Lord Brahmā	Daśaratha	Lord Śiva Drink
Bows and Arrows	Jaya	Bridge
Tortoise	Bhakta	Vāsuki
Śūrpaṇakhā	Tusks	Mandara Mountain
Vijaya	Nectar	Dhanvantari
Gates of Vaikuṇṭha	Demons for Lifetimes	Surabhi Cow
Hiraṇyākṣa	Jaṭāyu	Durvāsā Muni

ANSWERS

"Understanding the Story" (pages 65–66, multiple choice questions)
1) a, 2) b, 3) c, 4) b, 5) a, 6) b, 7) b, 8) c

Incarnation Word Jumble (page 74)

JUMBLED	UNJUMBLED
URARPASAMA	PARAŚURĀMA
ANVANTADHRI	DHANVANTARI
PIAALK	KAPILA
ALKIK	KALKI
ADANAR	NĀRADA
MAKUR	KŪRMA
AMVAAN	VĀMANA
ARUAKMS	KUMĀRAS
RAAHVA	VARĀHA
DHBAUD	BUDDHA
MRAA	RĀMA
TAMYSA	MATSYA

Connective Words (page 75)
2) but, 3) so, 4) When (the demons come), 5) and, 6) because

Keywords (pages 75–76)

KEYWORD	DEFINITION
remember	Bring to awareness something that one has already seen or heard
talk	Give information or express feelings by using spoken words
serve	Perform duties or services for someone or something else
worship	An act of showing reverance
about	On the subject of
always	For all future time; forever

Cryptogram (page 76)

T H E	S U P R E M E	E N J O Y E R	O F	A L L
18 24 25	3 13 9 12 25 20 25	25 16 5 4 23 25 12	4 11	10 1 1

S A C R I F I C E S	A C C E P T E D	T H E
3 10 8 12 26 11 26 8 25 3	10 8 8 25 9 18 25 22	18 24 25

I N C A R N A T I O N	O F	A	B O A R
26 16 8 10 12 16 10 18 26 4 16	4 11	10	19 4 10 12

Solution to Resource 3:

Kūrma	**Varāha**	**Rāma**
Mandara Mountain	Garbodhaka Ocean	Lakṣmaṇa
Vāsuki	Hiraṇyākṣa	Daśaratha
Churning	Earth	Sītā
Durvāsā Muni	Boar	Rāvaṇa
Nectar	Lord Brahmā	Kumbhakarṇa
Poison	Four Kumāras	Forest
Mohinī Mūrti	Jaya	Jaṭāyu
Tortoise	Vijaya	Hanumān
Dhanvantari	Curse	Bows and Arrows
Lord Śiva Drink	Demons for Lifetimes	Ayodhya
Surabhi Cow	Gates of Vaikuṇṭha	Śūrpaṇakhā
Demigods and Demons	Tusks	Bridge

4

The Appearance Of Śrī Nārada

Story Summary

The sages who had gathered at Naimiṣāraṇya had many questions to ask Sūta Gosvāmī. Śaunaka Ṛṣi, the leader of the assembled sages, asked, "Oh, Sūta Gosvāmī, please tell us all about the *Śrīmad-Bhāgavatam*. We want to know about Vyāsadeva who wrote the *Bhāgavatam* and what inspired him to write it. His son, Śukadeva Gosvāmī, was a pure devotee, but he looked like a madman and nobody knew that he was a pure devotee until he reached Hastināpura where King Parīkṣit was. How did they know that Śukadeva Gosvāmī was a pure devotee when no one else knew? And how did King Parīkṣit meet Śukadeva Gosvāmī for the *Bhāgavatam* to be sung to him?"

Śaunaka Ṛṣi had asked Sūta Gosvāmī many questions on behalf of all the sages present there. They'd also heard a lot about King Parīkṣit and had many questions about the king, too . . .

". . . and our dear Sūta," continued Śaunaka Ṛṣi, "we really want to know about King Parīkṣit. He was a great devotee and a great king. He was young, very strong and had the wealth of all his enemies . . . he had everything! Why did he choose to give up everything and sit on the banks of the Ganges and fast until death? It's not like he was attached to worldly things and had to detach himself, so why did he do this when others depended on him for shelter?"

The sages really wanted to know the answers to their questions. They wanted to learn about the *Śrīmad-Bhāgavatam* . . . especially Vyāsadeva the author, Śukadeva Gosvāmī his son, and also King Parīkṣit.

"We know that you know the answers and can clearly explain it all to us." Śaunaka Ṛṣi finished his questions then waited for a reply from the great Sūta Gosvāmī.

Sūta Gosvāmī then began his reply. "Once upon a time," he started, "on the bank of the Sarasvatī River, as the morning sun rose in the east, the great sage Vyāsadeva, son of Parāśara Muni and Satyavatī, bathed in the holy river before sitting alone to concentrate.

You see, Vyāsadeva had the mystic power of being able to see in the past and future . . . so he was looking into the future. All of a sudden, he was distraught as he saw what was about to happen to the people of the world as the gloomy age of Kali approached."

"'Oh my!'" he gasped to himself, "'I can see the world will get worse and worse! And most of the people will have no faith in God, and they won't live for very long, and . . . oh dear! They will be less in the mode of goodness so they will become more and more impatient!' He began to contemplate on what could possibly be done to help them . . ."

"'I know!'" he thought. "'The *Vedas* explain to people how they can purify their activities . . . so I just need to simplify this for them so they don't get too overwhelmed with the vast knowledge offered in these texts.'"

"So he split the *Vedas* up for the different types of people and appointed a teacher for each of the four *Vedas*. Vaiśampāyana would teach the *Yajur Veda*, Paila Ṛṣi would teach the *Ṛg Veda*, Jaimini would teach the *Sāma Veda*, and Sumantu Muni Aṅgirā would teach the *Atharva Veda*."

"Then he considered there were also a class of people that would like to learn through true stories like the *Mahābhārata*, so he wrote the *Purāṇas*, which were filled with stories, especially to help the people achieve the ultimate goal of life."

"My father Romaharṣaṇa was put in charge of the *Purāṇas* (which are called the fifth *Veda*)," Sūta told the sages, excitedly. "But . . . even though the great Vyāsadeva was really trying to help the people, he still felt unhappy!"

"'Why am I still feeling unhappy?'" wondered Vyāsadeva. "'I did everything properly. I worshiped the *Vedas*. I worshiped the spiritual master. I performed a fire sacrifice under very strict discipline and I'm in the disciplic succession – so what could possibly still be wrong?'" he thought to himself, scratching his head in doubt. "'Maybe it's because I didn't emphasize devotional service which really is the only process that can fully satisfy Lord Kṛṣṇa and the perfect souls.'"

"At the very moment Vyāsadeva was regretting his mistake, Nārada Muni – his dear spiritual master – arrived at the cottage. Vyāsadeva was very happy to see him! He immediately got up from his seat to respectfully welcome and worship him."

Key Messages

- Look them up in your *Śrīmad-Bhāgavatam.*
- Put them in your own words to help you memorize them.
- Discuss each one further.
- Apply them in your life.

Theme	References	Key Messages
Paramparā	1.4.1–1.4.2, Purport (pp) 1.4.23–25 1.4.28–29 1.4.33pp	A qualified teacher comes in a disciplic succession, representing the scriptures accurately and presents them in a suitable manner for the audience. This is what Vyāsadeva did when he broke down the *Vedas* and compiled the Purāṇic stories. Similarly, Śrīla Prabhupāda tailored the teachings for the people he preached to.
The position of *Śrīmad-Bhāgavatam*	1.4.3pp 1.4.7 1.4.13pp	The *Vedas* are all compiled by Vyāsadeva, namely the *Sāma, Arthava, Ṛg, Yajur, Purāṇas, Itihāsas, Upaniṣads*, etc. They originally came from the breathing of the Supreme Lord. *Śrīmad-Bhāgavatam* is the ripened fruit of all the *Vedas*. This means that it includes the most important messages from the Lord – in fact, it is the literary incarnation of the Lord Himself.
Spiritual vision	1.4.4–5 1.4.6pp	The way we assess spiritual life is different from that of material life. Śukadeva Gosvāmī seemed ignorant, but he was completely self-realized. A sage is not recognized by sight, but by hearing. One should approach a *sādhu* or great sage, not to see him, but to hear him. Devotees and materialists may look the same, but the devotee always thinks about how he can please the Lord and the materialist always thinks about how he can satisfy his own desires.
Devotees are truly compassionate	1.4.12 1.4.16–19 1.4.25–26	A devotee is truly compassionate; he is always thinking about how he can benefit others. True compassion is to give spiritual enlightenment through the teachings of the *Śrīmad-Bhāgavatam* and by the chanting of the Holy Names. Devotees can see that alleviating material suffering alone is temporary.

Character Descriptions

Have you heard of any of these characters before? What do you know about them? Share what you know with a partner, then read the descriptions below.

Nārada Muni

- An empowered incarnation of the Lord
- Son of Lord Brahmā
- One of the twelve *mahājanas*
- Immortal sage
- Carries a *vīṇā*
- Always chants the Lord's glories
- Spiritual master of Vyāsadeva, as well as many other special personalities such as Dhruva Mahārāja and Prahlāda Mahārāja.
- In his previous life, he was the son of a maidservant and, as a young boy, he would help his mother serve traveling sages. He would hear them speak on transcendental subject matters and eat their *prasāda* remnants.
- He received many blessings from them and thus became intoxicated with Kṛṣṇa consciousness.

Vyāsadeva

- Author of *Śrīmad-Bhāgavatam*
- Wrote down the 4 *Vedas* and the *Purāṇas*
- Son of Parāśara Muni and Satyavatī
- Also known as Kṛṣṇa-Dvaipāyana Vyāsa
- An empowered incarnation of the Lord
- Grandfather of the Pāṇḍavas and Kauravas
- His sons were Dhṛtarāṣtra, Pāṇḍu, and Vidura
- His son, Śukadeva Gosvāmī, spoke the *Śrīmad-Bhāgavatam* to Mahārāja Parīkṣit.

Understanding the Story

Now it's time to check how well you've understood the story with these questions. (Answers at the end of the chapter.)

1. Which sage asked Sūta Gosvāmī the questions?
   a) Śukadeva Gosvāmī
   b) Śrīla Vyāsadeva
   c) Śaunaka Ṛṣi
2. What did the sages want to know about Śrīla Vyāsadeva?
   a) What inspired him to write the *Śrīmad-Bhāgavatam?*
   b) Why did he call his son Śukadeva Gosvāmī?
   c) Where did he live?
3. What did the sages want to know about Śukadeva Gosvāmī?
   a) How did King Parīkṣit and the sages know he was a pure devotee while others thought he was mad?
   b) Why he did not wear any clothes and want to recite the *Śrīmad-Bhāgavatam?*
   c) Why did King Parīkṣit want to hear from Śukadeva Gosvāmī and no other sage?
4. What did the sages want to know about King Parīkṣit?
   a. Which state did he rule in?
   b. Why did he choose to leave everything and sit by the Ganges, if he was already a pure devotee and detached?
   c. How many children does he have?
5. Which river did Vyāsadeva bathe in before sitting down on its banks to concentrate?
   a) River Yamunā
   b) River Gaṅgā
   c) River Sarasvatī
6. What did Vyāsadeva see?
   a) People of Kali-yuga will want to chant the holy names everywhere.
   b) People of Kali-yuga would become atheistic, short-lived and overcome with passion and ignorance.
   c) People of Kali-yuga would become demons with tantric powers, whereby they could live for thousands of years.
7. Why did he want to write the *Vedas* and the *Purāṇas?*
   a) To engage the people of Kali-yuga in pure devotional service

b) To guide the people of Kali-yuga in purifying their activities
c) Because he didn't want to think about the people of Kali-yuga anymore

8. Did Vyāsadeva feel satisfied after this?
   a) Yes
   b) No
9. What did Vyāsadeva feel was the cause of his dissatisfaction?
   a) His spiritual master hadn't blessed him
   b) He didn't emphasize devotional service
   c) He hadn't had enough rest
10. Who came to Vyāsadeva's cottage after he was thinking in this way?
    a) Nārada Muni
    b) Śukadeva Gosvāmī
    c) Śaunaka Ṛṣi
11. What did Vyāsadeva do when the great sage came to the cottage?
    a) Respectfully welcomed and worshipped him
    b) Nothing. He was too upset.
    c) Ran away because he was too ashamed

Higher-Thinking Questions

Now it's time to deepen your understanding of Chapter 4 by delving into Śrīla Prabhupāda's purports for this chapter and reflecting upon the following questions.

1. Why did Śrīla Vyāsadeva divide the *Vedas* into four parts?
2. Why didn't Vyāsadeva write about *Śrīmad-Bhāgavatam* to begin with?
3. Why did Śukadeva Gosvāmī not stay for very long with householders? What should renunciates be careful about when they visit the *gṛhasthas?*
4. Why was Śrīla Vyāsadeva dissatisfied even after writing the four *Vedas?*
5. Why did *Bhagavad-gītā* appear in the *Mahābhārata* even though it was meant for the less intelligent classes of people?
6. In *Śrīmad-Bhāgavatam* 1.4.12, it says, "Those who are devoted to the cause of the Personality of Godhead live only for the welfare, development and happiness of others." Explain and expand upon this sentence. Can you think of any relevant examples of devotees who faithfully follow this example?

ACTIVITIES

In this section you will find many exciting things to do! They will get you thinking, moving, drawing, acting, and most importantly, having loads of fun!

Action Activities . . . to get you moving!

VYĀSADEVA'S JUMP ROPE

Description: Vyāsadeva's rope chant – how long can you say it while jumping, without touching the rope? You will need a long rope and three people, two to turn the rope and one to jump!

Vyāsadeva is very kind,
People of Kali-yuga are so blind.

Vyāsadeva is feeling sad,
'Cause Kali-yuga is so bad.

He can foresee suffering,
Because this age is declining.

He split the Vedas into four,
Ṛg, Sāma, Artharva and *Yajur,*

But he was feeling incomplete,
Though accomplishing a major feat.

He felt that he had done some wrong,
but then Nārada came along . . .

Analogy Activities

. . . to bring out the scholar in you!

OUR ŚRĪLA PRABHUPĀDA – FRIEND OF ALL!

"The great sage Vyāsadeva could see this by his transcendental vision. As an astrologer can see the future fate of a man, or an astronomer can foretell the solar and lunar eclipses, those liberated souls who can see through the scriptures can foretell the future of all mankind. They can see this due to their sharp vision of spiritual attainment." (Purport 1.4.17–18)

Children should be able to . . .

- Begin to understand what an astrologer does and compare an astrologer with someone with transcendental vision.
- Understand what Vyāsadeva saw for the future.

PROPHECIES

Instructions: Do you know what an astrologer does? He is someone who can tell you what will happen in the future by looking at the stars. Do you think you know what will happen tomorrow?

Did you know that Śrīla Prabhupāda's life was predicted by an astrologer? Śrīla Prabhupāda was named Abhay Charan when he was born. This means 'one who is fearless,' having taken shelter of Kṛṣṇa's lotus feet. He is never scared.

The astrologer said that, at the age of seventy, Abhay would cross the ocean, become a very important religious teacher and open 108 temples. Yes, so many wonderful temples where Rādhā and Kṛṣṇa will be dressed so beautifully.

So, just like this astrologer could see what would happen in Śrīla Prabhupāda's life, special souls with Kṛṣṇa conscious vision can also see what will happen to mankind in the future.

Śrīla Vyāsadeva could see that things unrelated to Kṛṣṇa are temporary. He could also see that people in general would be impatient and they would have short lives.

Let's sing this song to help us understand how this special soul, Śrīla Prabhupāda, is our very dear friend and teacher:

(Song is sung to the "Yankee Doodle Went to Town" melody)

Prabhupāda went to Boston with a trunk of books,
He taught us Hare Kṛṣṇa so that we might become good!

(Chorus) Prabhupāda – our grandfather, Prabhupāda – you shelter us,
Chanting Hare Kṛṣṇa is the process that he gave us.

Prabhupāda opened one-hundred-and-eight temples,
The astrologer said he would take Kṛṣṇa to the people!

(Chorus) Prabhupāda – our grandfather, Prabhupāda – you shelter us,
Chanting Hare Kṛṣṇa is the process that he gave us.

Prompt Questions:

- What was Prabhupāda's name when he was born?
- What does an astrologer do?
- How many temples did Prabhupāda open?
- How did he cross the ocean? What form of transport do you think he used?

Critical Thinking Activities

. . . to bring out the spiritual investigator in you!

GUESS-THE-SCRIPTURE QUIZ

Description: We are so fortunate that by the grace of Śrīla Prabhupāda, who is a representative of Śrīla Vyāsadeva, we have so many wonderful scriptures to guide us. Organize a quiz, using the clues on **Resource 1**. One person can read the clues out loud, while others can try to guess the name of the scripture.

Introspective Activities

. . . to bring out the reflective devotee in you!

VYĀSADEVA'S FEELINGS

Description: Let's try to understand Vyāsadeva's feelings by matching the picture to the feeling in **Resource 2**.

Extension: Find synonyms for the feelings.

HOW IS VYĀSADEVA THINKING AND FEELING?

Learning Objective:

- Describe and recognize a range of complex feelings.
- Show understanding of Vyāsadeva's feelings.

Description: Using **Resource 3** draw or write down in complete sentences (using the thought and speech bubbles) Vyāsadeva's thoughts and feelings in this chapter. Think about how he felt before and after dividing up the *Vedas*.

Writing Activities . . . to bring out the writer in you!

PUNCTUATION PRACTICE

Description: The following passage is from the Story Summary, but someone forgot to punctuate it! Edit it, using punctuation marks: periods, commas, apostrophes, and quotation marks. Add capital letters. Check it against the edited version in the answer section.

Why am I still feeling unhappy wondered Vyāsadeva I did everything properly I worshiped the *Vedas* I worshiped the spiritual master I performed a fire sacrifice under very strict discipline and im in the disciplic succession – so what could possibly still be wrong he thought to himself scratching his head in doubt maybe its because I didnt emphasize devotional service which really is the only process that can fully satisfy Lord Kṛṣṇa and the perfect souls

KEYWORD SCRAMBLE

Description: Unscramble these words that have been used in the Story Summary.

MIXED-UP KEYWORD	UNSCRAMBLED
oomygl	
staf	
agecott	
alweht	
comwlee	
yenem	
btuod	

KEYWORDS

- Define the following keywords from the story.
- Use each word in a sentence (either in oral or written form).
- Complete a New Word Map for any new words.

KEYWORD or PHRASE	DEFINITION
fast	
gloomy	
wealth	
welcome	
spiritual master	
cottage	
enemy	
doubt	
disciplic succession	
emphasize	

WORD SEARCH

A	F	P	U	R	A	N	A	U	V	A	F	P	U
E	N	H	E	J	H	Y	K	S	E	E	G	H	R
X	C	G	Y	X	C	R	Z	U	D	X	C	I	Y
P	M	A	I	P	M	G	X	C	A	P	M	A	R
O	A	H	N	R	U	I	N	Y	E	O	A	H	N
I	H	H	J	V	A	C	S	U	M	A	N	T	U
K	A	K	O	Y	E	Z	A	Q	P	M	A	Y	S
H	B	I	S	A	M	A	T	X	O	A	H	P	A
J	H	Y	K	S	X	C	Y	U	A	N	T	E	R
T	A	P	E	A	P	M	A	K	N	I	O	K	A
V	R	E	Q	D	H	H	V	Y	A	J	U	R	S
D	A	K	G	E	A	K	A	U	R	A	K	O	V
F	T	I	B	V	B	I	T	M	A	B	I	S	A
C	A	E	C	A	J	B	I	B	D	H	Y	K	T
U	H	W	X	D	R	T	H	N	A	A	P	E	I

RG	
SAMA	
YAJUR	
NARADA	
VYASADEVA	
ANGIRA	

VEDA	
SUMANTU	
SATYAVATI	
SARASVATI	
MAHABHARATA	
PURANA	

Theatrical Activities

. . . to bring out the actor in you!

MONOLOGUE

Description: Write a monologue for Vyāsadeva. A monologue is presented by a single character, most often to express their mental thoughts aloud.

VYĀSADEVA'S FEELINGS

Vyāsadeva is very kind,
People of Kali-yuga are so blind.

Vyāsadeva is feeling sad,
'Cause Kali-yuga is so bad.

He can foresee suffering,
Because this age is declining.

He split the *Vedas* into four,
Ṛg, Sāma, Artharva and *Yajur,*

But he was feeling incomplete,
Though accomplishing a major feat.

He felt that he had done some wrong,
But then Nārada came along . . .

Resource 1

GUESS-THE-SCRIPTURE QUIZ

SCRIPTURE	CLUES
BHAGAVAD-GĪTĀ	Kṛṣṇa shows His universal form.
	It was spoken on a battlefield.
	It has 18 chapters.
	It is a conversation between Kṛṣṇa and Arjuna.
	It is contained in the *Mahābhārata*.
KṚṢṆA BOOK	It describes all of Kṛṣṇa's pastimes.
	It was sponsored by George Harrison.
	It has 90 chapters.
	It describes the killing of Kaṁsa.
	It is the Tenth Canto of the *Bhāgavatam*.
MAHĀBHĀRATA	It is the story of the five Pāṇḍavas.
	It contains the *Bhagavad-gītā*.
	It contains the story of the house made of lac.
	Some of the story is set in Indraprastha.
	The story describes a terrible game of dice.
THE NECTAR OF DEVOTION	It was written by Rūpa Gosvāmī.
	It lists the five most potent items of devotional service.
	It describes all of the offenses to be avoided.
	It describes all of the qualities of Śrī Kṛṣṇa.
THE NECTAR OF INSTRUCTION	It was written by Rūpa Gosvāmī.
	It has 11 verses.
	It discusses the 6 loving exchanges for devotional service.

(*continued on the next page*)

Resource 1: GUESS-THE-SCRIPTURE QUIZ (*continued*)

SCRIPTURE	CLUES
RAMĀYANA	Rāvaṇa appears in this scripture.
	It was written by Vālmīki Muni.
	The story has a monkey warrior named Hanumān.
	The demon lived in Laṅkā.
	It tells the story of the Prince of Ayodhyā.
	One of the characters is Jaṭāyu, the eagle.
ŚRĪ CAITANYA-CARITĀMṚTA	It is made up of the *Ādi-līlā, Madhya-līlā,* and *Antya-līlā*.
	It is all about a golden *avatāra*.
	It contains descripions of the following personalities: Advaita Ācārya, Haridāsa Ṭhākura, and Mother Śacī.
	It contains the *Śikṣāṣṭakam* prayer.
	It was written by Kṛṣṇadāsa Kavirāja Gosvāmī.
ŚRĪMAD-BHĀGAVATAM	It was written by Vyāsadeva in his maturity.
	It is contained within 12 cantos.
	It describes the story of King Parīkṣit, who was cursed to die in 7 days.
	It was spoken by Śukadeva Gosvāmī.
	It contains 18,000 verses.

Resource 2

VYĀSADEVA'S FEELINGS

Poor Vyāsadeva really needs help. Discuss the meanings of these feelings and then match the feelings to the picture to help you understand Vyāsadeva.

Incomplete

Dissatisfied at heart

Compassion

Dissatisfied mind

Reflective

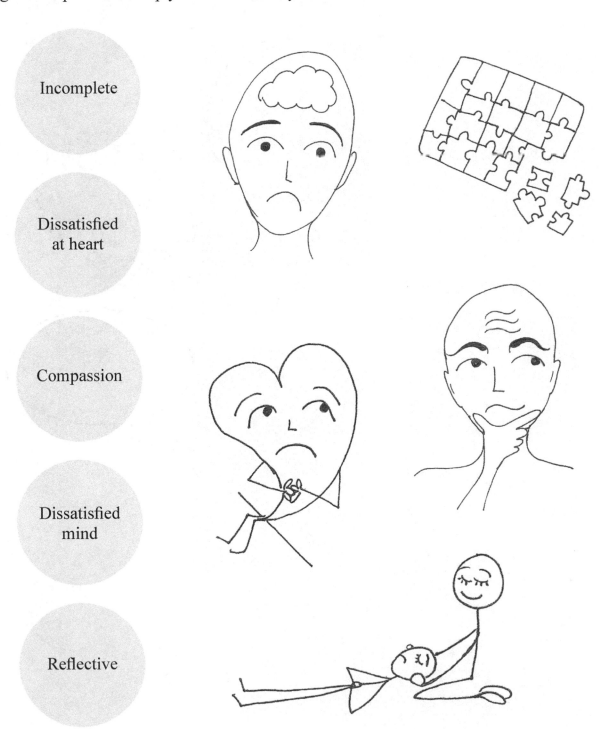

Resource 3

HOW IS VYĀSADEVA THINKING AND FEELING?

Draw or write down in complete sentences (using the thought and speech bubbles) Vyāsadeva's thoughts and feelings in this chapter. Think about how he felt before and after dividing up the *Vedas*.

ANSWERS

"Understanding the Story" (pages 106–107, multiple choice questions)
1) c, 2) a, 3) a, 4) b, 5) c, 6) b, 7) b, 8) b, 9) b, 10) a, 11) a

Punctuation Practice (page 111)

"Why am I still feeling unhappy?" wondered Vyāsadeva. "I did everything properly. I worshiped the *Vedas*. I worshiped the spiritual master. I performed a fire sacrifice under very strict discipline and I'm in the disciplic succession – so what could possibly still be wrong?" he thought to himself, scratching his head in doubt. "Maybe it's because I didn't emphasize devotional service, which really is the only process that can fully satisfy Lord Kṛṣṇa and the perfect souls."

Keyword Scramble (page 112)
gloomy, fast, cottage, wealth, welcome, enemy, doubt

Keywords (page 112)

KEYWORD or PHRASE	DEFINITION
fast	To avoid eating all or some kinds of food or drink, especially as a religious observance
gloomy	Causing or feeling depression or despondency; dark or poorly lit, especially so as to appear depressing or frightening; hopeless or despairing
wealth	A lot of money, valuable possessions, property, or other riches
welcome	To greet the arrival of (a person, guest, etc.) with pleasure or kind courtesy
spiritual master	A spiritual guide who gives personal religious instruction
cottage	A small house, typically in the countryside, near a lake or a mountain
enemy	A person who is actively opposed or feels hatred towards someone or something
doubt	To be uncertain about
disciplic succession	A succession of spiritual teachers passing down pure knowledge to disciples who will in turn become spiritual teachers and pass the knowledge onto their disciples
emphasize	To give special importance or value to (something) in speaking or writing

Word Search (page 113)

A		P	U	R	A	N	A		V				
	N								E				
		G				R			D				
	M		I			G			A				
	A			R									
	H			V	A		S	U	M	A	N	T	U
	A			Y			A						S
	B		S	A	M	A	T						A
	H			S			Y						R
	A			A			A		N				A
	R			D			V	Y	A	J	U	R	S
	A			E			A		R				V
	T			V			T		A				A
	A			A			I		D				T
									A				I

5

Nārada's Instructions On Śrīmad-Bhāgavatam For Vyāsadeva

Story Summary

The great sage Sūta continued to retell the story to the sages:

Nārada Muni was now comfortably seated in Vyāsadeva's *āśrama*. He had a slight smile on his face because he knew why Vyāsadeva was feeling troubled, and what exactly was missing from his endeavors to help the people. In this way, Nārada began to prod him with questions.

"Are you feeling satisfied now?" began Nārada to Vyāsadeva. "You've written so many religious scriptures showing people how to become materially happy and eventually to merge with Lord Kṛṣṇa's light . . ."

This was a hint by Nārada to his disciple, Vyāsadeva, of where he had gone wrong.

Nārada then continued speaking to Vyāsadeva, "You researched and studied the *Vedas* fully and your work was very thorough, and your *Mahābhārata* compilation – wonderful – it entirely explains the *Vedas*. It was all very scholarly and you've revealed to everyone the light of impersonal Brahman. So why do you feel so despondent despite all this? Tell me, why do you still feel incomplete, my dear *prabhu*?"

Vyāsadeva sighed, "Yes, my dear spiritual master. All you have said is correct. Despite all this work, I'm still feeling unhappy. Please, tell me what's causing my unhappiness? You know everything because you worship Lord Kṛṣṇa, so you're spiritually perfect. This means you can really understand people's hearts, so please tell me why I'm feeling deficient, even though I'm strictly following all the rules and regulations of the scriptures."

"Oh, Vyāsadeva," replied Nārada Muni shaking his head sympathetically. "You haven't described the glories of Lord Kṛṣṇa. You see, any philosophy, even from the *Vedas,* that doesn't give pleasure to Lord Kṛṣṇa, is considered worthless. You've thoroughly explained the four principles of righteousness: religion, economic development, sense gratification and liberation – but you haven't described the glories of Lord Kṛṣṇa!"

"Let me explain," continued sage Nārada to Vyāsadeva. "Pure devotees like to live in spiritual places, and any words that don't glorify Lord Kṛṣṇa are like a place where crows live. So saintly devotees don't like to go there because it's not a nice spiritual place for them. On the other hand, my dear Vyāsadeva, any words that describe the glories of Lord Kṛṣṇa, even if they are imperfectly composed, are very powerful. They are so powerful that they can change impious people into saints. The pure honest men like to hear, sing and accept these words that glorify Lord Kṛṣṇa."

"So you see, if even Vedic scriptures don't carry much value if they don't glorify Lord Kṛṣṇa, what is the value of ordinary activities which people do every day? If their activities aren't pleasing Lord Kṛṣṇa, they are temporary by nature and they just bring about pain eventually."

"Vyāsadeva, you are qualified to write

scriptures for the people, but you've cheated the people by making them think that real religion is meant for pleasing their own senses. The people of Kali-yuga like to enjoy, so as these instructions are coming from you, a great sage, they will enjoy without any prohibitions. Anything you describe that is separate from Kṛṣṇa disturbs the mind, just like wind disturbs a boat that isn't properly anchored. The thing is, you must write about Kṛṣṇa so it can act like medicine for the materialistic people. Eventually this will clear away their material desires and then they will deserve to know Lord Kṛṣṇa fully and be truly happy. Because you're an expert and unattached to material happiness, you are qualified to write about Lord Kṛṣṇa."

"Those wise men who want to know the truth should try this path of Kṛṣṇa consciousness. Even if they fall from the path, there's no chance of failure because they will always remember the sweetness of Lord Kṛṣṇa.Those people, however, who do all their material duties perfectly, but don't serve Kṛṣṇa, gain nothing. Vyāsadeva, don't worry about people's material happiness. It comes to every-

one, just like distress comes to everyone, even though we don't desire it."

"Vyāsadeva, you're an incarnation of Lord Kṛṣṇa and came here especially for this purpose of helping people, so please write about Lord Kṛṣṇa more clearly."

Sage Vyāsadeva now knew why he was feeling despondent after writing these scriptures. It was because he hadn't told people the glories of Lord Kṛṣṇa. He was very thankful to his spiritual master, Nārada Muni.

"Let me give an example of my own past life," said Nārada to Vyāsadeva.

"Oh, that would be nice!" exclaimed Vyāsadeva excitedly. He was very eager to hear about Nārada's past life.

"In a previous life, I was the son of a maidservant," began Nārada. "I was a good boy. I was never naughty and I never spoke more than necessary. At one time, I personally served some *brāhmaṇas*,who were living together during four months of the rainy season, and they blessed me with their mercy. One day, with their permission, I even ate their *prasāda* remnants and something very special happened … all my sins just disappeared and my heart became pure. I kept hearing the *brāhmaṇas* describe the activities of Kṛṣṇa, and oh, Vyāsadeva, the more I heard about Kṛṣṇa, the more I wanted to hear about Kṛṣṇa! That's when I realized who I really was. I wasn't this little boy, but rather a spirit soul inside the body of a boy. So I served these *brāhmaṇas* with my body and mind, without listening to my senses. I had a lot of faith in these *brāhmaṇas* and I became very attached to them. As the kind *brāhmaṇas* were leaving, they told me the most confidential and sublime secret . . ."

"What was the secret?" piped Vyāsadeva with enthusiasm.

"The secret," replied Nārada, "was that devotional service to Lord Kṛṣṇa will make us the happiest – and nothing else. It will end all our troubles and miseries if we are always serving Lord Kṛṣna."

"How is that?" asked Vyāsadeva, as he scratched his head with confusion.

"You see," explained Nārada. "Whatever we do in this material world will bind us more to the material world, but whatever we do for Kṛṣṇa, will bind us more to our dear Lord Kṛṣṇa. Eventually, this will break the rope that binds us to this material world. So please, my dear Vyāsadeva, write about the Almighty Lord's wonderful activities and, in this way, ease the suffering of the common people. Help them by showing them that devotional service is the only way to get out of the miseries of this material world."

Key Messages

- Look them up in your *Śrīmad-Bhāgavatam.*
- Put them in your own words to help you memorize them.
- Discuss each one further.
- Apply them in your life.

Theme	References	Key Messages
Instructions of the spiritual master	1.5.5–6 1.5.29–32 1.5.40	One must approach a bona fide spiritual master and inquire from him submissively. If we are willing to hear and follow his instructions, we can perfect our lives.
Directly glorify the Lord	1.5.8–16 1.5.21	Only by directly glorifying the Lord can we be truly satisfied. Even discussing other spiritual topics will not satisfy us as much as the direct glorification of the Lord will.
Mundane literature versus the Lord's glories	1.5.10–11 1.5.13–16	Mundane literature is written and read by people who have a materialistic mentality; they identify with the body and mind. Literature that directly glorifies the Lord, even if it is not perfectly composed, is very spiritually potent because devotees, who are inspired by the Lord, write it. They have the power to spiritually transform people's lives because they are non-different from the Lord.
Serve the servants of the Lord	1.5.23	The service of the Lord's servant is greater than His personal service. Such a pure devotee is the transparent medium by which to visualize the Lord, who is beyond the conception of the material senses. By service of the pure devotee, the Lord agrees to reveal Himself in proportion to the service rendered.
Qualify ourselves to receive mercy	1.5.24 1.5.29	We should try to cultivate good habits by becoming humble and submissive. When we approach pure devotees in this attitude, they will be very happy to impart knowledge unto us and allow us to serve them.
The power of *mahā-mahāprasāda*	1.5.25	The *prasāda* that has been tasted by the pure devotees is very spiritually potent. By taking the remnants of such *prasāda* we can advance very quickly in devotional service.
Kṛṣṇa is present in sound – connect by hearing	1.5.26–28 1.5.36–40	Nārada Muni personally experienced that the best way to get relief from all miseries of life is to submissively hear the activities of the Lord from the devotees. By hearing the narration of the pastimes of the Lord, we contact the Lord directly.

Understanding the Story

Now it's time to check how well you've understood the story with these questions. (Answers at the end of the chapter.)

1. Why was Nārada Muni slightly smiling?
   a) He felt nice and comfortable.
   b) He knew why Vyāsadeva was disturbed.
   c) He was pleased with how Vyāsadeva received him.
2. Nārada had said Vyāsadeva's work would help the people . . .
   a) be materially happy and eventually merge with Kṛṣṇa's light.
   b) be materially happy and eventually love Kṛṣṇa.
   c) be materially happy and eventually go to heavenly planets.
3. Why did Nārada congratulate Vyāsadeva for his work?
   a) It was scholarly and thoroughly written.
   b) It revealed the glories of Lord Kṛṣṇa.
   c) It revealed devotional service.
4. What did Nārada Muni say was the cause of Vyāsadeva's distress?
   a) He hadn't remembered to glorify his spiritual master.
   b) He hadn't fully explained the four principles of righteousness.
   c) He hadn't directly written about the glories of Lord Kṛṣṇa.
5. Any place where Lord Kṛṣṇa's glories are not chanted, is a place where . . .
   a) crows gather.
   b) devotees gather.
   c) scientists gather.
6. Singing, hearing and accepting the words that glorify Lord Kṛṣṇa has the power to turn . . .
   a) impious people into saints.
   b) impious people into God.
   c) devotees into demons.
7. Any activities that don't please Lord Kṛṣṇa (whether recommended in the *Vedas* or just ordinary activities) will eventually bring . . .
   a) happiness.
   b) money.
   c) pain.

8. Why did Nārada say Vyāsadeva had cheated the people?
    a) He made them pay too much money for the *Vedas.*
    b) He made them think real religion is pleasing their own senses.
    c) He made them think real religion is meant for pleasing Kṛṣṇa's senses.
9. How does hearing about Kṛṣṇa act like a medicine?
    a) It treats sinful material desires so people can have good material desires.
    b) It treats material sins so people can enjoy life freely.
    c) It treats material desires to make people qualified to know Kṛṣṇa fully.
10. Why is Vyāsadeva qualified to write about Kṛṣṇa?
    a) He has no material desires and is expert.
    b) He came before Kṛṣṇa.
    c) He could go without sleep.
11. Who benefits more?
    a) Someone who tried practicing Kṛṣṇa Consciousness, but fell away.
    b) Someone who carries out their material duties perfectly.
    c) Someone who carries out their material duties imperfectly.
12. Why did Nārada instruct Vyāsadeva not to be concerned with making people materially happy?
    a) Nārada wants the people to suffer.
    b) Happiness comes to everyone anyway, just like distress comes to everyone.
    c) The people will never be unhappy.
13. Vyāsadeva had come to help the people of Kali-yuga. Who was he an incarnation of?
    a) Śukadeva Gosvāmī.
    b) Lord Kṛṣṇa.
    c) Lord Śiva.
14. Who did Nārada Muni serve in his last life?
    a) Some animals.
    b) Some kings.
    c) Some *brāhmaṇas.*
15. What happened when he heard from the *brāhmaṇas* about the glories of Kṛṣṇa?
    a) He wanted to hear more and more and then got bored.
    b) He wanted to hear more and more and realized he was a spirit soul.
    c) He wanted to hear more and more and realized he was Kṛṣṇa.
16. What was the secret the *brāhmaṇas* told Nārada?
    a) Devotional service to Kṛṣṇa will make you the happiest and end all miseries.
    b) The heavenly planets will make you the happiest and end all miseries.
    c) Merging with Lord Kṛṣṇa will make you the happiest and end all miseries.

17. How does this secret work?
    a) We stop thinking about everything that makes us miserable.
    b) We love ourselves more and this makes us happy.
    c) Whatever we do for Kṛṣṇa will bind us more to Kṛṣṇa, while, at the same time, break our bondage to the material world.

Higher-Thinking Questions

Now it's time to deepen your understanding of Chapter 5 by delving into Śrīla Prabhupāda's purports for this chapter and reflecting upon the following questions.

1. Vyāsadeva wrote the *Mahābhārata* which talks about Kṛṣṇa, so why did Nārada say he hasn't glorified Kṛṣṇa? (See the Purport of Verse 9.)
2. Why are saintly persons compared to swans, and fruitive workers to crows?
3. Even if someone falls away from the path of Kṛṣṇa consciousness, why is there no chance of failure?
4. What was the solution that Nārada Muni offered to Vyāsadeva? Do you think that it was correct? Explain your answer.
5. To what extent can a spiritual master help us in our life? Name some key examples of personalities that have accepted spiritual masters who have helped them.

ACTIVITIES

In this section you will find many exciting things to do! They will get you thinking, moving, drawing, acting, and most importantly, having loads of fun!

Action Activities . . . to get you moving!

ASSOCIATION, ASSOCIATION, ASSOCIATION!

Description: Your task this week is to be a real eager-beaver to get the association of devotees! Start by writing a plan of the week of how you can meet and serve devotees. Here are some ideas to start you off:

- Serving the devotees – *prasāda*, other menial tasks.
- Serving with devotees – cooking, cleaning, and any other temple services.
- Attending morning program – chanting with devotees, singing, worshiping together, hearing class together
- Engaging in preaching activities with devotees – *harināma,* book distribution, etc.

At the end of your association marathon, think about some of the following questions: Did you meet anyone new? What have you learned? What or who has inspired you the most and why?

Analogy Activities
. . . to bring out the scholar in you!

THE CROW AND THE SWAN

"Crows and swans are not birds of the same feather because of their different mental attitudes. The fruitive workers or passionate men are compared to the crows, whereas the all-perfect saintly persons are compared to the swans. The crows take pleasure in a place where garbage is thrown out, just as the passionate fruitive workers take pleasure in wine and woman and places for gross sense pleasure. The swans do not take pleasure in the places where crows are assembled for conferences and meetings. They are instead seen in the atmosphere of natural scenic beauty where there are transparent reservoirs of water, nicely decorated with stems of lotus flowers in variegated colors of natural beauty. That is the difference between the two classes of birds." (SB 1.5.10 Purport)

Learning Activity (Topic: Vaiṣṇavas are like Swans)
Children should be able to . . .

- Explain the difference between a crow and a swan.
- Understand and discuss why the comparison may be made between a swan and a saintly person.

Resources:

- Swan from **Resource 1** printed on cardstock
- Glue or glue stick
- Black felt tip for the eye
- White or grey feathers
- White or cream fabric
- Silver foil paper

Instructions: With the swan template on **Resource 1**, create a beautiful collage of a swan using a range of materials. Once the collage is complete, write down or draw something to represent Kṛṣṇa, showing the idea that just as swans are attracted to beautiful things in nature, similarly, saintly people are attracted to the glories of the Lord. (For example, a lotus flower or a *Bhagavad-gītā* book.)

Prompt Questions:

- Why are those who enjoy literature that glorifies the Lord compared to swans?
- What is it that makes the swan beautiful? What is it that makes a Vaiṣṇava beautiful?

Conclusion (discuss): Saintly people are compared to swans. The swans do not take pleasure in the places where crows gather. They are attracted to nature and beauty, as saintly people are attracted to the glories of the Lord.

Critical Thinking Activities

. . . to bring out the spiritual investigator in you!

LITERATURES ACTIVITY

Description: It is important that we are aware of what we read. Reading certain literature can help us to advance very quickly in devotional service, whereas others may have undesirable effects on our consciousness.

Read verses 1.5.10 and 1.5.11 of the *Śrīmad-Bhāgavatam.* Then complete the table in **Resource 2** to analyze different types of literature and how they may affect your consciousness.

PURE DEVOTIONAL SERVICE – A PRACTICAL EXAMPLE

Description: The description given of the process of purification that Nārada Munī went through correlates with the process that is described in Chapter 2, Verses 1.2.16–1.2.21.

Read both of the descriptions in detail and try to find the similarities between the two descriptions.

What have you learned by this exercise that you can apply in your own life?

IT'S NEVER TOO EARLY!

Description: Can you imagine that at the age of only 5, Nārada Muni took to serving the sages and became completely purified by their association! This must be a very powerful process that he is describing.

What would you say to a person who said, "Spiritual life is for when you are old. Don't waste your time being bored now. Enjoy life!"

Try to back up your answer by giving scriptural references. (Hint: Prahlāda Mahārāja's teachings and example.)

NĀRADA'S SPIRITUAL PROCESS

Description: Nārada Muni carried out some very important devotional activities. In **Resource 3**, match the correct activity with the clues given.

Introspective Activities

. . . to bring out the reflective devotee in you!

LETTER & GIFT OF APPRECIATION

Description: Are there any devotees you know who really inspire you? Write a letter of appreciation to them, thanking them and letting them know how they have influenced and inspired you.

You can also make a gift of appreciation – using one of the ideas given previously – or bake some cookies for them to show your gratitude.

DEAR DIARY

Description: Write a diary entry for Nārada Muni in his previous life as the son of a maidservant. Explain how he is feeling just after the sages have left. What impressions did they make on him?

Writing Activities . . . to bring out the writer in you!

REPORT WRITING

Description: Read the following sequence of events in Nārada Muni's life:

1. Some *brāhmaṇas* stay with Nārada Munī and his mother. Nārada Muni serves the sages.
2. Nārada Muni takes the remnants of the sages' *prasādam.*
3. Nārada's sins are eradicated and his heart purified.
4. Nārada Muni hears instructions from the sages and develops a taste for hearing.
5. The sages tell Nārada Muni a special secret: devotional service will make us the happiest.

Write a report about what Nārada learned from the sages, using the past tense. Use the word lists on the following page to help you.

Describing words (adjectives):	Action words (verbs):	Naming words (nouns):
small	blessed	*prasādam*
kind	served	mercy
pure	ate	instructions
		brāhmaṇas
		mind
		body
		soul

KEYWORDS

- Explain the meanings of the following keywords from the story.
- Use each word in a sentence (either in oral or written form).
- Complete a New Word Map for any new words.

KEYWORD	DEFINITION
attached	
desire	
previous	
past	
distress	
eager	
senses	

WORD SEARCH

S	O	K	G	V	N	P	R	A	S	A	D	A	M
D	E	V	Y	I	K	H	I	K	L	S	A	R	F
I	V	R	T	E	K	A	Y	J	Q	T	K	C	E
N	E	Q	V	I	U	N	Y	T	K	G	V	H	A
S	I	K	L	I	J	H	O	E	V	Y	I	A	P
T	Y	J	Q	W	C	H	B	W	R	T	E	N	R
R	G	L	O	R	I	E	S	K	L	H	J	T	E
U	K	I	K	L	Y	A	Y	J	A	E	R	I	O
C	G	Y	J	Q	N	R	I	F	K	Y	D	N	K
T	F	A	I	T	H	I	U	H	J	H	M	G	B
I	I	K	L	E	O	N	N	G	I	K	L	B	E
O	Y	J	Q	S	A	G	E	S	Y	J	Q	R	G
N	W	R	H	Y	B	P	U	R	I	F	I	E	D
S	A	E	A	D	A	R	A	N	U	H	F	R	I
R	E	M	E	M	B	E	R	I	N	G	B	H	L

SERVICE	
HEARING	
SAGES	
NARADA	
PRASADAM	
CHANTING	

GLORIES	
KNOWLEDGE	
PURIFIED	
REMEMBERING	
INSTRUCTIONS	
FAITH	

NĀRADA

In my previous life I was a maidservant's son
That is when my devotional service was once again begun.

I was innocent, self-controlled, quiet and not naughty.
So some traveling sages gave me their mercy.

Once, when they agreed, I took the remnants of their food.
I was purified in my heart and attained their saintly mood.

In their association I increased my desire to hear.
As my taste developed, the lower modes of nature disappeared.

If there is anything you can learn from my past life's narration,
It is to seek out the mercy of saintly association.

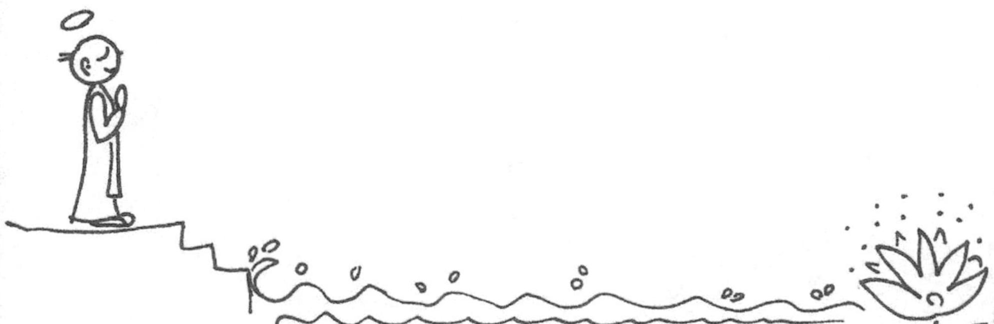

Resource 1

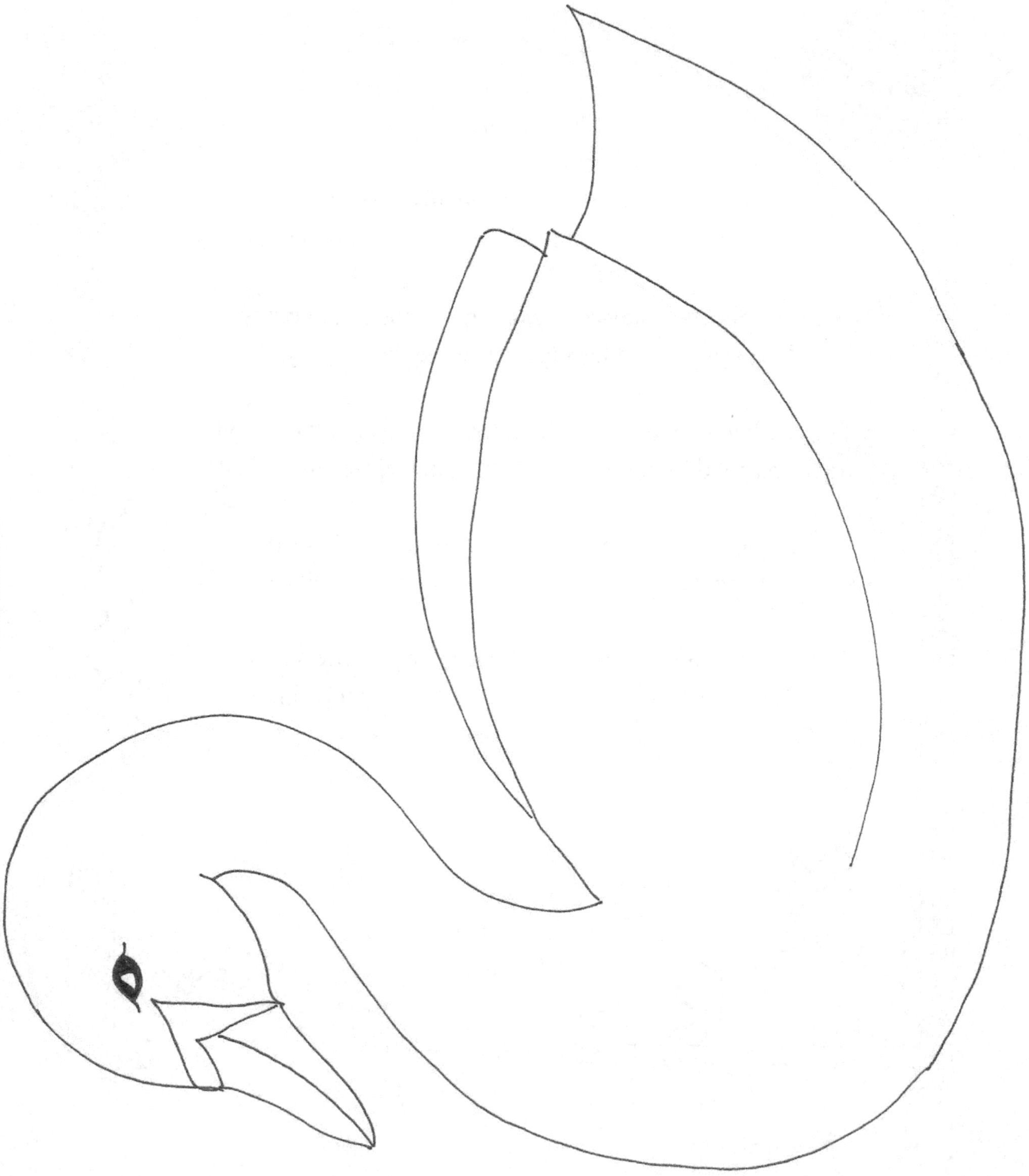

Resource 2

LITERATURE	WHO WROTE IT?	WHAT IS IT ABOUT?	IS IT BENEFICIAL FOR SPIRITUAL LIFE, OR CAN IT BE USED INDIRECTLY IN THE SERVICE OF THE LORD?
EXAMPLE: *Bhagavad-gītā*	Compiled by Vyāsadeva, translated by Śrīla Prabhupāda.	A conversation between Kṛṣṇa and Arjuna.	Yes, it can be directly used because it contains Kṛṣṇa's instructions. These are nondifferent from Him and, if we follow them, we can become Kṛṣṇa conscious and return back to Godhead.
EXAMPLE: Newspapers	Non-devotees	Daily life, incidents that happen, sad stories, happy stories, advertisements.	Not really. By reading this kind of literature we begin to relate more to this material body and start thinking that the material world is reality. It can also influence our desires and create impressions in our mind. However, sometimes it may be beneficial to read some headlines to keep up-to-date on a basic level for preaching purposes.
Back to Godhead magazine			
Reader's Digest			
Nectar of Devotion			

(*continued on the next page*)

Resource 2 (*continued*)

Harry Potter			
Caitanya-caritāmṛta			
School textbooks			
Śrīmad-Bhāgavatam			
Dictionary			
Novel about a famous pop star			

Resource 3

NĀRADA'S SPIRITUAL PROCESS

Nārada Muni carried out some very important devotional activities.
Match them up with the correct images.

Served devotees

Took their *prasādam*

Heard the sages attentively

Took instruction

Controlled senses

Strong faith

Well-behaved

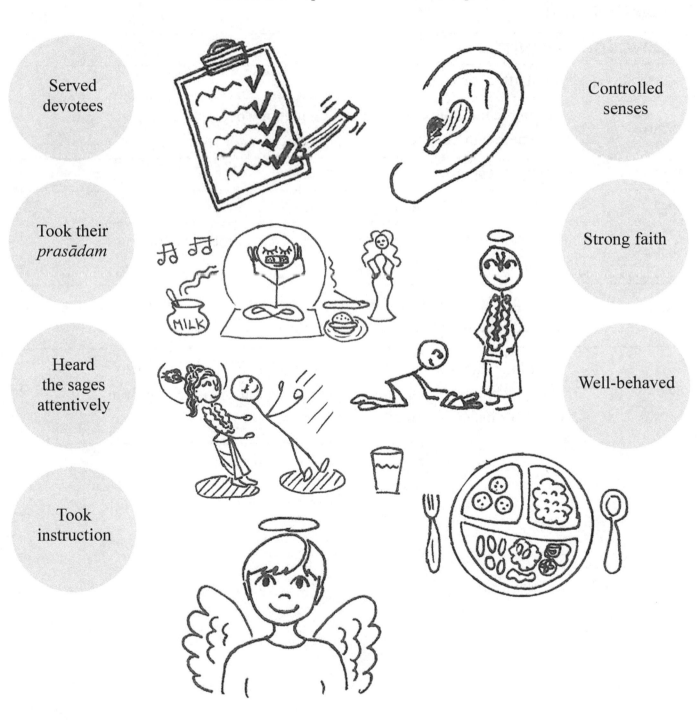

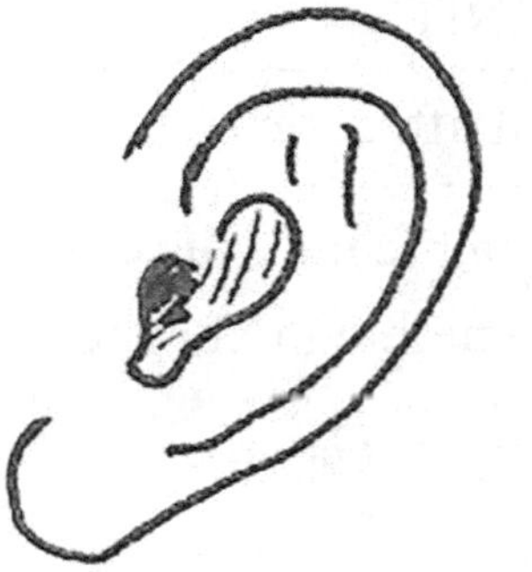

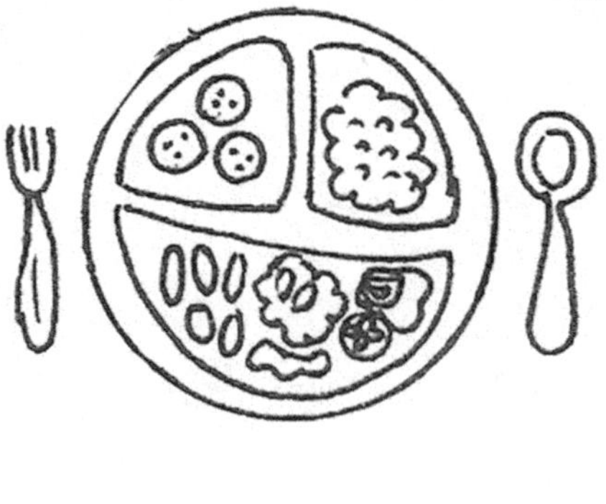

ANSWERS

"Understanding the Story" (pages 126–128, multiple choice questions)

1) b, 2) a, 3) a, 4) c, 5) a, 6) a, 7) c, 8) b, 9) c, 10) a, 11) a, 12) b, 13) b, 14) c, 15) b, 16) a, 17) c

Keywords (page 133)

KEYWORD	DEFINITION
attached	Full of affection or fondness
desire	A strong feeling of wanting to have something or wishing for something to happen
previous	Coming or occurring before something else
past	Gone by in time and no longer existing
distress	Great pain, anxiety, or sorrow; acute physical or mental suffering; affliction; trouble
eager	Keen or ardent in desire or feeling; impatiently longing, strongly wanting to do or have something, keenly expectant or interested
senses	Any of the faculties, such as sight, hearing, smell, taste, or touch, with which humans and animals perceive stimuli, originating from outside or inside the body

Word Search (page 134)

S						P	R	A	S	A	D	A	M
	E												
I		R			K							C	
N			V			N						H	
S				I			O					A	
T					C	H		W				N	
R						E			L			T	
U						A				E		I	
C						R					D	N	
T	F	A	I	T	H	I						G	
I						N							E
O				S	A	G	E	S					
N						P	U	R	I	F	I	E	D
S			A	D	A	R	A	N					
R	E	M	E	M	B	E	R	I	N	G			

6

Conversation Between Nārada and Vyāsadeva

Story Summary

The great sage Sūta continued to retell the story to the sages. Vyāsadeva was captivated by Nārada Muni's story and wanted to know more.

"Please," he pleaded. "Can you tell me what happened after the *brāhmaṇas* instructed you up until the time you became Nārada Muni? And how is it that you remember what happened in your past life from another age? We all forget things over time, so how is it that you remember this all so clearly?"

"One time, though, my mother went out at night to milk a cow and was bitten on the leg by a deadly serpent. She left her body. I saw this as Kṛṣṇa's mercy, as He always wants the best for His devotees. Then I began to travel north and saw different lands I had never seen before."

"I passed through cities, towns, villages, farms, mines, valleys, flower gardens, and forests. Sometimes I came across places that were fit for heavenly beings, such as hills, mountains and different lands with lakes full of beautiful lotus flowers, surrounded by busy bees and singing birds; and sometimes I traversed through deep, dark and dangerous forests and caves which were difficult to travel through alone where snakes, owls and jackals played."

"After traveling all this time, I was exhausted and felt really hungry and thirsty, too, so I rested by a lake and drank some water. This made me feel much better."

"After that I sat under a banyan tree in a forest and began to meditate on Lord Kṛṣṇa, just as the *brāhmaṇas* had shown me. As I thought about His beautiful lotus feet, I felt so much love for the Lord that tears started to roll down my cheeks."

Nārada Muni exclaimed excitedly, "All of a sudden, I actually saw Lord Kṛṣṇa in my heart, and I felt so ecstatic!"

His excitement ended abruptly . . .

But then, he cried, "The form of Kṛṣṇa vanished! Where did Kṛṣṇa go? I jumped up in distress, like anyone would if they had just lost something very valuable. I tried again and again to see Him, but my Lord wasn't reappearing in my heart. Oh, Vyāsadeva, I became so miserable as I could no longer see my dear Lord! But Kṛṣṇa could see me, and He saw that I was upset and trying again and again to see Him in that lonely forest, so He spoke to me in such sweet words just to lessen my grief."

"My dear little boy," spoke Kṛṣṇa. "I'm sorry, but you won't be able to see Me again in this lifetime. It's very hard to see Me if you still have material desires, or if you're not always engaged in My service. I had let you see Me just this once so you can remember Me and want to see Me more and more. For the more you hanker for Me, the more you'll be free from material desires. By serving Me under a spiritual master, even for a few days, you get to be My associate in the spiritual world in your next life. By My mercy, you will remember Me even in the next age."

"When Lord Kṛṣṇa finished speaking to me, I paid my obeisances unto Him with heartfelt gratitude. I felt much better and, after that, I started traveling all over the world chanting the holy name of the Lord wherever I would go. I was now satisfied, humble and not envious. By the end of my life I had no material desires; I left my material body. At the end of the age, I entered into Lord Viṣṇu along with everything else in this world and, at the beginning of the new age, I appeared in my spiritual body as Nārada Muni. Since then, by Viṣṇu's mercy, I travel everywhere throughout the material and spiritual worlds because I'm fixed in unbroken devotional service, constantly singing the glories of Kṛṣṇa and vibrating this vīṇā, which has a spiritual sound. This was personally given to me by Lord Kṛṣṇa."

"As soon as I chant Kṛṣṇa's name, He sits in my heart as if I'm calling Him."

"So you see, Vyāsadeva, I have personal experience that those people, who are always anxious or troubled, can cross over this dark ocean by the bright boat of the holy name of Lord Kṛṣṇa. And, yes, my dear disciple, we can get some relief from miseries by changing our frame of mind, but our soul doesn't experience satisfaction. It doesn't become extremely happy this way – only devotional service can do this."

"'Vyāsadeva, I've told you my story because I know this will help you."

The sages at Naimiṣāraṇya were in awe, listening to this amazing story.

Nārada had now instructed Vyāsadeva, Sūta explained, and so picked up his *vīṇā,* started playing it and singing the glories of Lord Kṛṣṇa. As he left Vyāsadeva's *āśrama,* he wandered throughout the world at his free will. All glories and success to Nārada, who glorifies Kṛṣṇa, takes pleasure in it, and enlivens the distressed souls of the universe!

"Jai!" cheered the sages.

Key Messages

- Look them up in your *Śrīmad-Bhāgavatam.*
- Put them in your own words to help you memorize them.
- Discuss each one further.
- Apply them in your life.

Theme	References	Key Messages
Detachment is natural, not artificial	1.6.9 1.6.10	When we follow the process of devotional service our heart automatically becomes cleaned of our material attachments. In such a pure state, we will not be disturbed by what seems to be "unfortunate events"; instead, we will see these as the special mercy of the Lord.
He reveals Himself by His causeless mercy	1.6.16 1.6.19 1.6.20	There is no mechanical process to see the form of the Lord. When He is satisfied by the sincere attempt of the devotee, He bestows His causeless mercy by revealing Himself.
Try, try and try again	1.6.18–20 1.6.22	The process of devotional service requires a determined effort. Even if we aren't always successful in our attempts, we need to keep trying.
Be pure to understand	1.6.21	When we are materially contaminated, it becomes very difficult to understand the Lord. We must purify our hearts by chanting Hare Kṛṣṇa and performing devotional service, so that we can perceive Him clearly
Increase our desire for Kṛṣṇa	1.6.22	We must increase our desire to get the association of the Lord and serve Him. As soon as we try to develop this desire, automatically He appears. The more we hanker for Him, the more we will feel His presence.
Devotional service, our eternal wealth	1.6.23–24 1.6.35	The *prasāda* that has been tasted by the pure devotees is very spiritually potent. By taking the remnants of such *prasāda* we can advance very quickly in devotional service.
Chant, chant, chant	1.6.26 1.6.32–33 1.6.35 1.6.38	The Lord is non-different from His name, form and glories, so when we chant He is present with us. The highest duty of the devotee is to engage in devotional service by remembering the Lord's name, form and pastimes and to distribute this message for the welfare of others.

Understanding the Story

Now it's time to check how well you've understood the story with these questions. (Answers at the end of the chapter.)

1. Who was Nārada really attached to?
   a) His mother.
   b) The cow.
   c) the snake.
2. How old was Nārada?
   a) 2
   b) 5
   c) 15
3. How did his mother leave her body?
   a) Cursed by the sages.
   b) Kicked by a cow one night.
   c) Bitten by a snake while milking a cow one night.
4. How did Nārada see this incident?
   a) As his mother's *karma*.
   b) Serpents are bad creatures and must be punished.
   c) As Kṛṣṇa's mercy.
5. What did he do after that?
   a) Traveled north.
   b) Cried for five days.
   c) Searched for the *brāhmaṇas*.
6. After some time, he felt exhausted and rested by a . . .
   a) lake.
   b) cave.
   c) temple.
7. Thereafter, he sat under a banyan tree and began to . . .
   a) cry more.
   b) make a home for himself with the twigs and leaves.
   c) meditate on Lord Kṛṣṇa, as the *brāhmaṇas* had shown.

8. What did he meditate on that made him cry out of love?
    a) Kṛṣṇa's lotus feet.
    b) Kṛṣṇa's smile.
    c) Kṛṣṇa's flute.
9. What did Nārada Muni see?
    a) Lord Kṛṣṇa in his heart.
    b) Lord Kṛṣṇa in the tree.
    c) Lord Kṛṣṇa in the sky.
10. The Lord then disappeared. What did Nārada Muni do?
    a) Continued building a home.
    b) Tried to see Him again and again.
    c) Found something to eat and drink.
11. Did Kṛṣṇa reappear?
    a) Yes, every time Nārada called Him.
    b) No. He never saw or heard Kṛṣṇa again.
    c) Not visually, but He spoke to Nārada.
12. Why was it hard for him to see Kṛṣṇa?
    a) His eyes were blurred from crying.
    b) Because he still had material desires and wasn't always engaged in Kṛṣṇa's service.
    c) He was too young to engage in Kṛṣṇa's devotional service.
13. Why, then, did Kṛṣṇa let Nārada see Him at all if he still had material desires?
    a) So he could remember Him and would hanker to see Him more and more.
    b) Kṛṣṇa forgot that he still had some material desires.
    c) He didn't really see Kṛṣṇa.
14. Why did Kṛṣṇa promise that Nārada would join Him in the spiritual world?
    a) Because Nārada served Kṛṣṇa with devotion.
    b) Because Kṛṣṇa felt bad, seeing Nārada cry so much.
    c) Because Nārada had traveled so far.
15. How could Nārada remember Kṛṣṇa in his next life?
    a) Good memory.
    b) He would practice not being forgetful.
    c) Kṛṣṇa's mercy.
16. What did Nārada do after that?
    a) Chanted in palaces to please the royal families.
    b) Traveled everywhere chanting the holy names of the Lord.
    c) Traveled everywhere telling everyone that he'd seen Kṛṣṇa.

17. How did he feel?
    a) Sad, angry and envious of happy people.
    b) Proud that he'd seen Kṛṣṇa.
    c) Humble, satisfied and non-envious.
18. In this life, what happens when Nārada chants Kṛṣṇa's names?
    a) He sits in his heart.
    b) He dances on his tongue.
    c) Everyone starts to dance.

Higher-Thinking Questions

Now it's time to deepen your understanding of Chapter 6 by delving into Śrīla Prabhupāda's purports for this chapter and reflecting upon the following questions.

1. Nārada mentioned in verse 1.6.28 that he left his material body of five elements. What are those elements?
2. Investigate examples of other important devotees who went to the forest to meditate. How successful were they?
3. The Lord said to Nārada Muni, "Those who are incomplete in service and who are not completely free from all material taints, can hardly see Me." What do you think the Lord means by this? What could be some possible material taints?
4. What "material taints" do you have that you would like to get rid of? How are you going to achieve this?
5. Usually, when we think of going back to Godhead or getting liberated, we think of going back to Goloka Vṛndāvana and performing pastimes with the Lord. However, Nārada Muni travels around singing the glories of the Lord to enliven the distressed souls. Is this just as good? Why?
6. Have you lost anything valuable? Discuss the most valuable thing you've lost or that you might lose and how upset you'd feel – then think about Lord Kṛṣṇa who is unlimitedly valuable.
7. Nārada Muni explained that he was awarded a transcendental body. What is the difference between a material body and a transcendental body?

ACTIVITIES

In this section you will find many exciting things to do! They will get you thinking, moving, drawing, acting, and most importantly, having loads of fun!

Artistic Activities

. . . to reveal your creativity!

COLLABORATIVE PROJECT: A MURAL DEPICTING NĀRADA MUNI'S LIFE

Description: After reading about Nārada Muni's life, divide the children into 10 small groups of preferably two to three. Each group will be responsible for depicting one event in Nārada's life. (See the list of scenes below). Supply each group with one large sheet of paper. Students can paint or make collages of colored paper to create their scene. When each group has completed a scene, hang the images on the wall in chronological order and review Nārada Muni's life.

The scenes in Nārada Muni's life could include:

1. Nārada serving the sages.
2. His mother getting bitten on the leg by a deadly snake.
3. Nārada traveling in cities and villages.
4. Nārada in lotus gardens with birds and bees,
5. Nārada passing through hills and mountains, filled with gold.
6. Nārada passing roaring rivers.
7. Nārada in the forest with owls, snakes and jackals.
8. Nārada sitting under a banyan tree and meditating on Lord Kṛṣṇa.
9. Nārada seeing Lord Kṛṣṇa.
10. Nārada leaving his body like a strike of lightning and attaining a spiritual body.

NĀRADA MUNI PUPPET

Description: Make a puppet of Nārada Muni as a small boy. Walk him through each scene of his life, re-telling his story as he moves along.

NĀRADA MUNI THEATER PRODUCTION

Description: Design a poster for the theater production of *Nārada Muni, the Spiritual Spaceman.* The production will retell the story of Nārada Muni's life. Research the principles of effective poster design before you start.

ANIMAL MASKS

Description: Make masks of the animals Nārada Muni may have seen in the forest as he traveled north. These can be used to enact the pastime in a drama.

Critical Thinking Activities

. . . to bring out the spiritual investigator in you!

NĀRADA MUNI'S SPIRITUAL JOURNEY

Description: Let's analyze Nārada Muni's spiritual journey. Answer the questions on **Resource 1** first, then map out the events in Nārada Muni's life, in a visual form, using the template on **Resource 2**. Write the event along the path and then draw an illustration of the event.

Follow-Up Discussion: What can you learn from the life of the great sage Nārada Muni? How can you apply these lessons in your life?

NĀRADA MUNI QUIZ

Description: Now that you know everything about Nārada Muni's life, it's quiz time! This activity can be done with a partner or in a group. Write a 10-question quiz about the story, as contained in chapters 4, 5 and 6. You give the quiz to a partner or read them out as a quizmaster in a group. Remember to include the answers!

QUESTION TIME

Description: Think of 5 questions you would like to ask Nārada Muni and then answer them the way you think Nārada Muni would answer them.

REINCARNATION DEBATE

Description: This activity can be done in pairs or in a group. Do some research on the arguments for and against reincarnation. One side will be for reincarnation and the other, against. Both teams should prepare their arguments from the perspectives of:

- Science
- Real past-life experiences
- Religion/philosophy – many cultures originally incorporated reincarnation

Structure of a Debate:

1. The pro side can introduce their arguments first, speaking for 5–7 minutes.
2. Repeat step number 1 for the opposing side.
3. Give three minutes to confer.
4. Begin the rebuttals with the opposing side and give them 3 minutes to speak.
5. Repeat step 4 for the pro side.
6. Conclude and end.

Introspective Activities

. . . to bring out the reflective devotee in you!

MY PERSONAL JOURNEY

Description: Now that you have heard about Nārada Muni's spiritual journey, you can explore your own. Answer the questions on **Resource 3** to help you reflect on your own devotional life and current spiritual inspirations, influences and aspirations. Then map out your journey on **Resource 4**. You can write in key events and draw an illustration.

Alternative Interview Activity: You can also use the questions on **Resource 3** as a questionnaire and interview a friend, sibling, parent or other adult about his/her spiritual journey. Ask him/her the questions and write the answers down.

Writing Activities . . . to bring out the writer in you!

MAKING A BOOK ON NĀRADA MUNI'S PAST LIFE

Description: You will be creating your very own children's book. The target audience for the book is 3–5 years of age. You will need to think carefully about the illustrations and type of language that you use. You will also need to go through the story of Nārada Muni's past life to pick out the key events to include in your book, as it should be concise.

Resources and Preparation: Obtain 2 x A4 sheets of white paper, 1 x A4 sheet of white card, scissors, glue, and colored pencils or pens. Fold paper and card lengthwise and cut along the fold. Make a small oblong booklet with card on outside covers. Fold in center and staple. This should make a cover page with nine pages inside.

Instructions:

1. Write the title on the front cover: "My Past Life" by Nārada Muni and draw a picture to accompany this.
2. On each page of the book, include a caption describing each part of Nārada Muni's life.
3. On the page opposite the caption, draw a picture to illustrate the scene described.

ADJECTIVES ACTIVITY

Description: Make a list of adjectives in the summary story. Then use a thesaurus to find five other words for this adjective.

KEYWORDS

- Define the following keywords from the story.
- Use each word in a sentence (either in oral or written form).
- Complete a New Word Map at the back of the book for any new words.

KEYWORD	DEFINITION
deadly	
meditate	
relief	
vanished	
valuable	
constantly	
surrounded	

CROSSWORD

ACROSS

1) The occupation of Nārada Muni's mother
2) The Lord told Nārada to h___________ for Him
3) The instrument carried by Nārada Muni
4) The creature that bit Nārada Muni's mother

DOWN

5) The form of Lord Kṛṣṇa in the heart
6) The direction that Nārada Muni headed in
7) Nārada Muni travels the universe glorifying Lord K__________
8) The type of tree that Nārada Muni sat under to meditate

Theatrical Activities

. . . to bring out the actor in you!

DRAMA

Description: Enact the full pastime between Śrīla Vyāsadeva and Nārada Muni, as described in Chapters 4, 5 and 6. You can use the tips given in Chapter 3 about playwriting to guide you in planning your production.

NĀRADA MUNI

Nārada Muni,
Kṛṣṇa's devotee,
Who travels through the universes,
Chanting sweetly!

One lifetime ago he was a simple servant boy,
Serving great devotees with humility and joy.

One night his poor mother went outside to milk the cow,
But on her way home a serpent bit her leg and down she fell.

What was our young boy, all alone now, supposed to do?
Well, he walked all day and thought of Kṛṣṇa—that was all he knew.

Through great cities, tiny towns, farmlands and beautiful gardens,
Over hills and mountains, filled with gold, and many different lands

He passed lotus ponds with bees and singing birds high in the sky,
And through dangerous dark forests where both owls and jackals cry.

Feeling tired and hungry, he sat down under a banyan tree,
Then Kṛṣṇa appeared within his heart and told him, 'Think of Me!'

As lightning struck, he met with death and took his next body,
Now we know him by the name of Nārada Muni.

Hare Kṛṣṇa, Hare Kṛṣṇa, Kṛṣṇa Kṛṣṇa, Hare Hare,
Hare Rāma, Hare Rāma, Rāma Rāma, Hare Hare.

Resource 1

NĀRADA MUNI'S SPIRITUAL JOURNEY

Nārada Muni is such a special person and we can learn much from his life. Let's explore his spiritual journey. Answer the questions below to help you to think about what you should include in his spiritual journey. Then map out his journey with drawings on the next page.

1. What was Nārada Muni's background? (Give some details about his past lives).
2. What inspired Nārada Muni?
3. Who influenced him?
4. What were the challenges he had to deal with?
5. When did he feel that Kṛṣṇa was with him?
6. What does he love doing the most?
7. What were the main events in his life?

Resource 2

Resource 3

MY SPIRITUAL JOURNEY

Now that you have heard about Nārada Muni's spiritual journey, you can explore your own. Answer the questions below to help you to think about what you should include in your "spiritual journey" map on the next page.

Alternative Interview Activity: You can use the questions below as a questionnaire and interview a friend, sibling, parent or other adult about his/her spiritual journey. Ask him/her the questions and write the answers down. Listen carefully.

1. How did you become a devotee?
2. What made you want to become a devotee?
3. Who has influenced you?
4. Have you ever had any major challenges that were difficult for you to deal with? How did you deal with them?
5. Can you remember times when you really felt Kṛṣṇa's presence?
6. What do you love doing the most in your spiritual life?
7. What do you see yourself doing in the future?
8. What is your plan to help Śrīla Prabhupāda fulfill his mission to spread Kṛṣṇa consciousness ?

Resource 4

A MAP OF MY SPIRITUAL JOURNEY

ANSWERS

"Understanding the Story" (pages 147–149, multiple choice questions)

1) a, 2) b, 3) c, 4) c, 5) a, 6) a, 7) c, 8) a, 9) a, 10) b, 11) c, 12) b, 13) a, 14) a, 15) c, 16) b, 17) c, 18) a

Keywords (page 154)

KEYWORD	DEFINITION
deadly	Likely to cause or capable of producing death; (alternate meaning: extremely accurate and effective)
meditate	To give serious or careful thought to; to engage in contemplation or reflection
relief	A feeling of ease from grief or trouble; reduction of or freedom from pain
vanished	No longer existing
valuable	Precious; very useful or helpful; important and limited in amount
constantly	Occurring continuously; many times; again and again
surrounded	To be on every side of (something)

Crossword (pages 154–155)

ACROSS	DOWN
1) Maidservant	5) Supersoul
2) Hanker	6) North
3) Vina	7) Kṛṣṇa
4) Serpent	8) Banyan

7

The Son of Droṇa Punished

Story Summary

After instructing Vyāsadeva to write about Kṛṣṇa, Nārada Muni departed.

Vyāsadeva was feeling much more hopeful now, so he sat down in his *āśrama*, surrounded by beautiful berry trees, and began to meditate. While meditating, he thought of Lord Kṛṣṇa. Then, something amazing happened. He saw that Lord Kṛṣṇa was in control of the whole material world. He also saw that the people are actually really happy spirit souls, but the dark, cloudy, material world is covering them so much that they've forgotten who they are and they have become really miserable.

"I know!" thought Vyāsadeva. "The secret is that if the people serve Lord Kṛṣṇa, then He can protect them from the dark cloudy, material world. It's His external energy."

"Yes," he continued to think. "I will write about Kṛṣṇa and call the book *Śrīmad-Bhāgavatam*. Whoever hears these stories will surely love Kṛṣṇa so much that they will want to serve Him and then they will never feel sad, disillusioned or scared ever again."

Therefore, Vyāsadeva wrote down the pastimes of Lord Kṛṣṇa and then taught these to his own son, Śukadeva Gosvāmī, who was already free from the dark, cloudy, material world.

He was already happy, but hearing about Kṛṣṇa made him even happier.

Sūta Gosvāmī then said to the sages: "I shall begin the transcendental narration of the *Bhāgavatam*.

It all began when the battle of Kurukṣetra, between the evil Kauravas and the saintly Pāṇḍavas, had ended. The evil Duryodhana was lying on the ground with a broken spine and mourning because his Kaurava army had lost the battle.

Aśvatthāmā was the son of Droṇācārya, a *brāhmaṇa,* and he was also on the side of the Kauravas.

"I can't bear to see my master Duryodhana so defeated!" he thought while seeing Duryodhana lying on the ground. Aśvatthāmā angrily snuck into the Pāṇḍavas' camp and did something very terrible.

He saw the five poor defenseless sons of the Pāṇḍavas sleeping in their beds and he chopped off their heads. Then he ran back to Duryodhana and showed his master what he had done thinking that Duryodhana would be pleased. But, oh no, even Duryodhana disapproved this cowardly act, and he wasn't pleased in the least.

Meanwhile, Draupadī, the mother of the Pāṇḍavas, had just discovered that her sons were killed. She was so overcome with grief that she cried and cried. When her husband, Arjuna, learned about this, he was upset and he tried to comfort her. "My dear wife, Draupadī," he said. "I'm going to chase that Aśvatthāmā and sever his head and bring it back to you."

Saying this, he dressed in his armor, prepared his weapons and then set off in his chariot, with Lord Kṛṣṇa as his driver, to chase the evil Aśvatthāmā.

Aśvatthāmā saw Arjuna in the distance coming towards him with great speed and he started to panic. He quickly boarded his own chariot and tried to get his horses to gallop as fast as possible to save his very own life. But soon they became tired. What was he to do? Arjuna had almost caught up with him and he would definitely be killed because his horses didn't want to run anymore.

Aśvatthāmā was very desperate to save his life, so he foolishly chanted some mantras to invoke the most devastating weapon of all – the fiery *brahmāstra,* even though he didn't know how to withdraw it.

When this fiery *brahmāstra* arrow was released, a glaring light spread in all directions and began to burn the whole world. Arjuna became fearful, so he turned to his dear Lord Kṛṣṇa, "My Lord, only you can stop your devotees feeling scared, and I know You constantly protect the devotees who always think about You. Where is this burning light coming from? I don't understand what's happening."

Kṛṣṇa smiled at His dear devotee and explained, "This is Aśvatthāmā's foolish doing. He invoked the devastating *brahmāstra* weapon because he was scared for his life, but he doesn't know how to stop it. My dear Arjuna, you know how to stop it. If you release another *brahmāstra* to counteract it, you can then withdraw both of them."

So Arjuna circumambulated Lord Kṛṣṇa, and then shot another fiery *brahmāstra*. The two *brahmāstras* combined and created a great circle of fire around the whole universe and it was very hot. He then quickly with-

drew both the *brahmāstras* and all the danger had gone. The meek Aśvatthāmā was standing before him shivering in fright. There was nothing he could do now.

Arjuna looked at him angrily with eyes blazing like two red balls of copper. He grabbed the foolish son of a *brāhmaṇa* and bound him with ropes just like an animal.

"He killed your sleeping sons," Kṛṣṇa reminded him, "and he will have to pay back this karma in his next life if you don't punish him now. Also, you promised Draupadī you would sever his head. He even displeased his own master. I think you should kill this wretched Aśvatthāmā right now!"

Arjuna was angry, but he didn't feel like killing Aśvatthāmā so he dragged him back to his camp and presented the wretched Aśvatthāmā to his wife Draupadī. Aśvatthāmā looked just like an animal bound up with ropes and he stood silently before her.

The kind-hearted Draupadī couldn't bear to see him in this state. "Release him!" she cried with tears in her eyes. "He's still the son of a *brāhmaṇa* so we must respect him. After all, it was by the mercy of his father, Droṇācārya, that you learned the military art of throwing and controlling weapons. And besides"she sobbed, "I wouldn't want his mother to cry for the loss of her son, like I am now."

Everyone, including King Yudhiṣṭhira, Arjuna, Nakula and Sahadeva, agreed with her, except for Bhīma.

Bhīma shouted with great anger, "No, he didn't act like a *brāhmaṇa*! He should be killed!"

By now, Arjuna was very confused. He looked at Kṛṣṇa, Who smiled. "You both are right," Kṛṣṇa advised. "A son of a *brāhmaṇa* shouldn't be killed, but he didn't act as a *brāhmaṇa* so he can be killed – and the scriptures tell us that both ways are right. So you must now decide what to do to satisfy Me, your brother Bhīma and your wife Draupadī."

"Yes," thought Arjuna. "I know what to do."

He pulled out his sword and plucked the jewel from Aśvatthāmā's head, chopped off his hair, and then unbound him and drove him away out of the camp. Every last bit of Aśvatthāmā's honor was gone, which was a fate worse than death. In this way, the humiliated Aśvatthāmā was at the same time killed and not killed by the intelligence of Lord Kṛṣṇa and His dear friend Arjuna.

The Pāṇḍavas and Draupadī, overwhelmed with grief, then started the proper rituals for their deceased sons.

Key Messages

- Look them up in your *Śrīmad-Bhāgavatam.*
- Put them in your own words to help you memorize them.
- Discuss each one further.
- Apply them in your life.

Theme	References	Key Messages
A true *brāhmaṇa* has saintly qualities	1.7.19 1.7.33 1.7.35	A true *brāhmaṇa* has saintly qualities; if someone is born in the family of a *brāhmaṇa,* but doesn't act like one, then they cannot be called a *brāhmaṇa.*
Seek His shelter first	1.7.21–26 1.7.29	Devotees remember the Lord and seek His shelter before doing anything because it is by His mercy only that we are able to act.
Power of sound	1.7.20 1.7.27 1.7.44	Chanting mantras or Vedic hymns can have very powerful effects. In previous ages, sound vibration could create powerful weapons.
Kṛṣṇa tests his devotees	1.7.40	Kṛṣṇa tests His devotees by putting them in challenging situations to see what choices they make. In that way they become glorified and they set a perfect example for us.
Compassion and empathy	1.7.42–43 1.7.47	Devotees always seek to understand the suffering of others and develop deep compassion for them. They often put aside their own interests to see to the interests of others.
Thinking outside the box – the Vedic way	1.7.53–55	Devotees try to apply their intelligence to serve the Lord even when faced with so-called contradictions. They make their choices according to what is most favorable for serving Lord Kṛṣṇa.

Character Descriptions

Have you heard of any of these characters before? What do you know about them? Share what you know with a partner, then read the descriptions on the following page.

Lord Kṛṣṇa

- The Supreme Personality of Godhead
- Friend and chariot driver of Arjuna

Yudhiṣṭhira

- He was the king of the Earth 5,000 years ago, the eldest of the Pāṇḍava brothers, the son of Kuntī and is also Yamarāja, the Lord of death

Bhīma

- An expert club fighter, son of Kuntī and Vāyu, the wind God

Arjuna

- The famous archer of the Pāṇḍavas, his father was Indra, the king of heaven, and his mother was Kuntī Devī
- Lord Kṛṣṇa spoke the *Bhagavad-gītā* to him on the battlefield

Nakula and Sahadeva

- The youngest of the Pāṇḍava brothers, sons of Mādrī and the heavenly physicians, the Aśvinī Kumāras

Draupadī

- The wife of the Pāṇḍava brothers
- Daughter of King Drupada, of Pāñcāla, so is sometimes referred to as Pāñcālī
- She is known for her unflinching faith, surrender and devotion to Lord Kṛṣṇa

Aśvatthāmā

- The son of *brāhmaṇa* Droṇa; Aśvatthāmā was born with a jewel on his forehead, giving him strength, beauty and fame; a Kaurava general

Understanding the Story

Now it's time to check how well you've understood the story with these questions. (Answers at the end of the chapter.)

1. How can people be protected from the dark, cloudy material world?
   a) Serve Lord Kṛṣṇa.
   b) Use an umbrella.
   c) Hide under a banyan tree.
2. If we hear the stories from the *Śrīmad-Bhāgavatam,* we will love Kṛṣṇa and never again ever feel
   a) sad.
   b) disillusioned.
   c) scared.
3. Vyāsadeva taught the *Śrīmad-Bhāgavatam* to his son. What was his son's name?
   a) Śaunaka Ṛṣi
   b) Śukadeva Gosvāmī
   c) Vyāsadeva
4. Śukadeva Gosvāmī was already free from the material world so he was happy. So when he heard these stories about Kṛṣṇa he felt
   a) sad.
   b) even happier.
   c) angry.
5. What did Aśvatthāmā do that was so horrific?
6. Was Duryodhana happy with this?
7. Who chased Aśvatthāmā to kill him?
8. Did Aśvatthāmā stand and fight or try to run away on his chariot when he saw Arjuna coming after him?
9. When Aśvatthāmā's horses were tired, what did he do?
   a) Run
   b) Hide
   c) Shoot the fiery *brahmāstra* arrow
10. Who withdrew the fiery *brahmāstra* arrow?
    a) Aśvatthāmā
    b) Arjuna
    c) Kṛṣṇa

11. Who wanted Aśvatthāmā released?
    a) Bhīma
    b) Draupadī
    c) Kṛṣṇa
12. Who wanted Aśvatthāmā killed?
    a) King Yudhiṣṭhira
    b) Draupadī
    c) Both Lord Kṛṣṇa and Bhīma
13. What did Arjuna decide to do in the end, to satisfy Kṛṣṇa, Bhīma and Draupadī?

Higher-Thinking Questions

Now it's time to deepen your understanding of Chapter 7 by delving into Śrīla Prabhupāda's purports for this chapter and reflecting upon the following questions.

1. Śaunaka Ṛṣi asked the following question to Sūta Gosvāmī: "Śrī Śukadeva Gosvāmī was already on the path of self-realization, and thus he was pleased with his own self. So why did he take the trouble to undergo the study of such a vast literature?" What was the answer?
2. Explain what a *brahma-bandhu* is. How is this term significant in this chapter?
3. What does it mean to be a real *brāhmaṇa?* Research the qualities of a real *brāhmaṇa*. Use the following verses to help you (BG 18.42, SB 7.11.21).
4. Why did Aśvatthāmā kill the sleeping sons of the Pāṇḍavas?
5. Why do we have to be careful not to cause offenses to others? It is well-known that we should not offend devotees, but is it acceptable to offend non-devotees?
6. Why did Arjuna walk around Lord Kṛṣṇa before releasing the *brahmāstra* weapon?
7. How and why did Kṛṣṇa test Arjuna in this chapter?

ACTIVITIES

In this section you will find many exciting things to do! They will get you thinking, moving, drawing, acting, and most importantly, having loads of fun!

Action Activities . . . to get you moving!

WATER-BOMB BRAHMĀSTRAS

Description: Water-bomb *brahmāstras!* Two players are required for this re-enactment of the pastime of Arjuna and Aśvatthāmā. Each person can take a turn to throw a "water bomb," which is a water balloon filled with water.

Player One: Throw your water bomb as high up in the sky as possible.
Player Two: Try to hit player one's water bomb with your own.

Points can be calculated for how many water bombs get hit by each person.

WHAT GOES AROUND, COMES AROUND

Description: Prepare a Sunday Feast class on *karma*, entitled "What goes around, comes around." Remember these two helpful pointers:

- The "Authors PIE" – Persuade, Inform and Entertain your audience.
- A good speech structure: Open with a punch line, start with the main idea, then take the three most important points from your main idea and discuss them one after another. Conclude with an overall summary ending with your main idea and a punch line!

MANTRAS AND MUSIC

Description: The *brahmāstra* was such a powerful weapon it had the power to destroy everything! Can you believe that it was invoked simply by the sound vibration of *mantras*?

Do you know any other powerful mantras? Yes, that's right – the *mahā-mantra!* It has the power to awaken our love of God and take us to the spiritual world.

Share this most powerful mantra with others! Go on a *harināma* or perform *kīrtana* using lots of musical instruments. Make some shakers by placing rice, *dāhl,* small pasta shells or dry popcorn into suitable containers and sealing the tops or lids with cellotape. Decorate the containers.

Critical Thinking Activities

. . . to bring out the spiritual investigator in you!

MEMORY CARD GAME: THE PĀṆḌAVAS

Description: Match the correct Pāṇḍava brother! You will need to print out the cards on **Resource 1**, cut them out and color them in. Then turn all the cards face down in front of you and take turns with a friend to flip two cards over at a time. You can keep the pair of cards if they match. If they don't match, place them face down again and try to remember which Pāṇḍava brother was on each card. Whoever has the most matched pairs at the end of the game wins!

Extension: You can add a few more character cards of your own too, or play snap with them. Try to remember the spellings of the five Pāṇḍava brothers' names and remember that names begin with capital letters!

Introspective Activities

. . . to bring out the reflective devotee in you!

I'M SORRY

Description: Write a letter of apology from Aśvatthāmā for all of the terrible things that he has done. You will need to explain things from his perspective. Use the prompts below to help you.

- What did he do?
- Why did he do what he did?
- How does he feel about it all now?
- Who was he doing it for and were they pleased?
- What is he going to do now?

DECISIONS DECISIONS . . .

Description: Think about what you base your decisions on. Are your decisions based on what's best for you? Are they based on what is best for everyone? Are they based on morals – right and wrong things – even if that conflicts with your own interest? Above all, are they based on what guru and Kṛṣṇa want you to do? Think of decisions you have made and reflect on which factors influenced your decision-making. What were the outcomes? Now set some check-point targets to make sure that your decision-making is fairly based on doing the right things for the right reason.

Writing Activities . . . to bring out the writer in you!

A CHARACTER'S VIEWPOINT

Description: After reading the Story Summary, see **Resources 2** and **3**, the activity sheets entitled "Aśvatthāmā" and "Arjuna." Discuss each question and then complete the drawings in the spaces provided. You might need to review the Summary. You can use the questions below to guide you:

Aśvatthāmā

1. What does Aśvatthāmā see?
   - Who is chasing him?
   - What is he riding on?
   - Is Arjuna riding fast or slow?
   - What is Arjuna carrying?
   - How does Arjuna look?
2. How does he feel?
3. What does he hear?

Arjuna

1. What does Arjuna see?
2. How does he feel?
3. What does he do?

CHARACTER PROFILE

Learning Outcomes: Recall at least three facts about the characters in this pastime. Explain what the characters' main actions tell us about them.

Description: Choose a character from the pastime "The Son of Droṇa Punished" listed below:

a) Arjuna
b) Aśvatthāmā
c) Duryodhana
d) Draupadī
e) Bhīma
f) Kṛṣṇa

Read the story summary and the character descriptions. Complete the "Character Profile" on **Resource 4**, answering the questions about the six aspects of the character. Depending on age and ability, children can either draw or write their answers in the spaces provided on the template. (Answers are to be given orally first in a group discussion, and then followed by drawing or writing in the spaces.)

1. What does the character look like?
2. If relevant, does the character have a problem? What is the problem?
3. What are one or two main actions the character performs in this story?
4. Can you say what the character says in your own words?
5. What is this character like? What qualities does he/she have? Use some describing words. Can you give an example from the story to show this?
6. Who is another character that is important to your character? Why is that person important?

KEYWORDS

- Define the following keywords from the story.
- Use each word in a sentence (either in oral or written form).
- Complete a New Word Map at the back of the book for any new words.

KEYWORD	DEFINITION
surround	
meditate	
miserable	
lament	
defeat	
defenseless	
coward	
board	
invoke	
devastate	
withdraw	
honor	

WORD SEARCH

W	P	O	I	U	A	M	J	K	F	I	E	R	Y
B	R	A	H	M	A	N	A	G	H	J	A	N	B
Q	I	U	B	S	D	F	G	H	J	K	I	U	R
W	O	J	N	W	W	T	Y	H	O	T	O	J	A
R	P	K	M	S	E	N	A	Q	W	E	P	K	H
M	A	N	T	R	A	A	N	R	T	Y	U	I	M
Q	I	U	B	T	P	I	U	V	R	J	K	A	A
W	O	J	N	G	O	O	J	C	V	O	M	S	S
R	P	K	M	H	N	P	K	H	E	R	W	V	T
A	S	D	C	B	S	D	F	A	U	T	J	A	R
C	R	F	Y	O	V	S	D	S	K	L	E	T	A
D	B	D	P	C	W	I	B	E	A	N	W	T	C
Q	I	U	B	F	G	A	H	J	I	U	E	H	V
W	O	J	N	Z	X	C	R	F	O	J	L	A	B
R	P	K	M	A	S	D	B	D	P	K	G	M	N
W	I	T	H	D	R	A	W	P	O	I	U	A	M

BRAHMANA	
WEAPON	
COWARD	
JEWEL	
BRAHMASTRA	
ARROW	

HOT	
WITHDRAW	
MANTRA	
ASVATTHAMA	
FIERY	
CHASE	

BRAHMĀSTRA

Aśvatthāmā had a weapon so frightening;
When he set it off, it looked as bright as lightning.

Activated by Vedic sound,
It put fear in the hearts of all those around.
Brahmāstra, there's nothing faster!

Arjuna prayed to Kṛṣṇa for protection
So in his quest he would achieve perfection.

Activated by Vedic sound,
It put fear in the hearts of all those around.
Brahmāstra, there's nothing faster!

He counteracted the great force
And bound Aśvatthāmā just like a horse.

Cutting the hair and jewel from his head
Was as good for him as being dead.

Brahmāstra, Arjuna's faster!

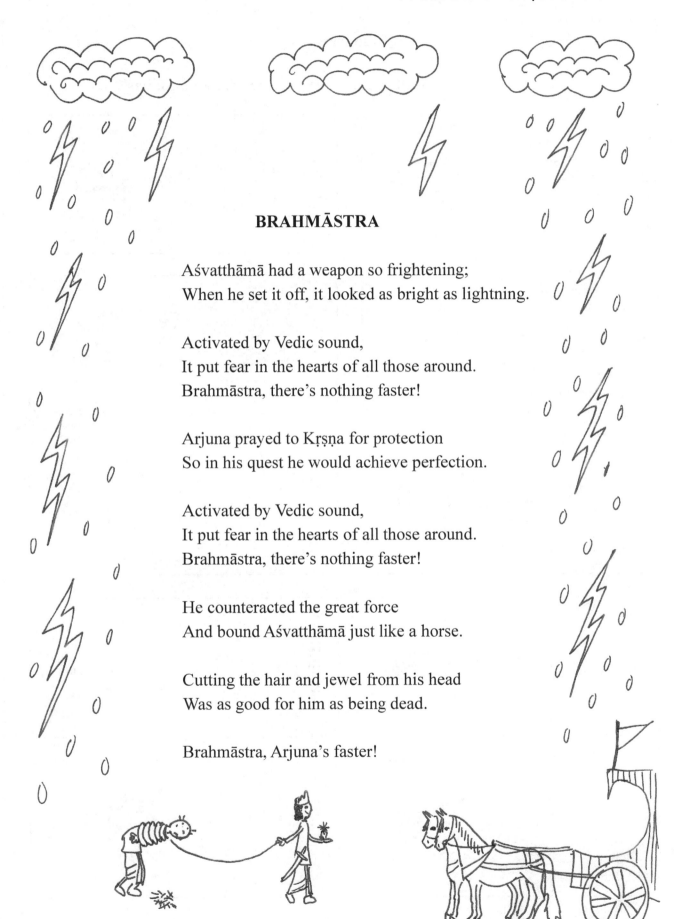

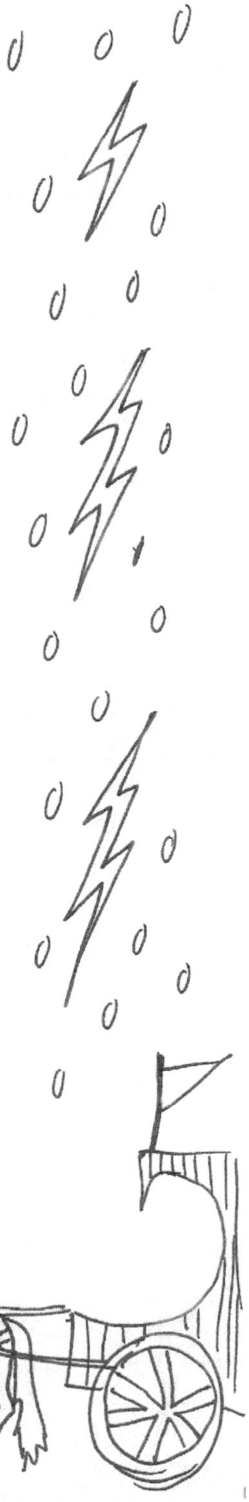

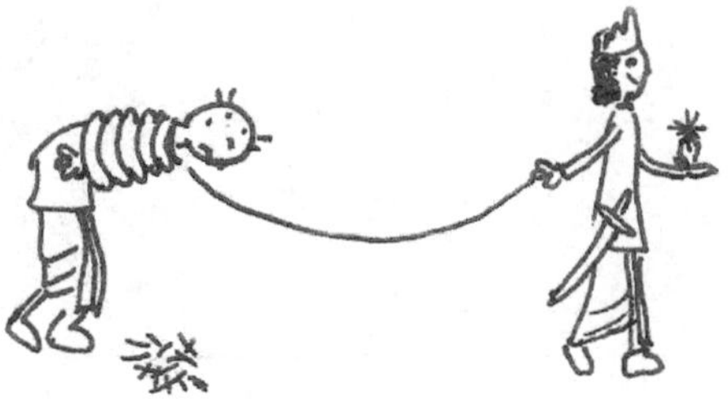

Resource 1

Cards for Memory-Matching Card Game, "The Pāṇḍavas"

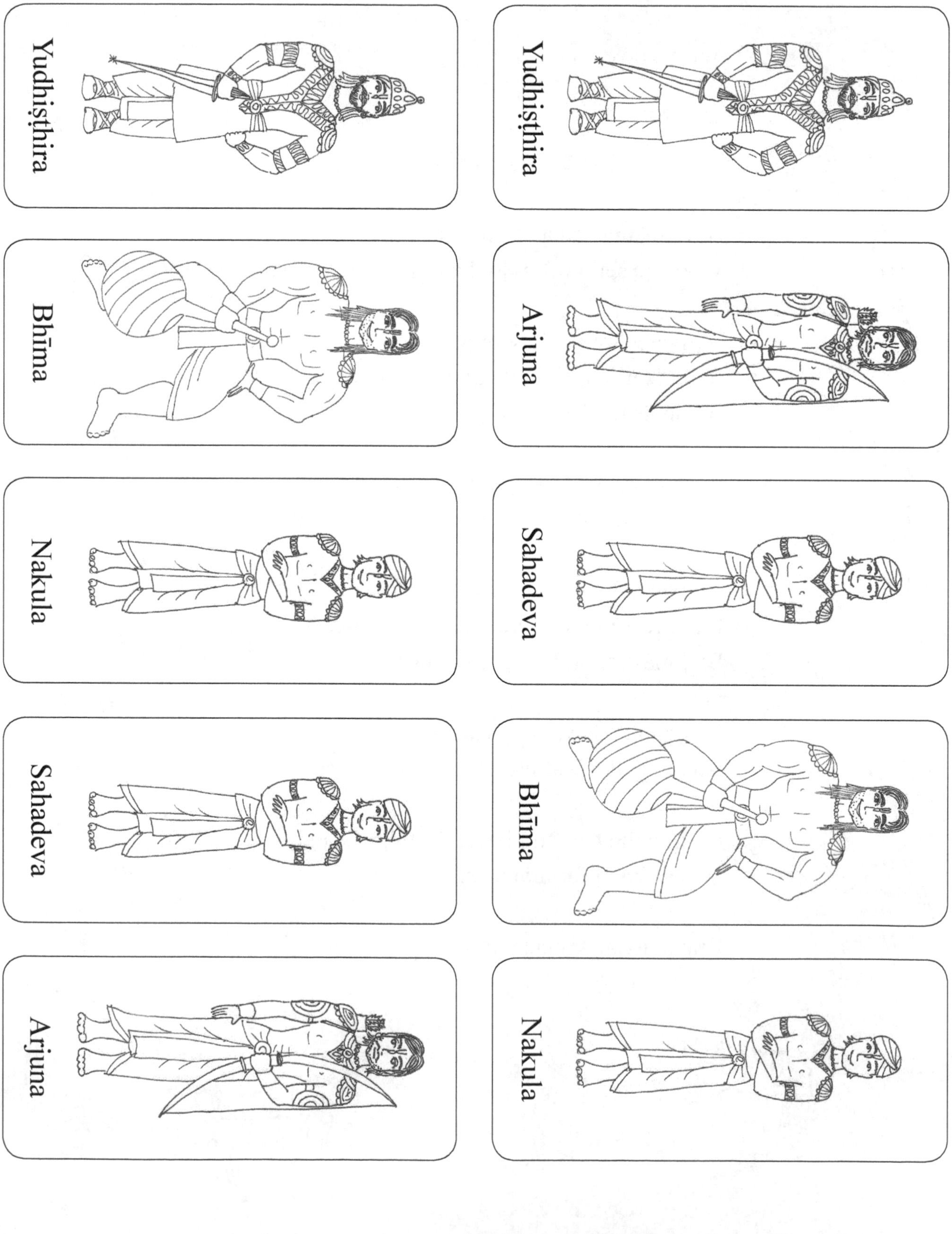

Resource 2

A Character's Viewpoint
(Aśvatthāmā)

What can Aśvatthāmā see from his chariot when Arjuna is chasing him? Draw it here:

How does Aśvatthāmā feel when he sees Arjuna chasing him?
Draw a face/faces showing how he feels:

What sounds does Aśvatthāmā hear from his chariot
when Arjuna is chasing him as he tries to escape?

Resource 3

A Character's Viewpoint
(Arjuna)

What does Arjuna see from his chariot when Aśvatthāmā releases the *brahmāstra* weapon? Draw it here:

How does Arjuna feel when he sees the *brahmāstra* weapon from his chariot? Draw a face/faces showing the feelings he has:

What does Arjuna do now? Imagine you are on the chariot with Arjuna when Aśvatthāmā releases the *brahmāstra* weapon. What do you see, hear, and feel?

Resource 4

Character's Profile

Name of character_________________________________

What does your character look like?
Draw a picture of your character here:

What does the character say?

What qualities are prominent
in the character?

What problem or difficulty
does the character face?

Which other character is important
to your character?

What does the character do?

ANSWERS

"Understanding the Story" (pages 169–170)

1) a, 2) d, 3) b, 4) b

5) He killed the five sleeping sons of the Pāṇḍavas.

6) No

7) Arjuna

8) He ran away

9) c, 10) b, 11) b, 12) c

13) Arjuna took off Aśvatthāmā's jewel and cut his hair.

Keywords (page 175)

KEYWORD	DEFINITION
surround	To be on every side of (something)
meditate	To give serious or careful thought to; to engage in contemplation or reflection
miserable	Very unhappy; very sick or unwell
lament	To express sorrow, regret, or unhappiness about something
defeat	To win a victory over someone or something; to cause someone or something to fail
defenseless	Without defense or protection; totally vulnerable
coward	Someone who is too afraid to do what is right or expected; someone who is not at all brave or courageous
board	(verb) To get into or onto something (e.g., an airplane)
invoke	To mention or refer to someone or something; to make use of (a law, a right, etc.)
devastate	To cause great damage or harm; to cause someone to feel extreme emotional pain
withdraw	To take back something that is spoken, offered, etc.
honor	Respect that is given to someone who is admired; good quality or character as judged by other people; high moral standards of behavior

Word Search (page 176)

									F	I	E	R	Y
B	R	A	H	M	A	N	A						B
													R
					W			H	O	T			A
					E		A						H
M	A	N	T	R	A			R					M
					P				R			A	A
					O			C		O		S	S
					N			H			W	V	T
			C					A			J	A	R
				O				S			E	T	A
					W			E			W	T	
						A					E	H	
							R				L	A	
								D				M	
W	I	T	H	D	R	A	W					A	

8

Prayers by Queen Kuntī And Parīkṣit Saved

Story Summary

Part I: Parīkṣit Saved

After chasing away the dishonored Aśvatthāmā, the Pāṇḍava family went to the holy Ganges River to offer water to their dead relatives. They mourned deeply for their loss and then bathed there before sitting on the river bank. Oh, they were so sad. Lord Kṛṣṇa and the sages tried to pacify them.

"Please don't despair," said Lord Kṛṣṇa and the sages to the Pāṇḍava family. "This is the material world. Your cousins were very immoral so their lives in these bodies ended earlier, but everyone is born and dies in this world. Nobody lives here forever. You can only live happily forever in the spiritual world if you always engage in loving devotional service." So they all got up and went back home.

The terrible war was over. The Pāṇḍavas now had their kingdom back, thanks to Lord Śrī Kṛṣṇa; and King Yudhiṣṭhira was famous throughout the entire world for being so virtuous after performing three (*aśvamedha-yajñas*) horse sacrifices.

Lord Kṛṣṇa was now ready to go back to His own city of Dvārakā. The *brāhmaṇas,* led by Vyāsadeva, worshiped Him as they bid Him farewell. Then Kṛṣṇa sat on His chariot, ready to leave.

All of a sudden, He saw Uttarā hurrying towards Him. She looked so scared. "Kṛṣṇa! Kṛṣṇa!" she cried. "Oh, Lord of the universe, You are all-powerful. Please protect me! There's a fiery iron arrow chasing me! If You want it to burn me, I don't mind, but please save my baby in my womb! Please do me this favor, my Lord."

Lord Kṛṣṇa, who is always very affectionate to His devotees, patiently heard Uttarā's humble request. "Hmmm!" He thought. "It is that Aśvatthāma who has released this fiery iron arrow. He is still trying to take revenge and kill the Pāṇḍavas' family."

The five Pāṇḍavas saw the fiery arrow (called the *brahmāstra*) coming towards them and so they took up their weapons to try to counteract it. When Lord Kṛṣṇa saw that His beloved devotees were in danger, He at once took up His Sudarśana disc to protect them.

The mystical Lord also went inside Uttarā's womb and personally covered and protected the baby.

They were all saved. Everyone was relieved and grateful to Lord Kṛṣṇa, especially Queen Kuntī. She offered Him many prayers.

Part II: Prayers by Queen Kuntī

As Mother Kuntī watched
Kṛṣṇa's wondrous act,
she worried now He would leave
and never again come back.
Indeed, His splendid chariot
stood ready to depart,
So approaching her beloved Kṛṣṇa,
Kuntī spoke her heart.

(Adapted from Kalākaṇṭha Dāsa's book, *Bhāgavata Purāṇa – Pastimes of the Supreme Person*)

"My dear Lord Kṛṣṇa," she said gently. "Please don't go. I know You're everywhere, but no one can see this because You're invisible. Even seeing You here, this material world is like a curtain. Therefore, some people foolishly can't even see that You're the Supreme Personality of Godhead."

She continued, "You came to this material world to teach the self-realized sages how to love You." Then, with tears in her eyes, she looked at Lord Kṛṣṇa and asked, "But how can I know You? I'm merely a woman."

Then, remembering Kṛṣṇa as a sweet little cowherd boy, she began to smile and prayed, "All I can do is simply bow down to You as the son of Vasudeva who brings happiness to His mother Devakī. Oh, Govinda, you are the darling of Vṛndāvana and You bring pleasure to the cows and to our senses."

She continued, "You're our hero, Kṛṣṇa! You rescued Your mother Devakī from that dark, cold prison cell of the evil King Kaṁsa, and You saved my sons and me so many times such as when my son Bhīma was given a cake with poison in it; and when our house was set afire; and when ghastly man-eating demons tried to eat us; and even when the Kurus tried to disrobe Draupadī! Even throughout this terrible battle You protected us, and now again, from Aśvatthāmā's fiery arrow."

She thoughtfully added, "I wish all these dangers could come to us again and again, because then we get to see You again and again, and then we will always be happy. But if we try to be happy in this material world, we won't be able to see You because we won't be able to approach You with the same feeling. Some people think that Your devotees are Your favorite people, but that's just their imagination because I know You love everyone equally and You give everyone Your loving mercy equally, too. They're probably confused because in Your pastimes You act like a normal human being, like when Mother Yaśodā bound You with ropes when You were a little boy. It was amazing, Kṛṣṇa, that You were crying and scared like a child but actually even 'fear' is scared of You. How can this be? You are truly amazing, my Lord."

Mother Kuntī could not stop glorifying her dear Lord Kṛṣṇa, "Anyone who continuously hears about You, talks about You, tells others about You or even feels happy seeing others do this, will definitely be able to see Your lotus feet and will never have to take birth or die again. Oh, Kṛṣṇa, are You really leaving us even though You know we need You and are completely dependent on Your mercy?

"There's no one else to protect us. Everything we have is because of You – when You leave, everything good we have will go. Our kingdom appears beautiful as it is being marked by the impressions of Your lotus feet, but if You leave it will no longer be so. Please cut my attachment to this world and let me be just attracted to You and nothing else, just like the Ganges River flows to the sea without anything stopping her!"

After hearing Mother Kuntī's loving prayers, Lord Kṛṣṇa simply smiled at her.

Oh, children, this smile was so enchanting and magical.

He then entered the palace to bid farewell to the other ladies. Then, as He was about to leave, He was stopped again, but this time by Yudhiṣṭhira Mahārāja.

Yudhiṣṭhira Mahārāja was still very upset because so many of his friends and relatives had to die on the battlefield. "Oh, Kṛṣṇa, I am so sinful!" he cried, "My body is meant to serve others, but I used it to kill so many people. There's nothing I can do to make everything better. You can't clean muddy water with mud or a wine-stained pot with wine. Therefore, I can't undo the killing of men by sacrificing horses."

Poor Yudhiṣṭhira Mahārāja felt very disturbed.

Key Messages

- Look them up in your *Śrīmad-Bhāgavatam.*
- Put them in your own words to help you memorize them.
- Discuss each one further.
- Apply them in your life.

Theme	References	Key Messages
The Lord's protection	1.8.8–11 1.8.13–14 1.8.24 1.8.36–37	In all circumstances, we must be fully dependent on the Lord and turn to Him for protection. Only He can save us from all danger.
True chastity	1.8.17 1.8.42	Devotees are chaste because they see Lord Śrī Kṛṣṇa as their only shelter. Therefore, the Lord is immediately willing to offer full protection to such chaste devotees.
Who knows Kṛṣṇa? Only those who have His mercy	1.8.19 1.8.20 1.8.29–31	The Lord is very difficult to understand, even by Vedic knowledge. But for one who is a devotee, and therefore has the mercy of the Lord, he can very easily understand the Lord.
Kṛṣṇa sends distress to increase our love	1.8.23 1.8.25	Lord Kṛṣṇa is our ultimate well-wisher. Sometimes He puts His devotees in distressful situations because in that condition of helplessness, the devotee becomes more attached to the Lord and takes exclusive shelter of Him.
Barriers to approaching the Lord	1.8.26–27	When one is eager to make advancement materially, one becomes proud of being born in a respectable family, of having great opulence, a high education and bodily beauty. These things can distract us and make it difficult to sincerely pray to the Lord.
The Appearance of the Lord	1.8.20–21 1.8.32–35	Lord Kṛṣṇa appears in this world to display His wonderful pastimes, to re-establish religious principles, to kill the demons and to please His devotees.
Offering Prayers in Humility	1.8.18–44	Offering humble prayers to the Lord, *vandanam*, is one of the 9 processes of *bhakti*. It is a wonderful way to glorify the Lord and express our loving feelings toward Him. When the Lord sees such humility He is pleased.

Understanding the Story

Now it's time to check how well you've understood the story with these questions. (Answers at the end of the chapter.)

1. From which river did the Pāṇḍavas offer water to their dead relatives?
   a) River Yamunā
   b) River Gaṅgā
   c) River Sarasvatī
2. What did the Pāṇḍavas do after reaching the bank of the river?
   a) Went for a bath.
   b) Went for a swim.
   c) Went boating.
3. Who tried to pacify the Paṇḍavas?
   a) Dhṛtarāṣṭra
   b) Śukadeva Gosvāmī
   c) Lord Kṛṣṇa and the sages
4. The cousins of the Pāṇḍavas are
   a) moral.
   b) immoral.
   c) saintly.
5. "Everybody born in this material world dies."
   a) True
   b) False
   c) Sometimes only
6. Who was very famous throughout the world after performing three horse sacrifices?
   a) Aśvatthāmā
   b) Arjuna
   c) King Yudhiṣṭhira
7. Lord Kṛṣṇa was ready to go to his own city,
   a) Vṛndāvana.
   b) Dvāraka.
   c) Mathurā.

8. Who worshipped Lord Kṛṣṇa when He was leaving for Dvāraka?
   a) Śrīla Vyāsadeva
   b) Śrī Śukadeva Gosvāmī
   c) Sūta Gosvāmī
9. Who was running towards Lord Kṛṣṇa when He was preparing to leave?
   a) Queen Kuntī
   b) Draupadī
   c) Uttarā
10. Who fired the iron arrow to kill the baby in the womb of Uttarā?
   a) Aśvatthāmā
   b) Kṛpācārya
   c) Kṛtavarma
11. What was the fiery iron arrow called?
   a) *nārāyaṇāstra*
   b) *brahmāstra*
   c) *paśupatāstra*
12. What did the Pāṇḍavas do when they saw they were all in danger?
   a) They ran away.
   b) Fired the *brahmāstra* on Aśvatthāmā.
   c) Took up their weapons to counteract it.
13. What did Lord Kṛṣṇa do when He saw the Pāṇḍavas were in danger?
   a) Took His Sudarśana disc to protect them.
   b) Took His club to protect them.
   c) Took a sword to protect them.
14. How did Lord Kṛṣṇa protect the baby in Uttarā's womb?
   a) He fired a *brahmāstra* at Aśvatthāmā.
   b) He went into Uttarā's womb and personally covered and protected the baby.
   c) He chanted some *mantras*.
15. Govinda means "one who brings happiness to the
   a) cows
   b) rivers
   c) sages
16. Kṛṣṇa saved His mother Devakī from
   a) the *brahmāstra.*
   b) the dark, cold prison cell of King Kaṁsa.
   c) the dark, cold prison cell of the Kauravas.

17. Who saved the Pāṇḍavas many times from different dangers?
    a) Lord Kṛṣṇa
    b) Lord Śiva
    c) Bhīṣmadeva
18. Why did Queen Kuntī want the dangers to come to her again and again?
    a) So that she could see Kṛṣṇa again and again.
    b) So that Kṛṣṇa could go away.
    c) So that the Pāṇḍavas could stay together.

Higher-Thinking Questions

Now it's time to deepen your understanding of Chapter 8 by delving into Śrīla Prabhupāda's purports for this chapter and reflecting upon the following questions.

1. If you met Mahārāja Yudhiṣṭhira at the time when he was feeling really guilty, what would you say to him?
2. Why do you think that Queen Kuntī mentioned in her prayers that one who is on the path of material progress, trying to improve himself with respectable parentage, great opulence, high education and bodily beauty, cannot approach the Lord with sincere feeling?
3. Give one incident in which Queen Kuntī's life was the most challenging? How did Kṛṣṇa save her family?
4. If Arjuna was convinced by Lord Kṛṣṇa that the battle of Kurukṣetra was necessary, why was Mahārāja Yudhiṣṭhira not convinced?
5. Why did Queen Kuntī wish that all those calamities would happen again and again?

ACTIVITIES

In this section you will find many exciting things to do! They will get you thinking, moving, drawing, acting, and most importantly, having loads of fun!

Action Activities . . . to get you moving!

SECRET SEVĀ!

Description: Have a go at imbibing Kuntīdevī's deep devotional humility by serving the Lord and his servants.

This is a really fun game that requires at least three people – but the more, the better. The aim is in the name – secretly serving! Write all the names on individual pieces of paper, fold and place them all in a bowl. Without looking, each devotee chooses one piece of paper. If someone gets their own name everyone has to put the papers back and try again until everyone has a different name.

Choose a time allowance –usually two weeks is good. Your task is to secretly serve that devotee in any way you can think of. You can clean their room, leave them a beautiful verse from *Bhagavad-gītā,* bake them some cookies, make them a preparation they like, fix something they have that is broken, or clean their shoes!

These are just some examples, but the list goes on. You can also serve the other devotees playing Secret Sevā so it becomes more difficult to guess who is serving who. After two weeks you can come together as a group and try to guess who was serving who – then reveal your Secret Sevā identities!

Critical Thinking Activities

. . . to bring out the spiritual investigator in you!

KṚṢṆA'S LOTUS FEET

Description: "O Gadādhara [Kṛṣṇa], our kingdom is now being marked by the impressions of Your feet, and therefore it appears beautiful. But when You leave, it will no longer be so." (SB 1.8.39)

Kṛṣṇa has many amazing marks on His lotus feet. This is one of the many ways we can tell that He is God. Some people think that they are God. If anyone ever tells you they are God, ask them to show you the symbols on their feet!

Point out 5 differences between the two sets of feet on **Resource 1**. Then match the word to the symbol on His lotus feet on **Resource 2**.

QUEEN KUNTĪ'S PRAYERS – PĀṆḌAVAS CALAMITIES

Description: Can you remember some of the terrible things that happened to the Pāṇḍavas? Use the clues in the table on **Resource 3** to help you remember. You may need to do some further reading in the *Mahābhārata* for this activity. Describe what happened, who was involved, and how Lord Kṛṣṇa helped.

QUEEN KUNTĪ'S FAMILY TREE

Description: Do you know what a family tree is? What is the technical name for it? Find out and research some examples of family trees. It can take some real detective work to find out about people's ancestors, but luckily Vyāsadeva detailed everything beautifully in the *Mahābhārata!* Start by listing all the members of Queen Kuntī's family. Answer the quiz questions on **Resource 4**, and then fill in Queen Kuntī's family tree on **Resource 5**.

MY FAMILY TREE

Description: You will already have completed Queen Kuntī's family tree. Now create your own! Start by writing down as many family members as you can think of. Who are the oldest people on your list? Who came before them? Research by asking your grandparents or great grandparents about their family members. Now use **Resources 6** and **7** to construct a family tree based upon your own family.

Writing Activities . . . to bring out the writer in you!

QUEEN KUNTĪ BIOGRAPHY

Description: Write a biography of Queen Kuntī. A biography is a written account of the series of events that make up a person's life.

Your first task is to research Queen Kuntī's life in detail. You can use some of the prompts below to guide you:

- Date and place of birth
- Family background
- What adjective would you use to describe this person?
- What examples from their life illustrate those qualities?
- Lifetime accomplishments
- Which major events shaped or changed this person's life?
- How has their life impacted future generations?
- Would the world be a better or worse place if this person hadn't lived? How and why?

Remember to add illustrations and a cover to make the biography complete.

SENTENCE COMPLETION

Resources: First read "The Prayers of Queen Kuntī" on **Resource 9**, and the answer page for "Remember Kuntī's Prayers" on **Resource 8**.

Children should be able to . . .

- Show understanding of events and important points from Kuntī's prayers.
- Use the linking word "because" in the context of a structured sentence.
- Write a sentence using "because."

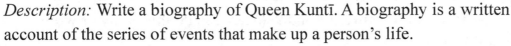

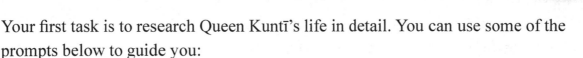

Task Instructions:

1. Print and cut out the sentence starters.
2. After reading the summary of Queen Kuntī's prayers (**Resource 9**), discuss why Queen Kuntī did not want Kṛṣṇa to leave. Encourage the answers to begin with the word "because." Adults can model how to respond using the sentence structure: "Queen Kuntī did not want Kṛṣṇa to leave because . . ." Ask for more answers and give value to answers that are given in the context of the sentence structure provided.
3. Show the first sentence starter and explain that this is just the beginning of the sentence, and that they are going to complete the sentence, using the word "because." The children can then complete each sentence, using their knowledge of the prayers from the Story Summary and **Resources 8** and **9**. (They can do this orally or write their answer on the strips.)
4. There could be a number of acceptable responses for some of these starters.
5. For a follow-up to this activity, the children can make up a "because" sentence of their own using their knowledge of the prayers or of the pastime of Parīkṣit being saved. They can write the beginning of their sentence on the first blank sentence strip and the end of their sentence on the second blank strip. They can then cut out the sentence strips and join them together. Ask them to show the beginning of their sentence to a friend to ask them to work out the ending, and vice versa.

SENTENCE STARTERS

(copy, cut out, and complete)

Queen Kuntī did not want Kṛṣṇa to leave *because*

Kṛṣṇa came to this world *because*

Some people cannot see that Kṛṣṇa is the Supreme Person *because*

Kuntī did not mind that so many bad things happened to her family *because*

Yudhiṣṭhira Mahārāja was very upset *because*

____

____ *because*

____

____

REMEMBER QUEEN KUNTĪ'S PRAYERS

Description: Queen Kuntī spoke such sweet prayers to Lord Kṛṣṇa. Can you remember the main points? Use the mind-map template on **Resource 8** to brainstorm what the key points were.

PRAYERS OF QUEEN KUNTĪ BOOK

Description: Churn the nectar of Queen Kuntī's prayers even more by compiling a book of her prayers! You will need to fold 6 pages of A4 paper together. Then bind with either 2 staples or, for a fancy effect, punch two holes and bind with some lace so that it's presented really nicely. Use the poetic verses on **Resource 9** as your text, writing on the left hand pages, then illustrate the right hand pages of your book. Remember to design a suitable front cover!

KEYWORDS

- Define the following keywords from the story.
- Use each word in a sentence (either in oral or written form).
- Complete a New Word Map at the back of the book for any new words.

KEYWORD	DEFINITION
dishonored	
despair	
ghastly	
virtuous	
revenge	
farewell	
disturbed	
enchanting	

WORD SEARCH

P	Y	J	C	W	Q	A	S	F	T	H	U	K	J
R	P	R	O	T	E	C	T	J	U	T	W	R	T
A	L	K	U	L	K	J	Y	U	E	O	V	S	G
Y	A	U	N	Y	I	N	K	O	R	D	B	N	F
E	S	C	T	S	H	A	I	R	F	G	C	A	D
R	Z	X	E	W	P	O	A	L	U	T	T	T	C
S	B	U	R	N	I	T	H	K	I	N	M	M	V
M	B	V	A	X	G	U	A	B	S	U	D	C	G
D	F	G	C	V	B	N	E	S	Q	R	W	T	W
F	U	T	T	A	R	A	T	Y	T	I	P	H	R
G	I	N	M	V	B	X	Z	W	Q	R	V	J	Y
Y	S	U	D	A	R	S	A	N	A	H	O	U	I
U	H	F	E	Y	U	I	P	O	A	S	F	N	O
I	Q	C	A	L	A	M	I	T	I	E	S	D	G
K	U	N	T	I	P	O	G	U	F	V	B	X	Z

PROTECT		CALAMITIES	
KRSNA		BURN	
STRONG		UTTARA	
KUNTI		ARROW	
COUNTERACT		KUNTI	
SUDARSANA		PRAYERS	

PRAYERS OF QUEEN KUNTĪ

Queen Kuntī couldn't bare to see
That her dearmost Kṛṣṇa would leave.

She loved Him so very much.
Thus, she prayed to Him as such . . .

"May my love for You always be,
Just like the Ganges flowing to the sea.

Strong and determined, never giving up,
Flowing to the ocean without any stop."

Kṛṣṇa smiled as Queen Kuntī prayed,
Forever in her heart, He promised He would stay.

Resource 1

Spot five differences between Lord Kṛṣṇa’s lotus feet.

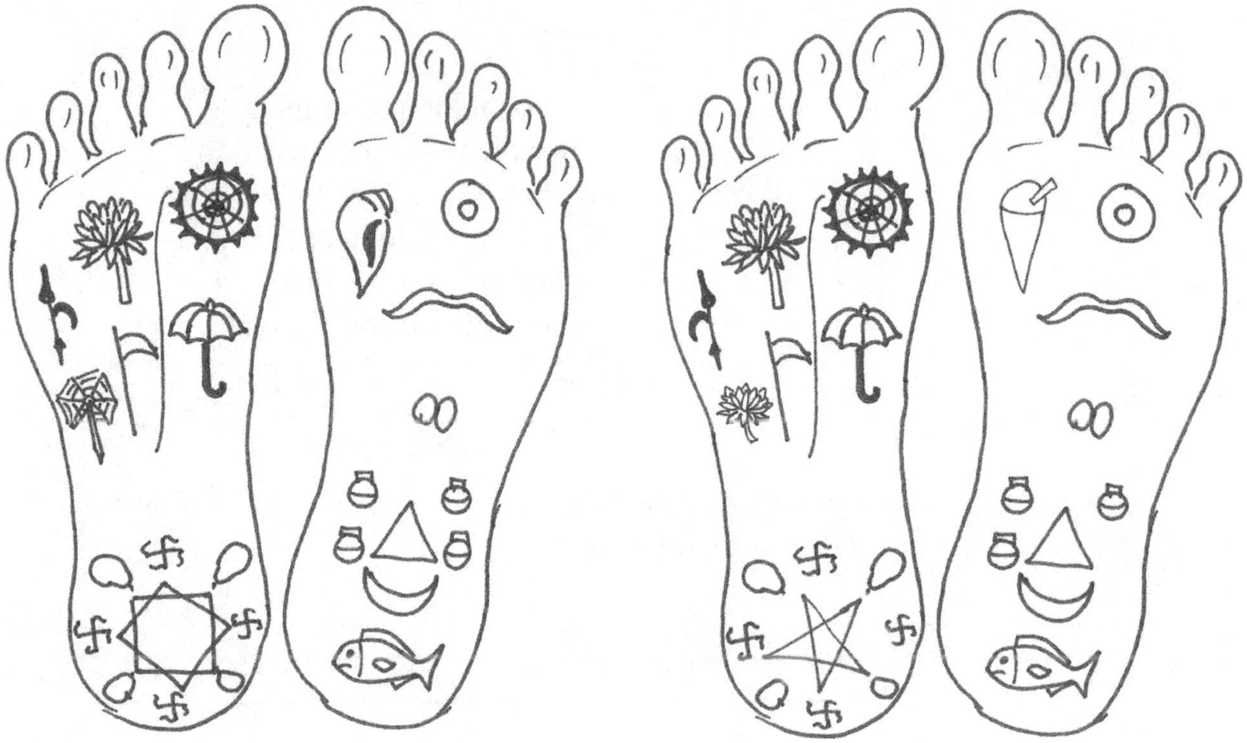

Resource 2

Match the picture to the word.

Lotus	
Moon	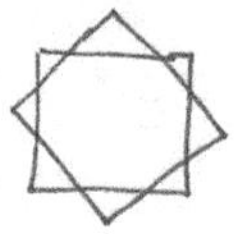
Flag	
Fish	
Star	
Fruit	

Resource 3

QUEEN KUNTĪ'S PRAYERS – PĀṆḌAVAS' CALAMITIES

Even though so many terrible things happened to my family, the Pāṇḍavas, I wish that they would happen again and again so that we can remember You, Kṛṣṇa!

Can you remember some of the terrible things that happened to the Pāṇḍavas?
Use the clues below to help you.

CLUE	Describe what you remember, who was involved, and how Kṛṣṇa helped.

Resource 4

QUEEN KUNTĪ'S FAMILY-TREE QUIZ

QUESTIONS	ANSWERS
How many children does Queen Kuntī have?	
Who is Kṛṣṇa's sister?	
Who is Uttarā married to?	
What are the names of the 5 Pāṇḍava brothers?	
Who is King Parīkṣit's grandfather?	
What are the names of two of Vasudeva's wives?	
What is the name of Kṛṣṇa's brother?	

What is the name of Arjuna's son?	
How many husbands does Draupadī have?	
Who are the two sons of Mādrī?	
Name the brother of Arjuna, known for his strength and love for eating.	
Who is Arjuna married to?	

Resource 5

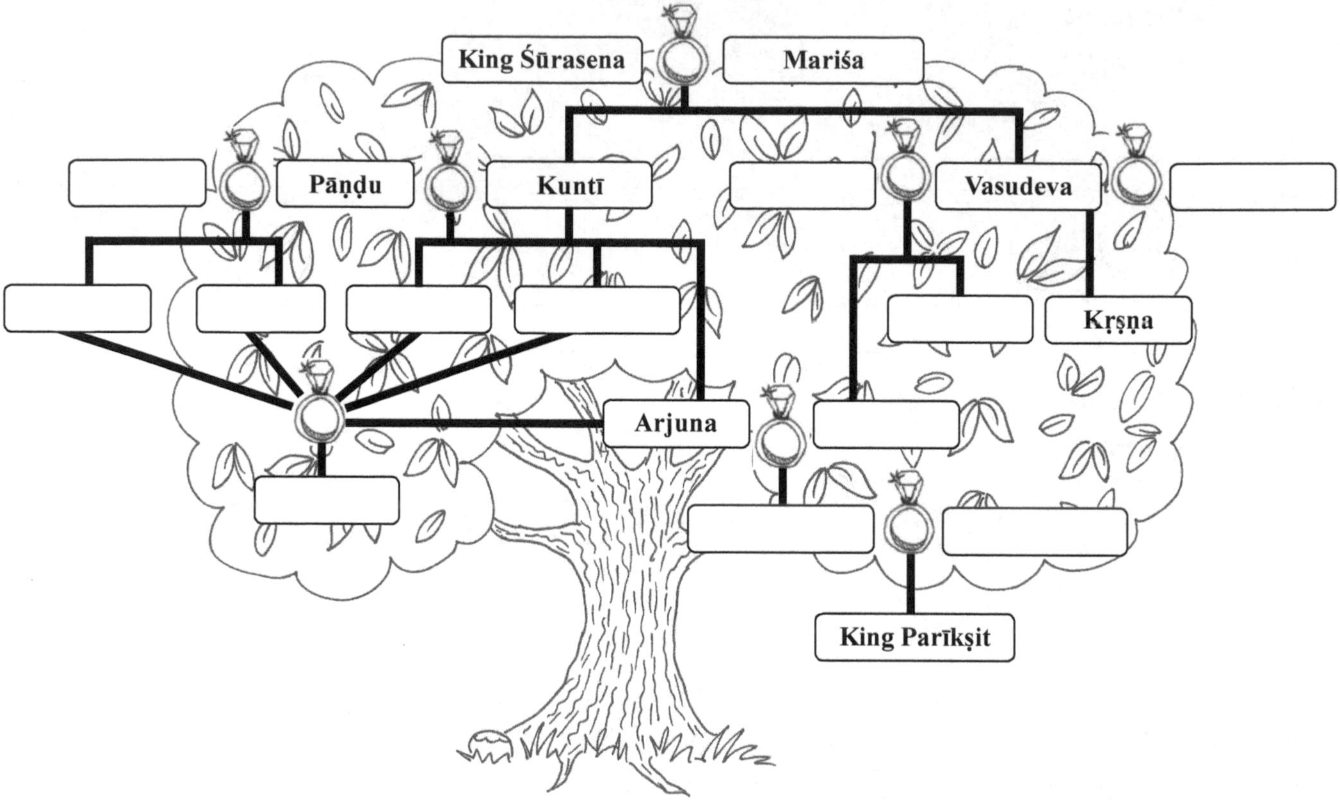

Resource 6

MY FAMILY TREE

Resource 7

Resource 8

Resource 9

THE PRAYERS OF QUEEN KUNTĪ

— A Children's Book Illustration Project —

Words for the book pages are given below in the form of a poem. Paste the words onto the left hand pages. The children can illustrate the right hand pages, using the accompanying text for inspiration.

Page 1	Kṛṣṇa, please accept my obeisances. You're the original personality, Not touched by material qualities. You're within and without everything we see.
Page 2	Beyond our understanding, You come, Giving devotional service to everyone, Like an actor on the stage who has such fun, Bewildering the audience with all he has done.
Page 3	*kṛṣṇāya vāsudevāya* *devakī-nandanāya ca* *nanda-gopa-kumārāya* *govindāya namo namaḥ* Let me offer my obeisances respectfully, To the son of Vasudeva and Devakī, Nanda Mahārāja and the Vrajavāsīs, Govinda, my Lord, from Vrajabhūmi. Your navel is sweet like a lotus flower; You're decorated by a lotus garland at every hour; Your cooling lotus glance is like a fresh spring shower; Your lotus-like feet are my greatest power.

Page 4	O Hṛṣīkeśa, My master and Lord of all, You saved Your mother Devakī from Kaṁsa, so cruel, My children and I, from dangers fearful, From poison and fire, only You heard our call. I wish that those dangers could all come again, As we were with You Kṛṣṇa, our dear most friend. If we can see You when our life is to end, We will reach out and tightly hold onto Your hand.
Page 5	My gentle Lord Kṛṣṇa, You are easy to approach, By those uninterested in material worth. You're eternal time, soul of the universe, Without beginning or end, You take Your birth.
Page 6	Equal and merciful to everyone, You appear to take birth as Yaśodā's son. You bewilder everyone when You come, With Your transcendental pastimes that have been done.
Page 7	Some say You have appeared to please Vasudeva and Devakī, Pious Kings and the Yadu Dynasty, Or the world overburdened like a boat at sea. As sandalwood in the Malaya hills appears, My Kṛṣṇa descends as Yaduvīra, To liberate conditioned souls filled with fear, By performing His pastimes for us to hear.
Page 8	Queen Kuntī prayed, "Dear Kṛṣṇa, please stay! Oh! Please don't leave us, never go away!" Queen Kuntī always wanted to see Sweet Kṛṣṇa before her, from His head to His feet.

Page 9	Our name, fame and fortune is finished, And our material body diminished, Along with our activities and families, If our kingdom is not tread on by Your lotus feet. Our beautiful lands and wealth in the sea, Our hills full of minerals and fruit on the trees, Is due to Your glance, oh, Lord of Mercy, Please sever my affection to my family.
Page 10	I pray my attraction for Kṛṣṇa will be As the Ganges forever flows to the sea, Without being diverted by anyone I see, I offer You my respectful obeisances.
Page 11	As Kṛṣṇa heard Queen Kuntī pray, He smiled and blessed her in every way. Although He had to leave that day, Deep in her heart He would always stay.

ANSWERS

"Understanding the Story" (pages 190–192)

1) b, 2) a, 3) c, 4) b, 5) a, 6) c, 7) b, 8) a, 9) c, 10) a, 11) b, 12) c, 13) a, 14) b, 15) a, 16) b, 17) a, 18) a

Keywords (page 198)

KEYWORD	DEFINITION
dishonored	Lost honor or prestige; disgraced; lost reputation
despair	To lose all hope; to lose belief that the situation will improve
ghastly	Horrible; shocking; very unpleasant or disagreeable
virtuous	Morally excellent; righteous; exhibiting virtue
revenge	To inflict harm or injury in return for a wrong done
farewell	Act of leaving; a formal occasion honoring a person about to leave
disturbed	Worried and unhappy; affected by a disturbance
enchanting	Charming; having great attraction

Word Search (page 199)

P			C									K	
R	P	R	O	T	E	C	T				W	R	
A			U							O		S	
Y			N						R			N	
E			T					R				A	
R			E				A						
S	B	U	R	N									
			A										
			C					S					
	U	T	T	A	R	A			T				
										R			
	S	U	D	A	R	S	A	N	A		O		
												N	
		C	A	L	A	M	I	T	I	E	S		G
K	U	N	T	I									

Resource 3 Answers (page 204–205)

CLUE	Describe what you remember, who was involved, and how Kṛṣṇa helped.
	Duryodhana arranged that a house be made out of material that can be very easily set on fire. He invited the Pāṇḍavas to stay there and then set it on fire. Luckily, Vidura, the Pāṇḍavas' uncle, gave them a clue that the house was going to be burnt, so they escaped via a tunnel leading to the forest.
	Duryodhana tried to kill Bhīma by giving him a poisoned cake to eat. After he ate it, Duryodhana, along with Duḥśāsana, his brother, threw Bhīma into the River Ganges. Bhīma sank under the water and was bitten by some snakes. The venom from the snakes neutralized the poison from the cake. Then he met the snakes' leader, Vasuki, and was given special powers by him to become as strong as 10,000 elephants.
	The Pāṇḍavas were tricked into being sent to the forest for 13 years. Then, in the final year, they had to live in disguise. While in the forest, they lived very simple lives and also came across demons and other difficulties. Kṛṣṇa was there to guide them.
	While in the forest, the Pāṇḍavas were attacked by a man-eating demon, called Hiḍimb. Hiḍimb asked his sister, Hiḍimbā, to capture the Pāṇḍavas so that he could eat them. When Hiḍimbā saw Bhīma, she thought he was very handsome and fell in love with him. When Hiḍimb found out that his sister did not want to capture and kill the Pāṇḍavas, he became angry and attacked them. Bhīma fought with the demon and killed him.

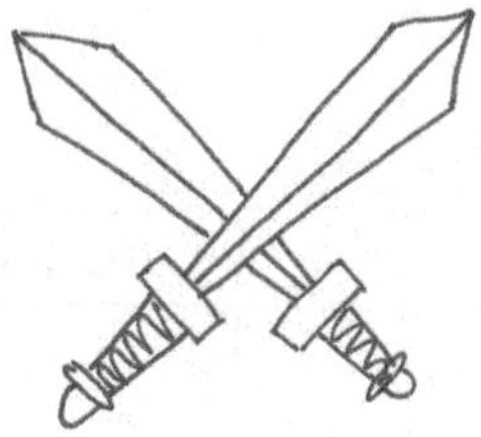	The Pāṇḍavas took part in the Battle of Kurukṣetra, against their cousins the Kurūs, headed by Duryodhana. When Arjuna became weak and didn't want to fight, Kṛṣṇa advised and encouraged him to not be afraid, but to do his duty. Kṛṣṇa was even willing to break His promise not to fight when He saw that His dear devotee, Arjuna, was in danger.
	The Pāṇḍavas were tricked into taking part in a gambling match. In this match, Duryodhana and his sneaky Uncle Śakunī cheated them out of their kingdom.
	The *brahmāstra* weapon was sent by Aśvatthāmā to kill King Parīkṣit in the womb of Uttarā. Uttarā ran to ask Kṛṣṇa for help, so Kṛṣṇa released His Sudarśana disc. He also appeared within the womb of Uttarā to personally protect Parīkṣit Mahārāja.
	Duryodhana's younger brother, Duḥśāsana, attempted to take Draupadī's *sārī* off in front of all the Kurū family members to embarrass her. She was terrified so she called out to Kṛṣṇa to save and protect her. Kṛṣṇa responded to Draupadī's prayer by sending an unlimited amount of *sārī* so that Draupadī could not be shown naked.

Resource 5 Answers (page 208)

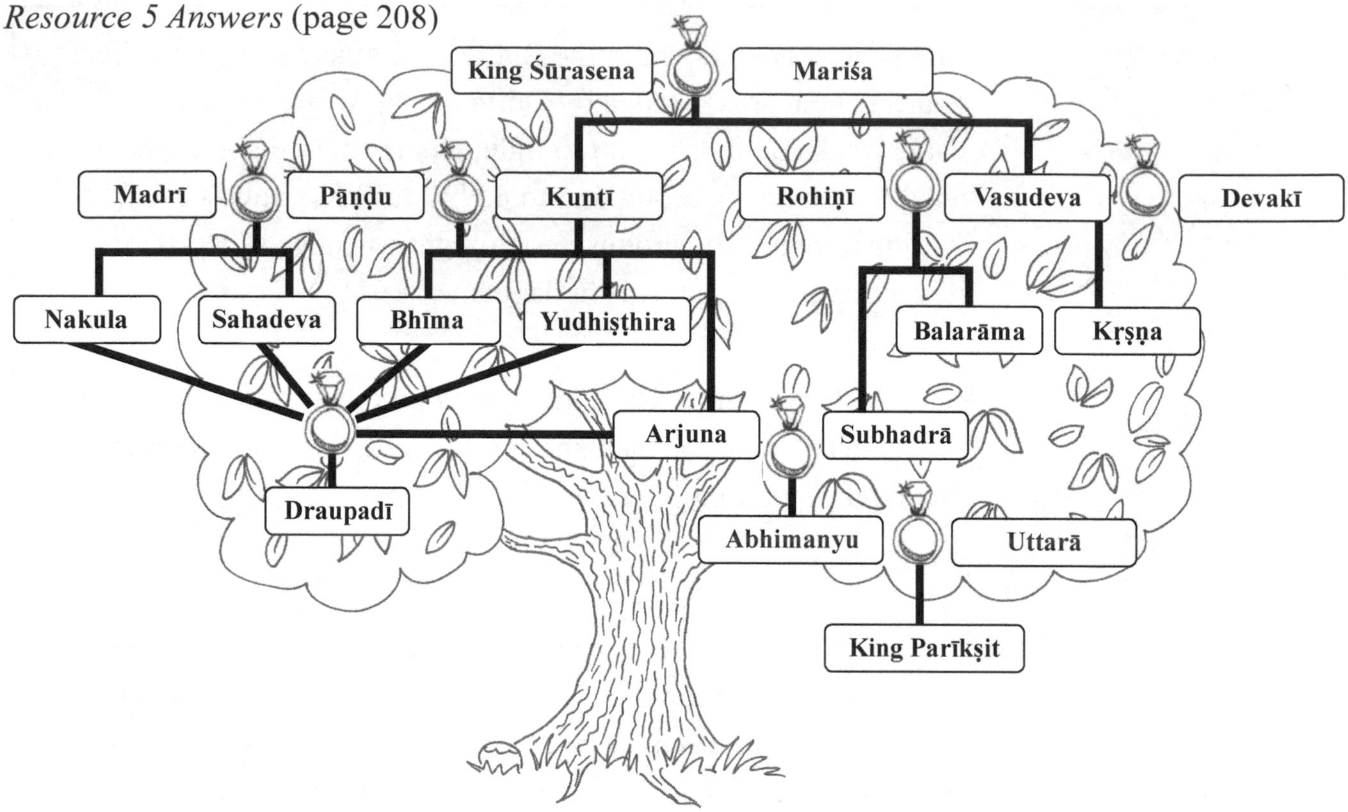

Resource 8 Answers (page 210)

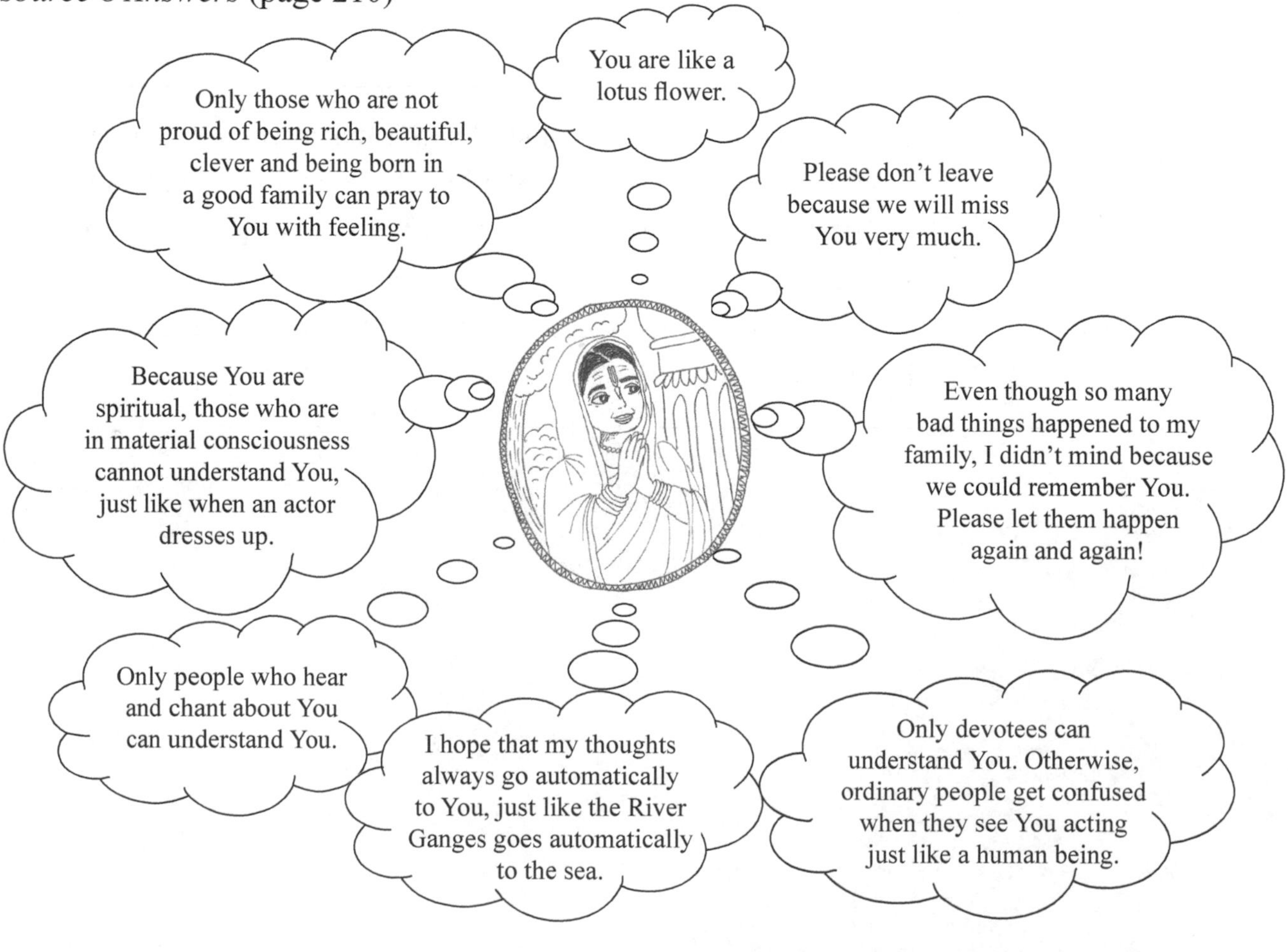

9

Bhīṣmadeva Passing Away

Story Summary

How would you feel if you had to do something really difficult for a higher good? The Pāṇḍavas had to kill many of their friends and relatives in battle just to protect the innocent people from evil rulers. It really wasn't easy for them because they loved their friends and relatives very much.

Poor Yudhiṣṭhira Mahārāja felt very afraid that he would have to pay for his sins of killing so many people. He decided to return to the battlefield to see how bad things were.

As he walked towards the Battlefield of Kurukṣetra, his brothers followed closely behind on splendid golden chariots, which were pulled by beautifully decorated horses. Lord Kṛṣṇa and many sages, including Vyāsadeva, also followed Yudhiṣṭhira Mahārāja, who looked like a very rich demigod followed by his entourage.

As they reached the battlefield, they saw their most dear Grandfather Bhīṣmadeva lying on a bed of arrows, and they all respectfully bowed down before him. He was about to leave his body. When Grandfather Bhīṣma saw them, he welcomed the sages and then worshiped Lord Kṛṣṇa. He saw his dear grandchildren, the Pāṇḍavas, sitting silently nearby. They seemed very upset, seeing him in this way, because they loved him so much.

"Oh my boys," spoke Grandfather Bhīṣmadeva with great affection, "Many bad things have happened to you and your mother Kuntī just because you tried to please Kṛṣṇa. You

could have died several times, but Kṛṣṇa and the devotees always protected you. You must remember that everything is Kṛṣṇa's plan so don't worry; accept the plan of the Lord and follow it. Dear Yudhiṣṭhira, you are now the appointed King and must take care of all of your subjects."

"Look at Śrī Kṛṣṇa standing next to you . . . ," continued Bhīṣmadeva. "You think He's just your cousin and your friend, but actually He's none other than the Supreme Personality of Godhead. He is in everyone's heart and treats everyone equally, but because I'm always His servant at all times, He has so mercifully come to me while I'm dying."

"Anyone who thinks of Kṛṣṇa and chants His name as they leave their body will go straight back to the spiritual world. Please, can my beautiful lotus-faced, smiling Kṛṣṇa be there for me when I leave my body?"

When Yudhiṣṭhira Mahārāja heard Grandfather Bhīṣma speak like this, he stepped forward and respectfully asked him: "Grandfather Bhīṣma, could you explain to us how one can follow religion properly?"

Bhīṣmadeva, seeing his grandson's eagerness to hear a reply, began to explain the answer about religion. He described the duties of devotees, and the occupational duties of the four orders of life. In this way Bhīṣmadeva told his grandsons the path through life, by which all human beings could realize their spiritual identity and become free from material life.

Soon it was time to leave his body, so Bhīṣmadeva stopped thinking about anything else and looked at Lord Kṛṣṇa standing before him. Lord Kṛṣṇa was standing with four hands and dressed in yellow garments that glittered and shined. All of a sudden, any bad luck just disappeared and he could no longer feel pain from the arrow wounds in his body. He then prayed to Lord Kṛṣṇa and thought only of Him.

Grandfather Bhīṣma then stopped breathing. His soul immediately left his body and traveled back to the spiritual world to be again with Lord Kṛṣṇa.

Everyone fell silent – like birds at the end of the day.

Then in honor of Grandfather Bhīṣmadeva leaving his body and returning to the spiritual world, drums resounded and flowers showered from the sky. What a wonderful scene! The sages turned to Kṛṣṇa and glorified Him before returning back to their own hermitages, while keeping Kṛṣṇa always in their hearts. Yudhiṣṭhira Mahārāja also returned home and began to rule His kingdom with fairness.

Key Messages

- Look them up in your *Śrīmad-Bhāgavatam.*
- Put them in your own words to help you memorize them.
- Discuss each one further.
- Apply them in your life.

Theme	References	Key Messages
Relationships with Kṛṣṇa; Kṛṣṇa plays the part for our benefit	1.9.4 1.9.20 1.9.34–40	Lord Kṛṣṇa is so kind, that He reciprocates the love of His devotees by engaging in loving relationships with them as a cousin, intimate friend, messenger, and counselor, etc. Although He performs all these services, it does not change His position.
Instructions of great souls	1.9.12–42	Senior devotees, who are experienced, can help us by imparting their instructions. By carefully hearing and applying these instructions, we can advance in devotional service.
Even devotees experience difficulties to teach us	1.9.12–13 1.9.15–16	The Lord teaches through His pure devotees that He is our only refuge. The suffering of his pure devotee is not due to past misdeeds.
Time	1.9.14–15	As long as we are in the material world, we must bear the actions and reactions of time. Time controls everything. But we shouldn't be disturbed by it, because time is Kṛṣṇa Himself.
Kṛṣṇa bewilders all – no one knows His plan.	1.9.16–18	It is impossible to understand the plan of the Lord. Even the great demigods cannot understand it, what to speak of us. The best policy is to accept His plan, having faith that He knows best.
How to live in this world	1.9.26–28	Religious principles direct us how to live in this world in such a way that we can gradually become free from identification with the material body. Then, in a purified state, we can start to recognize our true spiritual nature.
Fix the mind on the Lord	1.9.30–33 1.9.39–43	If we cultivate the strong desire to see the Lord by engaging in His loving service, at the time of death, by His grace, we will be able to fix our minds upon Him.
The art of dying	1.9.5–8 1.9.32 1.9.39 1.9.42–45	Pure devotees set an example of how to leave this material body. Following the example of Bhīṣmadeva, we should desire to leave in the association of devotees and focus our minds only on the Lord.

Character Description

Are you familiar with Bhīṣmadeva? What do you know about him? Share what you know with a partner, then read the descriptions below.

Bhīṣmadeva

- He is one of the 12 Mahājanas.
- He is the son of King Śāntanu and Gaṅgādevī.
- He is a disciple of Bṛhaspatī.
- He was known as Devavrata as a youth.
- His name, Bhīṣma, means "He who took a terrible vow."
- He took a vow to never marry.
- He fought on the Kaurava's side in the battle of Kurukṣetra.
- His nephews were Pāṇḍu, Dhṛtarāṣṭra and Vidura (sons of Vyāsadeva).

Understanding the Story

Now it's time to check how well you've understood the story with these questions. (Answers at the end of the chapter.)

1. Who did the Pāṇḍavas see lying on a bed of arrows on the battlefield?
   a) Aśvatthāmā
   b) Yudhiṣṭhira Mahārāja
   c) Grandfather Bhīṣmadeva
2. How did the Pāṇḍavas feel when they saw Grandfather Bhīṣmadeva?
   a) Happy
   b) Upset
   c) Scared
3. The Kauravas tried to kill the Pāṇḍavas many times. The Pāṇḍavas were always good, so who protected them?
   a) Kṛṣṇa and the devotees
   b) The demigods
   c) The demons
4. The Pāṇḍavas proceeded to see Bhīṣmadeva on the Battlefield of
   a) Kurukṣetra.
   b) Hastināpura.
   c) Dvārakā.

5. Who really is Kṛṣṇa?
   a) A demon
   b) A demigod
   c) The Supreme Personality of Godhead
6. Kṛṣṇa treats everyone equally, so why did He go to Bhīṣmadeva while he was leaving his body?
   a) Bhīṣmadeva was always His servant
   b) Bhīṣmadeva was an old man
   c) Bhīṣmadeva was very strong
7. What will happen to someone who thinks of Kṛṣṇa and chants His name as he/she leaves his/her body?
   a) Go straight back to the spiritual world
   b) Be born again as Kṛṣṇa
   c) Be born again as an ant
8. As Bhīṣmadeva was leaving his body, he looked at Kṛṣṇa. How many arms did Kṛṣṇa have?
   a) Two arms
   b) Four arms
   c) Six arms

Higher-Thinking Questions

Now it's time to deepen your understanding of Chapter 9 by delving into Śrīla Prabhupāda's purports for this chapter and reflecting upon the following questions.

1. Explain the phrase "higher or greater good." Refer to the part of the story summary describing how the Pāṇḍavas had to kill their family members and friends in order to protect innocent people from evil rulers.
2. How did Lord Kṛṣṇa fulfill the desire of Bhīṣma, while sacrificing His promise not to take up any weapon?
3. If Bhīṣmadeva was such a great devotee of the Lord and loved the Pāṇḍavas, why did he join the Kaurava army in the Battle of Kurukṣetra?
4. How did Bhīṣmadeva explain the essential principles of various religious duties?
5. Summarize Bhīṣmadeva's meditation on Kṛṣṇa before he passed away.

ACTIVITIES

In this section you will find many exciting things to do! They will get you thinking, moving, drawing, acting, and most importantly, having loads of fun!

Action Activities . . . to get you moving!

BHĪṢMADEVA SAYS!

Description: See how good you are at following instructions. This is a variation of the game "Simon Says" but instead it's "Bhīṣmadeva Says!" All of the commands which begin with "Bhīṣmadeva says . . ." must be followed – otherwise, you will be out. You are also out if you follow a command which does not start with "Bhīṣmadeva says . . ."

Here are some examples of commands you can give:

"Bhīṣmadeva says, 'pay obeisances.'"
"Bhīṣmadeva says, 'chant one *mahā-mantra.*'"

Remember to trick your players, so sometimes you should give a command without saying "Bhīṣmadeva says . . ." Instead, replace Bhīṣmadeva's name with another, like Arjuna or Yudhiṣṭhira. If someone responds to this trick command then they are out. If someone is out, call out his/her name and ask him/her to sit on the side. Play until you have a winner!

Variations on the above game include:

- Giving the orders quickly, one after the other
- Giving multiple orders at once, e.g. "Bhīṣmadeva says, 'touch your toes, jump up, and chant Hare Kṛṣṇa.'"

"BACK TO KṚṢṆA" BOARD GAME

You Will Need:

1. Dice and small token (e.g. button,etc.) for each person.
2. Print out the playing board on **Resource 1** and glue to cardboard. Older children

may wish to draw their own playing board directly on the cardboard.

3. Print out the questions on **Resource 2**, and cut and place them face down in a pile on one corner of the board.

How to Play:

1. Players place their tokens on **START**.
2. Each player takes a turn to roll the dice and move their token forward the number of spaces indicated on the dice. Follow the instructions on the place of landing.
3. If you land on an arrow with a number, move the token that number of spaces in the direction the arrow is pointing.
4. **?** means take a question from the top of the pile. If answered correctly, move forward 3 spaces. If answered incorrectly, the player does not move. Place the questions face down at the bottom of the pile.
5. A smiley face means to take another turn.
6. The winner is the one who reaches Kṛṣṇa first.
7. This game can be played using the discussion questions from any of the chapters.

Analogy Activities . . . to bring out the scholar in you!

THE ORDER OF THE DEVOTEE

"The Lord, being the supreme living being, is never the order supplier or order carrier of anyone, whoever he may be. But out of His causeless mercy and affection for His pure devotees, sometimes He carries out the order of the devotee like an awaiting servant. By executing the order of a devotee, the Lord becomes pleased, as a father is pleased to carry out the order of his small child. This is possible only out of pure transcendental love between the Lord and His devotees, and Bhīṣmadeva was quite aware of this fact." (SB 1.9.35 Purport)

Learning Activity:

Children should be able to . . .

- Comprehend how and why the Lord might follow the order of His devotee.
- Cite other examples from scripture where the Lord has followed the order of His devotee.
- Explain from their own experience why this is compared to a father and his child.

Resources: Below are some examples of quiz questions. The theme of the quiz is based on examples of when Kṛṣṇa carried out the order of His devotee just to please him. You can also add your own questions. You can also brainstorm other categories for additional questions to add.

Instructions: Each time you think you know the answer to the question being asked, ring a bell as fast as possible. The first to ring their bell can try to answer the question.

Arjuna's Charioteer

- The *Bhagavad-gītā* is a conversation between two people. Who are they? (a) Kṛṣṇa and Arjuna (b) Kṛṣṇa and Brahmā (c) Kṛṣṇa and Śrīla Prabhupāda
- Before going to battle, Arjuna wanted on his side (a) Kṛṣṇa (b) Kṛṣṇa's army (c) Kṛṣṇa's weapons
- To direct Kṛṣṇa in the right direction on the battlefield of Kurukṣetra, did Arjuna communicate (a) with his hands on Kṛṣṇa's head? (b) with his feet on Kṛṣṇa's shoulders? (c) by yelling left and right?

Sāndīpani Muni's Student

- Kṛṣṇa went to school at (a) Sāndīpani Munī's āśrama? (b) Sage Viśvāmitra's *āśrama*? (c) the *yogī's āśrama*?
- What did Sāndīpani Muni ask Kṛṣṇa to collect from the forest? (a) dry leaves (b) mud (c) firewood
- Who was with Kṛṣṇa when Sāndīpani Muni asked them to collect firewood from the forest? (a) Sudāmā (b) Advaita Ācārya (c) Lakṣmaṇa

Mother Yaśodā's Son

- Kṛṣṇa was punished by Mother Yaśodā for stealing (a) sugar (b) butter (c) milk
- When Mother Yaśodā tried to punish Kṛṣṇa by tying Him to the wooden mortar, the rope was always short by (a) 4 inches (b) 1 inch (c) 2 inches
- Kṛṣṇa allowed Himself to be tied to the wooden mortar with (a) rope (b) string (c) knitting yarn

Advaita Ācārya's Prayer

- Who prayed for the appearance of Lord Caitanya with Tulasī and Gaṅgā? (a) Nityānanda Prabhu (b) Gadādhara Paṇdita (c) Advaita Ācārya
- Advaita Ācārya prayed for the appearance of the Lord because (a) people were too materialistic (b) people were too happy (c) people were too spiritual
- Advaita Ācārya is considered to be an incarnation of (a) Lord Viṣṇu (b) Lord Śiva (c) both Lord Viṣṇu and Lord Śiva

King Daśaratha's Son

- Who did Queen Kaikeyī want to see coronated as King? (a) Lakṣmaṇa (b) Lord Rāma (c) Bharata
- How did King Daśaratha feel about sending Lord Rāma into exile? (a) happy (b) sad (c) heartbroken
- Lord Rāma was exiled for (a) 7 years (b) 14 years (c) 21 years

Preparation: Based on the above, prepare some quiz cards with the relevant questions. You can also research your own themes and questions. Below are some pastimes which you may want to discuss:

- Sākśī-Gopāla, bearing witness to the promise of the *brāhmāṇa*
- Kṛṣṇa creating Kusum Sarovara, upon the request of Rādhārāṇī
- Lord Brahmā approaching Lord Viṣṇu at the shore of the ocean of milk
- Lord Caitanya going back to Mayapur to fulfil the desire of Mother Śacī

Prompt Questions:

- Can you think of any other pastimes where the Lord has obeyed the orders of His devotee?
- What is your favorite pastime of the Lord, wherein He obeys the orders of His devotee(s)?

Conclusion (discuss):

- There are so many examples of the Lord reciprocating with His sincere devotees, and there are so many examples of this.
- The Lord does this out of compassion and mercy just to please the devotees.
- I have a favorite pastime that I turn to for inspiration.

Critical Thinking Activities

. . . to bring out the spiritual investigator in you!

BHĪṢMADEVA QUIZ

Description: Look at the questions below, and add more questions to form a Bhīṣmadeva Quiz. When you have a completed quiz, read your questions out either to a partner or, as a quizmaster, to two teams. For bonus points you can ask team members to elaborate on the details of their answers.

1. Whose side was Bhīṣmadeva on in the Battle of Kurukṣetra?
2. What was the terrible vow that he made?
3. How is he related to Arjuna?
4. Which famous river is his mother?
5. Name three great people that were present when Bhīṣmadeva was leaving his body.
6. Who shot the arrows that made Grandfather Bhīṣma's bed of arrows?
7. Why didn't Bhīṣmadeva leave his body right away? What was he waiting for?

BHĪṢMADEVA'S INSTRUCTIONS

Reference: SB 1.9.26 Purport
Description: Bhīṣmadeva imparted some amazing instructions on the nine qualities human beings must acquire to be called a civilized person, just before he left his body. Use the clues on **Resource 3** to try to guess what they are.

NAMES FOR KṚṢṆA – MATCH-UP ACTIVITY

While lying on his deathbed, Grandfather Bhīṣma remembered Kṛṣṇa in different relationships with His devotees:

- Speaking *Bhavagad-gītā* to Arjuna
- Fighting on the battlefield with himself
- Attracting the *gopīs*
- Being worshipped as the Supreme Lord during the Rājasūya sacrifice

Below are several names of Kṛṣṇa in different relationships with His devotees. Can you match each name to the appropriate meaning?

Puruṣottama	The master of the *gopīs*
Pārtha Sārathi	He who is affectionate to His devotees
Gopinātha	The Supreme Person
Bhakta-vatsala	Friend of the cows and calves
Gopāla	The chariot driver of Kṛṣṇa

Introspective Activities

. . . to bring out the reflective devotee in you!

SPIRITUAL INSTRUCTIONS INTERVIEW

Description: With a dictaphone, ask at least five devotees:

- What are the most memorable and important instructions they have received?
- Who gave these instructions?
- What effect it had on their lives?

Reflecting on the answers that they gave, did you hear any inspiring tales? Fill in the table in **Resource 4**.

INSTRUCTIONS OF DEVOTEES

Description: The instructions of senior devotees are invested with potency that can help to transform our hearts! Create a mind map of some key instructions that you have received. You can add how you have applied the instructions and the effects of following them. An example is given on **Resource 5**.

Writing Activities . . . to bring out the writer in you!

BHĪṢMADEVA BIOGRAPHY

Description: Write a biography of Bhīṣmadeva. A biography is a written account of the series of events that make up a person's life. Your first task is to research Bhīṣmadeva's life in detail. You can use the prompts below to guide you:

- Date and place of birth and when he left his body
- Family background
- What adjective would you use to describe this person?
- What examples from his life illustrate those qualities?
- Lifetime accomplishments
- Which major events shaped or changed this person's life?

- How has his life impacted future generations?
- Would the world be a better or worse place if this person hadn't lived? How and why?

Remember to add illustrations and a cover to make the biography complete.

ACROSTIC POEM

Description: Down one side of a sheet of paper, write the name Bhīṣmadeva. You can use the character description of Bhīṣmadeva at the beginning of the chapter for inspiration. Then, for each letter of the name, come up with qualities or traits that begin with the letter to describe Bhīṣmadeva. Example:

B rave
H
I
S
M
A
D
E
V
A

KEYWORDS

- Define the following keywords from the story.
- Use each word in a sentence (either in oral or written form).
- Complete a New Word Map at the back of the book for any new words.

KEYWORD	DEFINITION
entourage	
innocent	
honor	
resound	
subjects	
religion	

EXTENDED VOCABULARY

Here are some words describing Bhīṣmadeva's character. Match the word to the meaning.

Brave	Having good qualities and behavior
Heroic	Trained in a special area
Honest	Admired for his great qualities and acts
Skilled	Without fear
Virtuous	Always tells the truth

WORD SEARCH

P	O	I	Y	T	I	E	W	Q	G	F	D	A	S
A	D	T	R	L	G	H	J	K	L	C	B	M	E
S	E	G	A	J	H	E	A	R	T	Z	X	C	R
D	V	K	O	H	Q	S	F	G	I	Q	O	K	V
F	O	S	Y	G	W	H	G	D	O	K	B	N	E
R	T	C	H	F	R	E	E	S	Y	R	E	G	F
E	E	V	J	D	A	S	D	C	H	G	I	L	C
M	E	B	Q	U	E	S	T	I	O	N	S	T	Z
E	S	K	L	H	D	V	C	A	X	Z	A	G	I
M	F	U	N	Q	H	A	P	P	Y	Q	N	D	O
B	G	J	A	O	C	V	I	J	H	K	C	S	Y
E	H	B	D	S	T	T	O	H	Q	R	E	C	H
R	J	C	L	E	A	N	Y	G	W	G	S	P	O
I	K	O	Q	W	A	S	D	F	G	E	S	T	I
O	L	N	U	R	H	E	A	R	B	D	V	C	U

HEART		OBEISANCES	
KALI		FREE	
KNOT		QUESTION	
DEVOTEES		REMEMBER	
HEAR		CLEAN	
SERVE		HAPPY	

Theatrical Activities

. . . to bring out the actor in you!

KṚṢṆA FIGHTING WITH BHĪṢMADEVA

Reference: SB 1.9.37–39

Description: Characters / Arjuna, Bhīṣmadeva, Kṛṣṇa. Act out the following scenes using simple props:

1. Bhīṣma resolved to kill Arjuna on the battlefield one day.
2. He showered many arrows at Arjuna.
3. Kṛṣṇa realized that Arjuna was really in trouble so He got down from the chariot and picked up the chariot wheel. He spinned it around like His *sudarśana* disc and ran towards Bhīṣma, dropping His shawl along the way.
4. Seeing this, Bhīṣma at once gave up his weapons and stood to be killed by Kṛṣṇa, his beloved Lord.
5. Suddenly the sun went down and the fighting was finished for the day.

NEWS REPORT – BREAKING NEWS

Description: Imagine that you are a newspaper reporter at the scene of Bhīṣmadeva's passing and arc giving a report of what is happening live on TV. Give a minute-by-minute update of the current situation with the characters present and the events leading up to it. You can also interview some of the people after Bhīṣmadeva had passed away, such as one of the Pāṇḍavas – or even Lord Kṛṣṇa!

THE PASSING AWAY OF BHĪṢMADEVA

Bhīṣmadeva is lying on a sharp arrow bed;
He is not even crying and he does not feel sad.
Soon he will leave his body with Kṛṣṇa by his side,
Then he'll go back home to Godhead in the spiritual sky.

He was the mighty son of the great King Śāntanu;
His mother was the Ganges and brothers he had one and two,
The sage Vyāsa and the brave King Vicitravīrya,
Who had three sons Dhṛtarāstra, Pāṇḍu and Vidura.

Dhṛtarāstra had one-hundred sons and Pāṇḍu five Pāṇḍavas.
Bhīṣma taught them all how to fight and rule as honest Kṣatriyas.
The Kauravas never listened to Bhīṣmadeva's advice,
So during the Battle of Kurukṣetra the Kauravas paid the price.

The sons of Pāṇḍu always did just as Bhīṣma said;
They loved him very much and came to see him on his arrow bed.
They asked him many questions and he gave them good advice
On how to always love Kṛṣṇa, all throughout their life.

Bhīṣmadeva is lying on a sharp arrow bed,
His soul is eternal that's why we're not sad,
He has left his body, with Kṛṣṇa by his side.

Resource 1

BACK TO KRṢṆA

Resource 2

BACK TO KṚṢṆA GAME CARDS

TRUE or FALSE? Yudhiṣṭhira asked Bhīṣmadeva to explain how to win more battles.	**TRUE or FALSE?** Before Bhīṣmadeva left his body he looked at Lord Kṛṣṇa standing with four hands and dressed in yellow garments that glittered and shined.
TRUE or FALSE? When Bhīṣmadeva stopped breathing, his soul immediately left his body and traveled back to be again with Lord Śiva.	**TRUE or FALSE?** In honor of Bhīṣmadeva leaving his body and returning to the spiritual world, drums resounded and flowers showered from the sky.
TRUE or FALSE? Yudhiṣṭhira felt bad that he had killed so many people in the Battle of Kurukṣetra.	**TRUE or FALSE?** When Bhīṣmadeva looked at Lord Kṛṣṇa he felt even more pain in his body from the arrows.
TRUE or FALSE? We should practice devotional service in this lifetime so we can think of Kṛṣṇa at the time of death.	**TRUE or FALSE?** Bhīṣma was sad because he was hungry.
TRUE or FALSE? Bhīṣmadeva is the son of King Śāntanu and Yamunā devi.	**TRUE or FALSE?** Vyāsadeva was present at the time that Bhīṣmadeva was leaving his body.

TRUE or FALSE? Bhīṣmadeva took a vow to fast from grains.	**TRUE or FALSE?** "Bhīṣma" means one who has taken a terrible vow.
TRUE or FALSE? Bhīṣma fought on the side of the Kauravas.	**TRUE or FALSE?** Vidura was Bhīṣmadeva's nephew.
TRUE or FALSE? One of Bhīṣmadeva's instructions was to give charity on Tuesdays.	**TRUE or FALSE?** Bhīṣmadeva approved of Dhṛtarāstra and Duryodhana's actions.
TRUE or FALSE? Bhīṣmadeva left his body when the sun ran into the southern hemisphere.	**TRUE or FALSE?** Bhīṣmadeva was one of the nine Vasus.

Resource 3

BHĪṢMADEVA'S INSTRUCTIONS

CLUE	INSTRUCTION

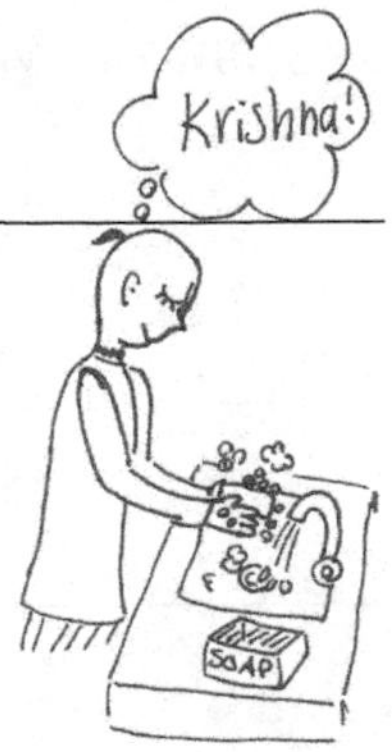	

The opposite of complicated.	

Resource 4

SPIRITUAL INSTRUCTIONS REFLECTION EXERCISE

Did you find out anything that inspired you? Explain what it was and why.

Describe the attitude that the devotees had when they were receiving
or following the instructions they were given.

Can you think of any reasons why a spiritual guide
may not give guidance to a person/disciple?

Imagine that someone new to Kṛṣṇa Consciousness asked you – "Why do you need to take instructions from others? I know what's best for me." How would you respond to them?

Who are the guides in your life that you take guidance from?

Resource 5

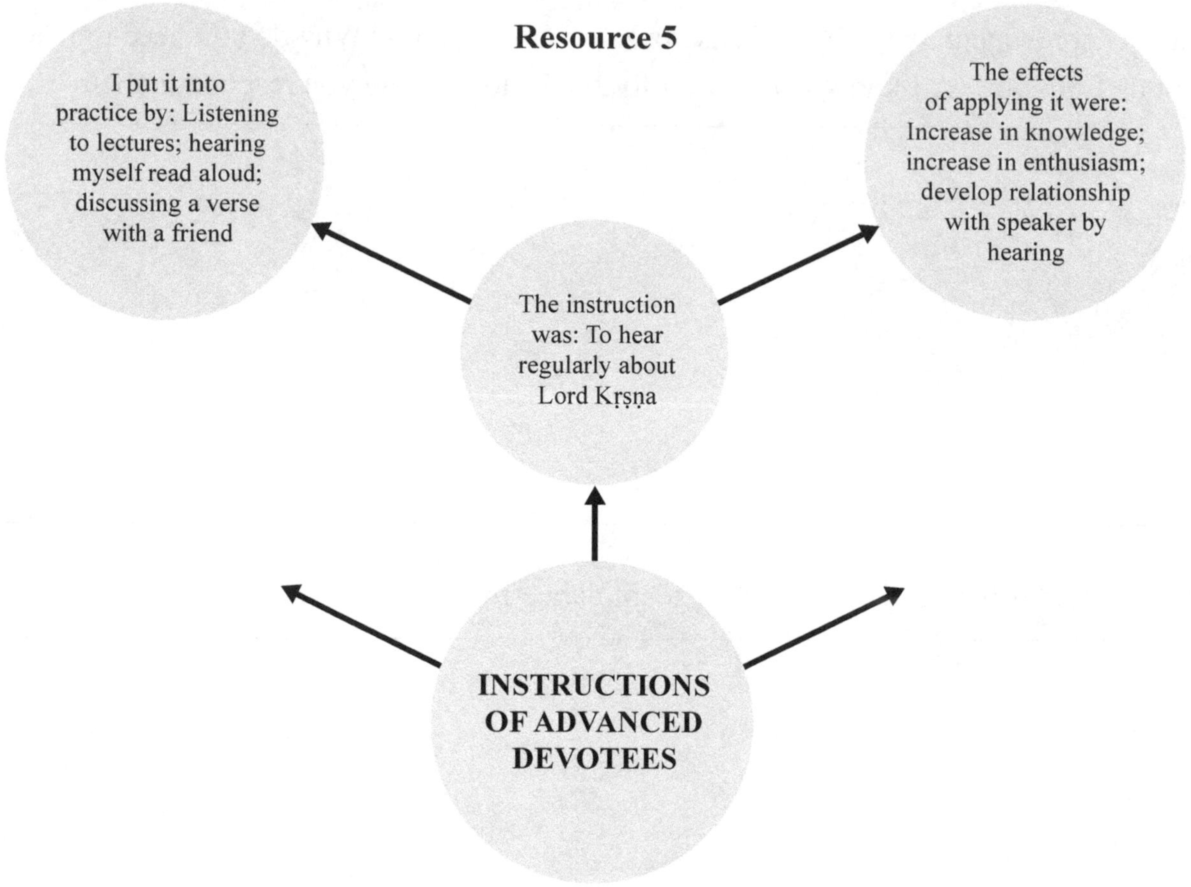

ANSWERS

"Understanding the Story" (pages 221–222): 1) c, 2) b, 3) a, 4) a, 5) c, 6) a, 7) a, 8) b

Keywords (page 229)

KEYWORD	DEFINITION
entourage	Attendants and associates; a group of people that usually accompany an important person
innocent	Free from guilt; free from sin; pure; harmless; unsophisticated
honor	Good name; reputation; show of respect; privilege
resound	To become filled with sound; to become renowned; to sound loudly
subjects	Persons under another's control or authority; person who owes loyalty to a monarch or state
religion	Service and worship of God; belief in religious faith or observance; a set or system of religious attitudes, beliefs, and ways of doing things

Word Search (page 232)

	R	E	L	I	G	I	O	N	B				
	A	Y	U	D	H	I	S	T	H	I	R	A	G
	R								I				R
B	R			S			K	R	S	N	A		A
A	O				O				H				N
T	W		L			U			M				D
T	S			Y			L		A				F
L					I				D				A
E						N			E				T
F		B	O	D	Y		G		V				H
I									A				E
E													R
L	I	N	S	T	R	U	C	T	I	O	N	S	
D													
							B	E	D				

10

Kṛṣṇa Leaves For Dvārakā

Story Summary

Yudhiṣṭhira Mahārāja was now back in his kingdom ruling the world. He ruled his kingdom only to please Lord Kṛṣṇa and his late grandfather, Bhīṣma. He still felt so guilty that he had killed so many of his friends and relatives to become king. Thus, he really didn't feel he was the best person to rule the world. Nevertheless, he continued to rule because he desired to do whatever Lord Kṛṣṇa wanted him to do.

Lord Kṛṣṇa saw this, and He also saw that His family members at the palace were still very much upset. "Hmmm…" Kṛṣṇa thought. "I can't leave when I see everyone is still so sad."

At that moment, his sister, Subhadrā, approached Him. "My dear brother, Kṛṣṇa," she said, "I'd really like it if You stayed here in Hastināpura a little while longer."

"Yes, My dear Subhadrā, I'll stay a little longer," replied Kṛṣṇa, wanting to pacify His sister, who had lost her only son, Abhimanyu.

During His stay in Hastināpura, Kṛṣṇa pleased His family members and spent some time with His sister, Subhadrā. But before long, a few months had passed and Kṛṣṇa felt it was time to return to Dvārakā.

He saw that His cousin Yudhiṣṭhira Mahārāja was a very good king. There was always enough rain and nobody on earth ever went hungry because there was enough fruit, vegetables and grains growing. Even the cows were happy because Yudhiṣṭhira Mahārāja was king. There was always enough milk. In fact, so much that it dripped on the ground from their udders. Yudhiṣṭhira Mahārāja's reign also pleased the rivers, oceans, hills, mountains, forests, plants and medicinal herbs, so they all served their king by appearing beautiful and offering the best service.

The people were also very happy, and nobody ever got sick or ever felt too hot or too cold.

One day, Lord Kṛṣṇa approached Mahārāja Yudhiṣṭhira in the palace and paid obeisances to him. "Kṛṣṇa!" Yudhiṣṭhira Mahārāja exclaimed excitedly. "How can I serve You, my Lord?"

"I've come to seek your permission," replied the Lord.

Yudhiṣṭhira Mahārāja was very confused, "Permission for what, my Lord?"

"Permission to leave," said Kṛṣṇa, "and return back to Dvārakā."

Yudhiṣṭhira Mahārāja and the royal family – the Pāṇḍavas, Mother Kuntī, Subhadrā, Draupadī, Uttarā, Mother Gāndhārī and Dhṛtarāṣṭra all gasped in shock – how could they possibly live without Kṛṣṇa?

Yudhiṣṭhira Mahārāja let out a sad cry and quietly replied: "So be it. Yes, Lord Kṛṣṇa, of course You may leave," while tightly embracing Him.

The royal family instantly ran up to Lord Kṛṣṇa and, while some paid their obeisances to Him, others embraced Him with affection. Then all of them walked Him to His awaiting chariot.

Yudhiṣṭhira Mahārāja clapped his hands and ordered, "Bring horses, elephants, an entire army and many chariots to escort Lord Kṛṣṇa back to Dvārakā. I want to make sure my Lord is safe on His way home." This was a sign of Yudhiṣṭhira Mahārāja's affection for Kṛṣṇa.

Lord Kṛṣṇa boarded His chariot ready to leave, while the Pāṇḍavas stared at Him with unblinking eyes. They moved about here and there, not knowing what to do. They all nearly fainted because they couldn't bear the thought of being separated from their dear Lord.

If people simply hear about Kṛṣṇa and keep devotee friends, they just want to hear more and more about Him. Imagine how the Pāṇḍavas felt, having had so much contact with Kṛṣṇa. They saw Him, touched Him, sat with Him, spoke with Him, ate with Him and even slept near Him.

"How?" they wondered hopelessly. "How are we possibly going to live now without Kṛṣṇa?"

It was very difficult for the female relatives to hold back their tears. "No, we can't cry," they said. "We don't want to cause misfortune as He leaves. We must bid Him a very happy farewell."

Many different types of drums and flutes began to play. "Quick!" said the palace ladies. "The chariot's about to depart! Let's run to the palace rooftop and shower flowers on Kṛṣṇa as He leaves!" So up they ran to the rooftop of the palace, and, smiling with shyness and affection, showered many fragrant flowers over Kṛṣṇa's chariot.

Arjuna opened a beautifully decorated jeweled umbrella and used it to shade the Lord, while Uddhava and Sātyaki fanned Him from both sides. Kṛṣṇa then sat on the seat of His chariot which was decorated with scattered flowers.

"Let's go!" commanded the Lord.

As Lord Kṛṣṇa passed through the city on His majestic chariot, the ladies on the rooftops of their homes began to talk about the Lord. This talk was said to be more attractive than the Vedic hymns, as they directly spoke of the glories of the Lord. Kṛṣṇa saw this and smiled at them as He passed, while the Pāṇḍavas followed closely behind.

Lord Kṛṣṇa left the city and was now on His journey back home, but the Pāṇḍavas were still behind Him. "You can go back now," He said to them, smiling.

"We'll come with you a little further," they replied. They really didn't want to be separated from Him, so they continued to follow Him.

A little while later, Kṛṣṇa saw they were still with Him. "You can go back now," He said to them again, smiling.

"We'll come with you a little further," they replied again, but by now, Lord Kṛṣṇa had traveled far away from Hastināpura. So this time, He convinced them to finally return while He continued His homeward journey with His dear companions.

While traveling through different lands, He was welcomed and worshiped by many and given many presents wherever He went. Each day after sunset, He would rest wherever He was and begin His journey the following morning until He finally reached the city of Dvārakā at last.

Key Messages

- Look them up in your *Śrīmad-Bhāgavatam.*
- Put them in your own words to help you memorize them.
- Discuss each one further.
- Apply them in your life.

Theme	References	Key Messages
Separation	1.10.9–14 1.10.33	The devotees of the Lord cannot tolerate being separated from the Lord. The more intense a devotee's love is for the Lord, the more that devotee feels the pain of separation.
Good leadership makes for a well-cared for society.	1.10.4–6	When the king is a devotee of the Lord, he can rule his citizens very well and provide for them. All of the necessities will be taken care of because there is cooperation with the Lord's will.
Special transcendental relationships	1.10.7–8 1.10.11–12 1.10.20 1.10.26 1.10.28 1.10.32	The Lord's relationships are transcendentally wonderful. Even though He is the Supreme Lord, He takes pleasure in being treated as younger than His devotee.
Devotees' glorification of the Lord versus Vedic hymns	1.10.20	The talks of devotees about the Lord are better than the hymns of the Vedas. These talks directly glorify the Lord and, thus, are pleasing to the heart.
The cause of all causes	1.10.21–22 1.10.24	Kṛṣṇa is the Supreme Lord; He creates, maintains and destroys everything. Kṛṣṇa existed first and everything in creation was created from Him.
The Lord descends	1.10.25–26	The Lord descends to this world to manifest His supreme power, to show mercy to the faithful devotees and perform His wonderful activities.
The Lord teaches by example	1.10.36	The Lord sets an example by performing religious principles, even though He does not require to do so. He does it to set a good example for us to follow.

Understanding the Story

Now it's time to check how well you've understood the story with these questions. (Answers at the end of the chapter.)

1. Yudhiṣṭhira Mahārāja didn't feel he should be ruling as King, but why did he continue to rule?
   a) To please Lord Kṛṣṇa
   b) To please Mother Kuntī
   c) To please Grandfather Bhīṣmadeva
2. Who asked Kṛṣṇa to stay a little longer in Hastināpura?
   a) Mother Kuntī
   b) Subhadrā
   c) Abhimanyu
3. How was Yudhiṣṭhira Mahārāja's character as a king?
   a) Good
   b) Lazy
   c) Demoniac
4. Were the cows happy that Yudhiṣṭhira Mahārāja was king?
5. Was there enough food for the people in the world?
6. Were the rivers and lakes all dirty and dried up?
7. How did the royal family feel when they heard Kṛṣṇa was about to leave for Dvārakā?
8. Name four personalities that were present while the Lord was departing.
9. Who is Lord Kṛṣṇa's sister?
10. Which instruments were played during the Lord's departure?
11. Who kept following Lord Kṛṣṇa while He was traveling home?
    a) Pāṇḍavas
    b) Dhṛtarāṣṭra
    c) Bhīsmadeva
12. Why did the Pāṇḍavas follow Kṛṣṇa while He was going home?
    a) They couldn't bear the thought of being separated from Him
    b) They were scared that demons might attack
    c) They wanted to make sure Kṛṣṇa was definitely going home

Higher-Thinking Questions

Now it's time to deepen your understanding of Chapter 9 by delving into Śrīla Prabhupāda's purports for this chapter and reflecting upon the following questions.

1. The relatives of Kṛṣṇa were very sad when Kṛṣṇa was leaving them. Discuss how the pure devotees' feelings of separation from Kṛṣṇa are much stronger than our own feelings for people whom we love. Details may include:

    a) Nearly fainting
    b) Not blinking (staring) while looking at Kṛṣṇa
    c) Tears flooding from their eyes
    d) Moving about here and there

2. It is described that Mahārāja Yudhiṣṭhira was the enemy of no one, however he fought in the Battle of Kurukṣetra. Is this a contradiction?
3. In SB 1.10.20, it describes how the talks of the residents of Hastināpura were more attractive than the hymns of the Vedas. How is this so? Do you think that it is an exaggeration?
4. Describe the living conditions at the time when Yudhiṣṭhira Mahārāja ruled the world. Contrast them with the present day conditions.

ACTIVITIES

In this section you will find many exciting things to do! They will get you thinking, moving, drawing, acting, and most importantly, having loads of fun!

Action Activities . . . to get you moving!

DUTIES

Description: Yudhiṣṭhira Mahārāja was made king by Kṛṣṇa after the Battle of Kurukṣetra, but he did not try to enjoy the kingdom for himself. Instead, he ruled the kingdom as a matter of duty.

Let's try to follow in the footsteps of Yudhiṣṭhira Mahārāja by developing a sense of "duty consciousness." Think of some duties that you could perform around the house such as cleaning the altar, helping with chores around the home or in the classroom, etc.

Write down three duties that you will do every day without fail for a week!

KṚṢṆA IN THE CENTER LECTURE

Description: Prepare a Sunday feast class on the topic of spiritual affection and family attachment, with Kṛṣṇa in the center. Use examples from this chapter.

Remember these helpful pointers:

- The authors' "PIE" – Persuade, Inform and Entertain your audience.
- A good speech structure: Open with a punch line, proceeding to the main idea. Then take the three most important points from your main idea and discuss them, one after another. Conclude with an overall summary ending with your main idea and a punch line!

Analogy Activities . . . to bring out the scholar in you!

FOREST FIRE

"This world is compared to a forest fire caused by the cohesion of bamboo bushes. Such a forest fire takes place automatically, for bamboo cohesion occurs without external cause. Similarly, in the material world the wrath of those who want to lord it over material nature interacts, and the fire of war takes place, exhausting the unwanted population. Such fires or wars take place, and the Lord has nothing to do with them." (SB 1.10.2 Purport)

Learning Activity:
Topic: What would you do?
Instructions: Another word for "wrath" is "anger." Create your own acrostic poem with the word "anger." An acrostic poem uses the letters in a given topic/word to begin each line of the poem. Each line should relate to the given topic/word. In this way, you will create your own acrostic poems on "anger."

Here is an example:

- Always try to serve the devotees instead of trying to be bossy
- Never get angry
- Good solutions help people who feel angry
- Express angry emotions in a nice and helpful way
- Real service to the Lord helps us to deal with our anger

Prompt Questions:

- What makes you angry?
- How do you feel when you are angry?
- Do we often blame others when we feel angry?
- If we pray to Kṛṣṇa, do you think He can help us with our anger?
- What happens when two angry people come together?
- Why do you think we become angry?

Conclusion (discuss):

- Sometimes when we want too many things, and we don't get them, we can become angry
- We can try to find nice ways of expressing how we feel when we are angry

- If we spend too much time with angry people, we will also slowly start to feel angry more often

Artistic Activities
. . . to reveal your creativity!

NATURAL WEALTH OF THE LAND

Description: Mahārāja Yudhiṣṭhira is such a glorious King! Color in the picture, showing the natural wealth of the land during Mahārāja Yudhiṣṭhira's reign. See **Resource 1**.

FAREWELL CARD

Description: Imagine that you are a resident of Hastināpura who is present when Lord Kṛṣṇa is leaving the city. Make a farewell card and gift for the Lord that you can give to Him before He departs.

MAKING A FAN

Description: "Uddhava and Sātyaki began to fan the Lord with decorated fans, and the Lord, as the master of Madhu, seated on scattered flowers, commanded them along the road." (SB 1.10.18)

You Will Need: 2 popsicle sticks, glue, tape, paper (40 inches by 6 inches), water colors or colored pens/pencils.

1. Decorate your piece of paper with watercolors or colored pens/ pencils.
2. Glue a popsicle stick at either of the short ends of your paper so that the full size of the stick is covered with paper, leaving 1.5 inches of popsicle stick sticking out above the top of the paper and 1 inch of paper sticking out at the bottom. Do the same with the other popsicle stick at the opposite end of your paper. Pleat the paper, each pleat being the same width as the popsicle stick.
3. Gather the pleated paper at the bottom of the fan and tape it together.
4. Now you can open out your fan by bringing the popsicle sticks all the way around so that they meet.
5. Remember to fan the Lord!

Critical Thinking Activities

. . . to bring out the spiritual investigator in you!

KṚṢṆA'S JOURNEY GEOGRAPHY TASK

Description: Using the map on **Resource 2**, plot out the places of Lord Kṛṣṇa's pastimes during His time on Earth. Attach the flags provided on **Resource 3** to the map, or draw your own pictures to show what Kṛṣṇa did at each place.

Next, fill in the table on **Resource 4**. You can note down details about what Lord Kṛṣṇa did in each place, who He was with and what His reason was for leaving there. This activity can also be extended outdoors or in a larger indoor area. Adults can help to plot out the map. The relevant places can be plotted using the smaller map. Paths can be created between the places, using stones or other objects and, at each relevant place, different objects that represent that particular area can be used. For example: Ujjain – pens/pencils, books, etc.; Kurukṣetra – homemade weapons (bow and arrows, *gadā,* sword, etc.).

Once you have your larger-than-life map set up, you can then use the objects to role-play a pastime at each location.

Extension: Look at other present-day maps to see if those places of Kṛṣṇa's pastimes can still be identified.

Prompt Questions:

- Can you find any pictures of what those places look like now?
- How have the places changed?
- Why/how did the change take place? Look in the history books!
- Have some of the names of the places changed?
- What are the actual distances between the places?
- Can you write down directions for the Lord, using a compass? Which way should He head?

Introspective Activities
. . . to bring out the reflective devotee in you!

EVENING PRAYERS

Description: In the evening, after sunset, in all the places He went, He would stop to perform evening prayers. Although the Lord did not need to do this, He did it so that others would follow Him. (See SB 1.10.36)

Follow Kṛṣṇa's example and choose some prayers to sing in the evenings at home with your family.

DEAR DIARY

Description: Imagine that you are King Yudhiṣṭhira. Write a diary entry to describe how you are feeling about seeing the Lord leave.

Writing Activities . . . to bring out the writer in you!

SEQUENCING TASK

Learning Outcomes:

Children should be able to . . .

- Recall events from the pastime of Kṛṣṇa leaving for Dvārakā
- Place events in chronological order

Description: Read the story summary first, and then photocopy and cut out each event and picture on **Resource 5** and **6**.

1. A basic version for younger children (ages 3–4): Read each event in order, and then ask the children to match the event to the picture.
2. Ages 4 and up: Put events in order and match them to the pictures. Use the Story Summary to help, if needed. The first one is done for you.

Mini-Dictionary Task: Now complete the "definitions" activity on **Resource 7** to create a mini-dictionary of the words in this lesson. See if you can spell the words correctly.

KEYWORDS

- Define the following keywords from the story.
- Use each word in a sentence (either in oral or written form).
- Complete a New Word Map at the back of the book for any new words.

KEYWORD	DEFINITION
rule	
desire	
embrace	
affection	
permission	
instantly	

WORD SEARCH

W	Q	H	O	R	S	E	S	P	I	U	Y	R	P
E	H	T	P	C	H	A	R	I	O	T	S	T	A
R	A	H	D	F	G	H	J	K	T	M	U	Y	N
T	S	S	E	S	C	O	R	T	Y	Y	B	U	D
Y	T	A	W	E	G	H	D	A	U	U	H	I	A
U	I	D	V	A	R	A	K	A	I	D	A	O	V
I	N	S	K	J	G	F	Q	W	N	H	D	P	A
O	A	D	F	Q	W	C	A	D	C	I	R	U	S
P	P	T	D	L	T	M	S	U	S	S	A	A	R
Q	U	G	Q	L	U	B	D	Y	D	T	Y	D	T
A	R	V	J	D	R	T	T	S	T	I	U	S	Y
S	A	Z	G	T	E	W	E	A	G	R	I	D	Q
D	R	U	M	S	R	P	I	S	V	A	N	T	A
T	O	X	R	Y	Q	L	A	X	L	Y	C	L	S
G	P	C	F	N	W	H	X	R	N	H	Z	Z	D
V	J	O	U	R	N	E	Y	M	T	K	H	J	T

HASTINAPURA		DVARAKA	
CHARIOT		YUDHISTHIRA	
JOURNEY		SUBHADRA	
DEPART		ESCORT	
PANDAVAS		DRUMS	
HORSES		FLUTES	

PRAYERS OF THE LADIES OF HASTINĀPURA

The ladies of Hastināpura
Went onto the rooftops to see Kṛṣṇa,
As He left that day in a great parade
For His home in Dvārakā far away.

Flower petals they threw on their Kṛṣṇa, dark blue.
And they smiled and they prayed and how they wished He could stay,
But to Dvārakā He went, so much time He had spent
Away from His family who wanted Him back.

Kṛṣṇa greets His wives with His sweet lotus smile,
And sons such as Pradyumna and Sāmba.
How blessed they all are, in Dvārakā with Kṛṣṇa,
Headed by His queens Rukmiṇī and Satyabhāmā.

Of His glorious acts, all the ladies thought back;
He was bound by His mother when she caught Him stealing butter.
He is the Supersoul, in the heart of us all,
And He gives His special mercy to all those faithful.

The ladies could see Kṛṣṇa smiling so sweet
As they offered their prayers unto His lotus feet.
He accepted their love, from the rooftops above,
Then away He left for Dvārakā, their Lord Mādhava.

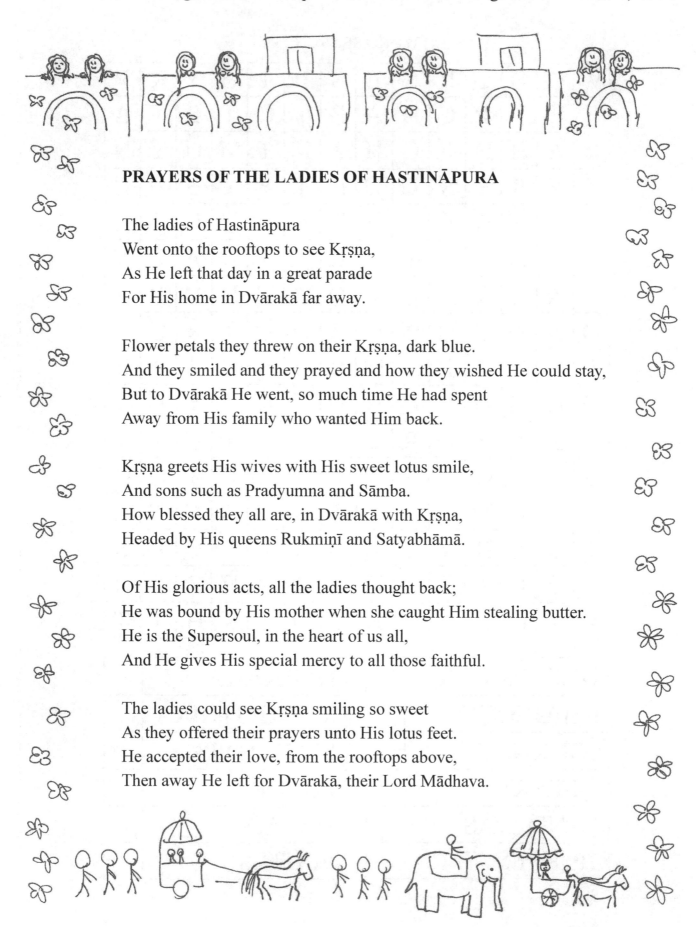

Resource 1

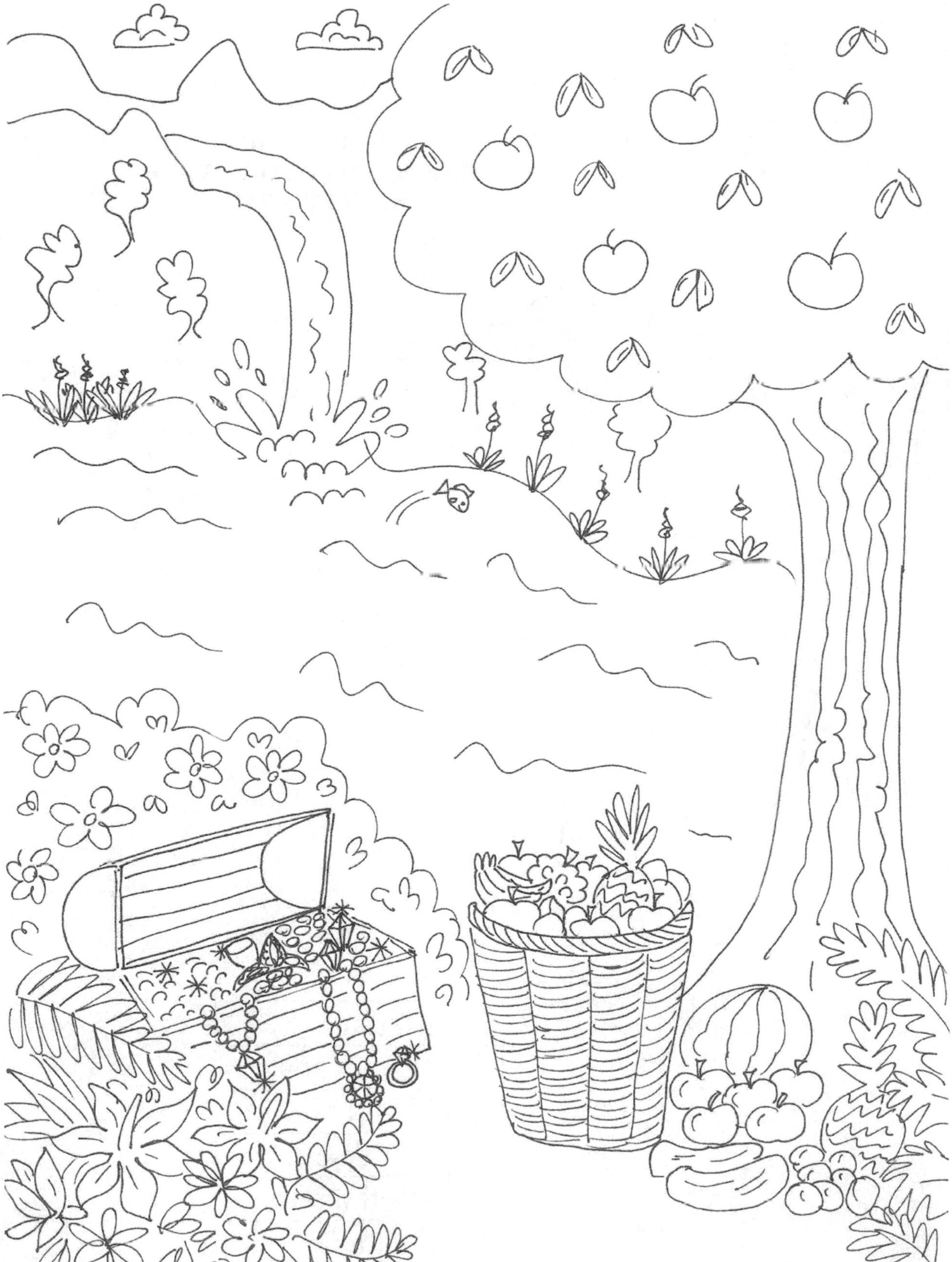

Resource 2

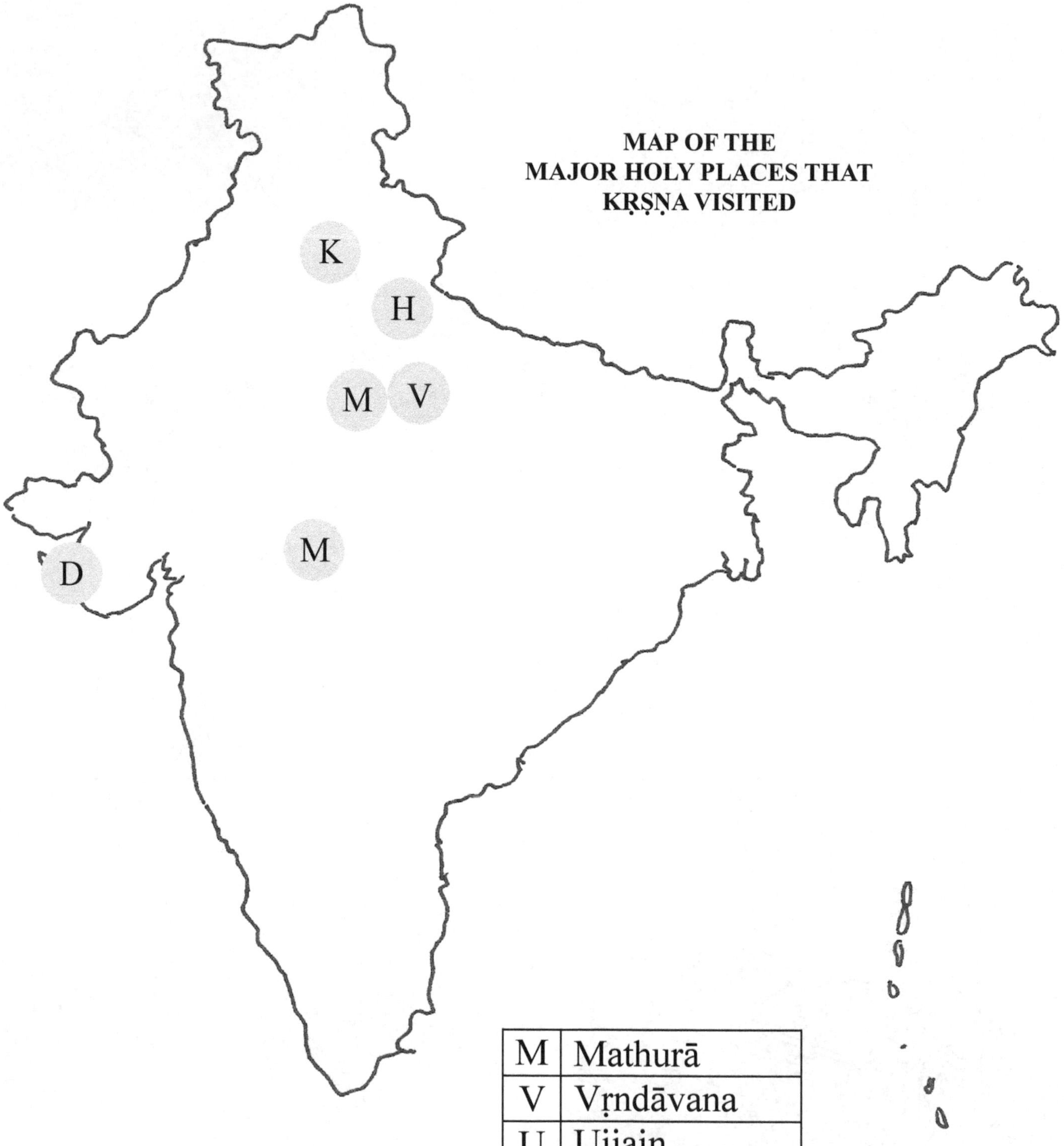

M	Mathurā
V	Vṛndāvana
U	Ujjain
K	Kurukṣetra
H	Hastināpura
D	Dvārakā

Resource 3

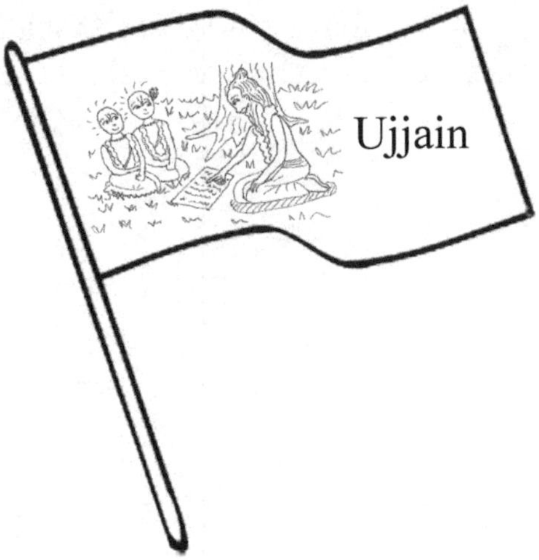
Ujjain

Vṛndāvana

Kurukṣetra

Mathurā

Dvārakā

Hastināpura

Resource 4

PICTURE AND NAME OF PLACE	What did Kṛṣṇa do there?	Who was with Kṛṣṇa?	Why did Kṛṣṇa leave?
 Mathurā			
 Ujjain			
 Vṛndāvana			
 Hastināpura			
 Kurukṣetra			
 Dvārakā			

Resource 5

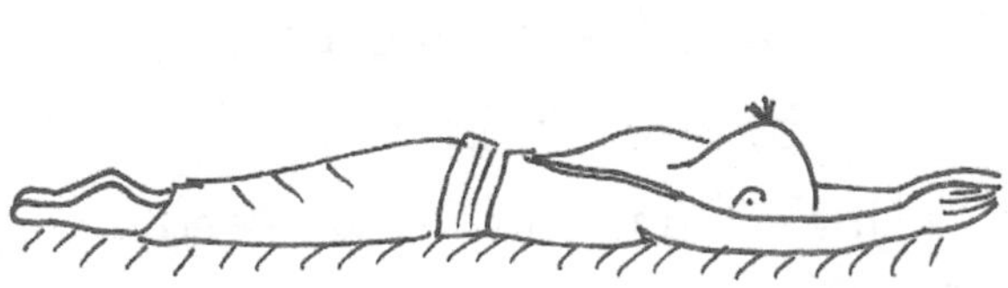

Resource 6

After Lord Kṛṣṇa asked Yudhiṣṭhira for permission to leave, the Lord's relatives gasped in shock.	Then different types of drums and flutes sounded as Lord Kṛṣṇa left the palace.
Then Kṛṣṇa sat on the seat of His chariot which was decorated with scattered flowers.	Then Yudhiṣṭhira ordered horses, elephants, an entire army and many chariots to go with Lord Kṛṣṇa back to Dvārakā.
Then the royal family ran up to Lord Kṛṣṇa. Some paid their obeisances to Him and some hugged Him with affection. Then they all walked Him to His chariot.	Then Uddhava and Sātyaki fanned Him from both sides.
Then the royal ladies showered flowers on Kṛṣṇa.	Then Arjuna opened a beautifully decorated jewelled umbrella and used it to shade the Lord.

Resource 7

OBJECT	Write a description of each object. Include details of how it is used and what it looks like/sounds like/feels like.
	A fan is . . .
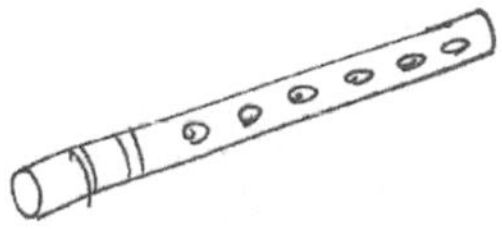	A flute is . . .
	A cow is . . .
	A drum is . . .
	A piece of grain is . . .
	Rain is . . .
	An umbrella is . . .
	A flower is . . .

ANSWERS

"Understanding the Story" (pages 247): 1) a, 2) b, 3) a, 11) a, 12) a

4) Yes
5) Yes
6) No
7) Very sad, couldn't bear the thought of being separated from Him
8) The Pāṇḍavas, Mother Kuntī, Subhadrā, Draupadī, Uttarā, Mother Gāndhārī, Dhṛtarāṣṭra, Uddhava, Sātyaki
9) Subhadrā
10) Different types of drums and flutes

Keywords (page 254)

KEYWORD	DEFINITION
rule	To exercise authority over (something); to have power over (something)
desire	A strong wish; longing
embrace	To hug; to clasp in the arms; to enclose on all sides
affection	Feeling of liking or caring for someone or something; feeling of fondness
permission	Authorization; consent of someone in authority
instantly	Immediately; without delay; at once

Word Search (page 257)

		H	O	R	S	E	S						P
	H			C	H	A	R	I	O	T	S		A
	A										U		N
	S		E	S	C	O	R	T		Y	B		D
	T									U	H		A
	I	D	V	A	R	A	K	A		D	A		V
	N									H	D		A
	A		F							I	R		S
	P			L						S	A		
	U				U					T			
	R			D		T				I			
	A				E		E			R			
D	R	U	M	S		P		S		A			
							A						
								R					
	J	O	U	R	N	E	Y		T				

New Word Map

KEY WORD

Definition of key word and synonyms

Use it in a sentence

Antonym
(opposite meaning)

CONTEXT: If the key word was used
in the story, explain what it meant in the story

Draw a picture of it here

CPSIA information can be obtained
at www.ICGtesting.com
Printed in the USA
LVHW020736200819
628263LV00019B/1214/P

9 781733 927215